The Fiction of the I

Contemporary Austrian Writers and Autobiography

Edited by
Nicholas J. Meyerhofer

ARIADNE PRESS
Riverside, California

Ariadne Press would like to express its appreciation to the Austrian Cultural Institute, New York for assistance in publishing this book.

Library of Congress Cataloging-in-Publication Data

The fiction of the I : contemporary Austrian writers and autobiography / edited by Nicholas J. Meyerhofer.
                    p.   cm. -- (Studies in Austrian literature, culture, and thought)
    Includes bibliographical references and index.
    ISBN 1-57241-080-9
    1. Austrian prose literature--20th century--History and criticism. 2. Biography as a literary form. 3. Autobiography. 4. Autobiographical fiction, Austrian--History and criticism. 5. Authors, Austrian--20th century--Biography. I. Meyerhofer, Nicholas J. II. Series.
PT3822.F53   1999
838'.91408099436--dc21
                                          98-54312
                                            CIP

Cover Design:
Art Director, Designer: George McGinnis

Copyright ©1999
by Ariadne Press
270 Goins Court
Riverside, CA 92507

All rights reserved.
No part of this publication may be reproduced or transmitted in any form or by any means without formal permission.
Printed in the United States of America.
ISBN 1-57241-080-9

The Fiction of the I

Contemporary Austrian Writers and Autobiography

Studies in Austrian Literature, Culture, and Thought

Contents

Nicholas J. Meyerhofer
Foreword   vii

Nicholas J. Meyerhofer
Introduction: Autobiographical Variants in
Frischmuth, Handke, Henisch, Hilsenrath, Jelinek,
Rosei, Roth, and Wander   1

Gerald Chapple
Will the Real Barbara Frischmuth Please Stand Up?
On Autobiography and Literary Creation   10

Michael Ossar
Amy or the Metamorphosis as a Bildungsroman   34

Ingeborg Hoesterey
Autofiction: Peter Handke's Trilogy of Try-Outs   47

Linda C. DeMeritt
Identity as Schizophrenia: The Autobiography
of Peter Henisch   61

Jennifer Michaels
An Experiment with Himself: Peter Henisch's
Autobiographical Writing in *The Small Figure of My
Father*, *May Is Gone*, and *Stein's Paranoia*   80

Bianca Rosenthal
Autobiography and the Fiction of the I: Edgar Hilsenrath   101

Imke Meyer
The Trouble with Elfriede: Jelinek and Autobiography   116

Alfred Barthofer
Vanishing in the Text: Elfriede Jelinek's Art of Self-
Effacement in *Die Klavierspielerin* and *Die Kinder der Toten*   138

Pamela S. Saur
Guiltless Confessions in Gerhard Roth's *Archives of Silence*   164

Helga Schreckenberger
Personalizing Fiction—Fictionalizing the Personal:
Gerhard Roth's *The Investigating Judge*   184

Robert Acker
Autobiographical Elements and the Search for Meaning
in Peter Rosei's Novel *Persona*   200

Geoffrey C. Howes
Rosei's I's: The (De)Composition of the Self in
Peter Rosei's Fiction   210

Jörg Thunecke
Fred Wander's Semi-Autobiographical Narrative,
The Seventh Well—"Such stories I never heard again"   242

Nicholas J. Meyerhofer and Karl Doerry
The I as Fiction: A Conversation with Peter Rosei   259

Contributors   284

Foreword

In his reflections on the genre of autobiography, Günter de Bruyn (1995, 61) is careful to draw a distinction between subjective and objective truth. Citing autobiographers as diverse as St. Augustine, Rousseau, Goethe and Bismarck, de Bruyn makes the fairly obvious point that the essence of any autobiography is the attempt to reveal the past of one's life, considered from the vantage point of the present. But what is interesting about such an attempt, de Bruyn goes on to posit, has little if anything to do with the problem of time eroding memory, or even with the desire for objectivity as such; rather, what is fascinating and idiosyncratic about any autobiographical text is its relationship to subjectivity, that is, its relationship to the manner in which an individual chooses to present himself or herself to the reader (62).

If one accepts de Bruyn's premise, many theoretical questions detailed in lengthy examinations of the autobiographical as genre become superfluous.[1] As the present volume does not purport to be an investigation into fundamental epistemological issues related to the autobiographical narrative, it will be content to accept de Bruyn and his approach. This does not mean, however, that *The Fiction of the I: Contemporary Austrian Writers and Autobiography* is devoid of theoretical considerations. The volume is intended as an English introduction to a limited number of contemporary Austrian writers, all of whom have been critically recognized as important, but not all of whom have an overtly autobiographical approach in their writing. Because of this latter point, certain questions recur in the essays on these writers and their individual approaches: In what sense is this autobiographical fiction? To what extent is this apparently other-centered narration in fact an example of self-reflexive writing, perhaps even a search for self-identity or the attempted articulation of an "I"? Does gender modulate the expression of this autobiographical voice?

As will be clear from my colleagues' contributions, the nexus of "the autobiographical" in contemporary Austrian fiction is not straightforward and naive, nor is it uncomplicated. It is my hope, however, that this thematic introduction will make the reader want to enjoy first-hand the writing of these various authors, all of whom either have been or are now being translated into English.

As with any project of this length, it would not have been realized without assistance. In my case, I am especially grateful to Ms. Louella Holter of Northern Arizona University's Bilby Research Center; her patience, editorial advice, and professional manner were simply invaluable.

Nicholas J. Meyerhofer
Flagstaff, Spring 1998

Introduction: Autobiographical Variants in Frischmuth, Handke, Henisch, Hilsenrath, Jelinek, Rosei, Roth, and Wander

Nicholas J. Meyerhofer

The Frankfurt Book Fair is the largest annual commercial gathering of book dealers in the world. For the 47th fair, held October 11–16, 1995, the chief subject of the exhibition was the history of Austrian thought in the twentieth century. A plethora of books and displays covered seven distinct themes and fields of Austrian literature, art, and science for visitors to browse through. One was titled "The Inner World," which is the general subject of this volume. Specifically, *The Fiction of the I: Contemporary Austrian Writers and Autobiography* focuses on a limited number of significant contemporary Austrian writers and their relationship to autobiographical writing. The goal is to introduce the English-speaking reader to authors who have already been critically recognized in Austria, but whose often complex relationship to the topic of autobiography has to date not been given its critical due.

It was no less a commentator than Theodor Adorno who, in his famous volume on aesthetic theory, pronounced that autobiographical writing worthy of the term should maintain something approaching objective alignment with nonpsychological reality.[2] This position, however, is countered by the literary meditation of the great Argentinean writer Jorge Luis Borges, whose brief but brilliant "Borges and I" concludes with the assertion that "I do not know which of us has written this page"

(1962). While acknowledging the validity of Adorno's "common sense" position, surely Borges's statement also touches on a feeling shared by any writer who has engaged in the task of self-representation. Is the self-reflective author ultimately an operator or a spectator? That each of us is the final and unimpeachable arbiter of what it is to be us seems beyond dispute. Yet this statement should presume nothing about self-representation in prose. Is the autobiographical author in fact attempting an unmediated hermeneutic mastery of the cognitive object, that is, one's own self? Or does the author feel that such an essentially Hegelian aesthetic, the accurate articulation of the self in standard discourse, is no longer possible? Does the author in fact posit, as many contemporary, postmodern authors do, the irrecuperability of traditional subjectivity, a Lacanian fragmentation of the self? And even if the object of scrutiny, the authorial self, is not viewed as a problematic entity as such, should this imply that language will be an adequate tool in attempting to realize its 'photographic' depiction? Or does the inherent inadequacy of language automatically radicalize any narrative project, thus making the task of subjective accuracy even more daunting?

These issues, and ancillary questions related to authorial intention (Is this text serious or ludic? Should it be seen as accurate or as off-kilter posturing? Is it intentionally autobiographical, or is it rather unintentionally self-revealing?) are arguably as old as literature, since they have occupied agile authors and truly critical readers throughout Western culture. That Miguel de Cervantes well appreciated these concerns is clear from the hermeneutic thematics of his *Don Quixote*, and Michel de Montaigne's *Livre de moi* is nothing if not the precursor to postmodern autobiographical texts that interweave threads of philosophy, psychology, epistemology, history, and erudition, in order to create a fascinating literary tapestry that may or may not overlap with the supposed narrative object, the authorial self.

The questions raised above with respect to autobiography are of particular relevance to the writers discussed in this volume, because each of them—Frischmuth, Handke, Hilsenrath, Henisch, Jelinek, Rosei, Roth, and Wander—has made an idiosyncratic contribution to the regeneration of certain genres in contemporary Austrian prose: myth, fairy tale, the *Bildungs*-

roman, the trilogy, the detective novel and, most notably, autobiographical variants. Ever since the publication of her first novel, an autobiographical *succès de scandale* called *The Convent School* (1968), **Barbara Frischmuth** has continued to write works that feature female protagonists and a subtle reworking of myths and fairy tales. Frischmuth's 1973 novel *The Shadow Disappears in the Sun* was just as overtly autobiographical as *Convent School*, yet it represents an experimental novel of sorts, hovering as it does between an anti-linear language experiment and a traditional narrative approach. In interviews, Frischmuth (1996, 42 f.) has stated that her works frequently represent an admixture of personal experience and literary imagination, and critics have often pointed out that her fiction is nothing if not multilayered. As Michael Ossar points out in his essay, one can read Frischmuth's trilogy *The Mystification of Sophie Silber* (1978) as a feminist *Bildungsroman*, but not necessarily as autobiographical; instead, the novels that comprise the trilogy can—and probably should—be read as representations of typical female biographies in our time and society. Gerald Chapple's treatment of the autobiographical as literary creation in Frischmuth touches on this issue, and on the problematics of fusing autobiographical horizons: the attempt to reanimate one's former self, to enter into the "other" of one's past from the perspective of today, can indeed assume many forms, since the difference between memory and imagination is epistemologically uncertain.

As the title ("Autofiction") of Ingeborg Hoesterey's essay indicates, **Peter Handke** has always written about writing under the guise of self-investigation. As early as 1966, Handke stated that he was not interested in writing about "so-called reality; rather, I choose to write about myself."[3] Indeed, one could argue that modern Austrian autobiography was invented by Handke and his rather more pessimistic counterpart, Thomas Bernhard. Born in Griffen in 1942, Handke is really of the generation just after Bernhard, who was born in 1931. Unlike Bernhard, Handke expands his autobiographical fiction to include personae other than himself, yet the reader soon understands that they are little more than self-extensions of the author, that is, metaphoric personages who mirror his own problems and semantic qualities. Although Handke's texts typically contain a multitude of spatial references, they also tend toward the quasi-mystical, centered and grounded as they are in the almost spiritual problematics of being an artist. A work such as *Absence* (1987), for instance, rather portentously follows the dreamlike journey of four representative types—the old man, the woman, the gambler, and the soldier—through a constantly metamorphosing landscape. Much of Handke's *oeuvre* also unfolds along the margin of silence. Although *Absence* is alive with movement, many of Handke's other works have only minimal action, although they do convey with a peculiar vividness something of what it is to be a writer: the feverishness, the boredom, the gradual wearing down of one's personality, and the bafflement and self-doubt connected to pursuing such a "profession" in an age of materialism, mass production, and mediocrity. What results from this sense of occupational singularity is, ineluctably, an isolation that is oppressive yet concomitantly liberating. Ingeborg Hoesterey's essay closes with Handke's reference to Hogarth's famous *Portrait of the Painter with his Pug*, with its quasi-emblematic "Line of Beauty and Grace." The S-shaped curve on the painter's palette furnishes the author with a symbol of his own quest for aesthetic perfection in the *Essay on the Successful Day*, and Hoesterey rather surprisingly states that this should not be seen as a pursuit of an impossible dream, despite Handke's literary subtitle: "A Winter's Daydream."

Peter Henisch, on the other hand, appears to be more traditionally autobiographical because, as Linda DeMeritt states, Henisch's entire literary production can be read as "one continuous text with returning figures and motifs drawn more or less from the author's own life." Her magisterial examination of the dynamics of construction and deconstruction in Henisch's *Negatives of My Father* points out, however, that the novel's intention is to cast doubt upon supposedly objective categories of identity. In similar fashion, Jennifer Michaels's essay on Henisch begins with a quotation from the author in which he states that writing is an experiment with himself. Yet immediately after this contention, Michaels maintains that Henisch in fact utilizes the autobiographical genre to address societal problems, and her analyses of *Negatives of My Father* (1975), *May Is Gone* (1978), and *Stein's Paranoia* (1988) makes it quite clear that this is indeed the case.

Of the eight authors in this volume, **Edgar Hilsenrath** is perhaps the least Austrian, but his writing is inarguably autobiographical. As Bianca Rosenthal's introduction to the author points out, Hilsenrath has actually spent more time in New York and Berlin than he has in Vienna, but he is still "Austrian" by dint of having been raised in the easternmost extension of the former Austro-Hungarian Empire, namely the Bukovina, in present-day Romania. Even in "exile," however, Hilsenrath has continued to gather together the elements of his own rather peripatetic and catastrophic life and to thematize identities from an Old World that has now disappeared: the traditions of the *shtetl* life and the sundry persecutions of East European Jewry. Interestingly, it was Hilsenrath's least autobiographical work, a novel called *The Fairy Tale of the Last Thought* (1989), that brought him his greatest literary recognition to date. The work depicts the genocide of the Armenians in World War I, and among other awards, it won for Hilsenrath the prestigious Alfred Döblin Prize that same year.

Of the authors discussed in this study, **Elfriede Jelinek** has certainly generated the most controversy. In making reference to Jelinek's having "aroused considerable controversy," Alfred Barthofer intentionally understates the case of a woman whose writing is frequently described as stridently feminist (Jelinek herself disavows the term), and who consistently thematizes sado-masochism and the impossibility of acceptable relations— in both senses of the term—between men and women. Jelinek's thematic preoccupation with female sexuality and her focus on the socioeconomic plight of women would be enough to make her unpopular in conservative Austria, but emotional interviews given early in her career only exacerbated the situation, due mainly to Jelinek's personal frankness and not infrequent allusions to "Austrian Fascism." But Alfred Barthofer's excellent introduction to Jelinek does not focus on this aspect of the author's career, as the early Jelinek—the veteran of a Berlin Maoist commune, the active member of the Austrian Communist Party, and the author of a feminist cult book such as *The Lovers* (1975)—should not be compared to or confused with the more recent Jelinek. This is appropriate, precisely because the early, overtly autobiographical Jelinek who thematized herself directly in a work such as *The Piano Player* (1983), this Jelinek—at least according to the author herself—has left the literary stage. As Alfred Barthofer illustrates, the Jelinek of *The Children of the Dead* (1995) is still essentially autobiographical in her approach, but only obliquely so, as her "self" is now radically transformed and abstracted, to the point of self-effacement. But that controversy will continue to pursue Jelinek is also apparent from her most recent work, *A Piece about Sports* (1998), which has just had its contentious premiere under the notorious Klaus Peymann at the Burgtheater. Jelinek admitted in a recent interview that sport is "one of my oldest hates," and the piece is a vitriolic attack on the phenomenon of sport in Austrian society. In *A Piece about Sports*, sport is presented as war-by-other-means, as energizing but mindless pabulum for the masses, and in general as a metaphor for humanity's basest instincts. Quoting a line from the play itself, one reviewer has described the work as "the tragedy of a risible woman,"[4] and other critics have been even less charitable.

Although controversial and at times unpopular in Austria, **Gerhard Roth** is certainly to be numbered among the country's most significant contemporary writers. In interviews, he has stated forthrightly that he continues to draw much inspiration for his prolific prose from the nightmares of his youth. Roth's childhood was marked by the end of World War II and its aftermath: harrowing escapes from Allied bombings, escalating confrontations with his father because of the latter's membership in the Nazi Party, and a growing conviction that Austria's refusal to confront or even acknowledge the anti-Semitism and crimes of its Nazi years was unhealthy—that it in fact was producing a collective sickness tantamount to a kind of national schizophrenia. It is hardly accidental, therefore, that Roth's works so often thematize insanity, convinced as he is that the phenomenon has much to reveal about society's dark side. Like Michel Foucault, Roth believes in the value of analyzing madness as an index of the oppressive nature of the normative. Noting these connections between Roth's life and his literary production, Pamela Saur delineates several of his novels as "nonfictional volumes," and she cites the author himself to this effect, as he states in the introduction to *The History of Darkness* (1991) that he wishes to "do away with the border between document and literature." One could also point to the jacket cover of Roth's 1991 publication, *A Journey into the Interior of Vienna*, which describes the collection of essays and photographs as "a travel guide through the abysses of Austria's psyche."[5] Helga Schreckenberger's essay expands on the connections between Roth and Foucault, and she posits that a work such as *The Investigating Judge* (1988) intends to break down traditional distinctions between self and society, subjectivity and reality, autobiography and fiction.

As the interview with him in this volume suggests, **Peter Rosei** is an author who has spent his entire career rejecting all literary teleologies save one: the dogged pursuit of—to quote Geoffrey Howes—"the question of what the self is." Rosei's novels, which are not without humor and are frequently satires of a consumer society gone mad, turn this question over and over like a literary prism. Is the self an integral reality, is it a fragmented multiplicity, or is it an utter fiction?[6] One must pay tribute to Rosei's literary talent, inventiveness, and tenacity in that he has traced this theme not only in such complex fashion, but also so elegantly: his fictional texts are among the most aesthetically rich and conceptually challenging in the German language today. The identity-quest of Rosei's prose is not a solipsistic exercise limited to his person, however, since it is clear that the author also intends to involve the perceptive reader in these dynamics of self-reflection. In his analysis of *Persona* (1995), Robert Acker appropriates both of these positions: although a virtual autobiography, the "so-called novel" is composed of shards and illusionary elements, and by fragmenting both the ontology of the self and the genre of the novel, it demands that the reader participate in the search for reassemblage, for meaning and identity. Geoffrey Howes's article, on the other hand, focuses not only on identity formation in Rosei's prose, but also—and most perceptively—on identity deformation, on self-decomposition as being thematically integral to most of the author's works. As he points out, in the novels *The Milky Way* (1981), the six books that comprise *15,000 Souls* (1984–88), *Rebus* (1990), and finally *Persona*, Rosei's protagonists actively seek redefinition—frequently by means of self-destructive behavior—due to their unhappiness with the status quo.

As described by Jörg Thunecke, **Fred Wander** is a "semi-autobiographical" author whose work has chiefly been given critical recognition in the context of postwar Holocaust writing. Beyond this appropriate description, however, works such as Wander's *The Seventh Well* are also arresting as the literary and emotional delineation of a twentieth-century experience shared by many, namely exile. Indeed, Wander could be accurately described as living in exile in Vienna even today. Having survived the concentration camp system, Wander made his way back to the Austrian capital after the war. Upon returning to his home, however, he was frequently confronted by blatant anti-Semitism due to his overtly Jewish birth-name, Fritz Rosenblatt. In order to avoid unpleasant questions such as how a Jew could have possibly survived in Buchenwald, Rosenblatt changed his name to Wander. The new surname, of course, suggests the rootlessness and itinerant destiny of the Jew in the modern world, a fate that is at least obliquely thematized in Wander's novels. Understood more generally, however, all of the authors in this volume identify with the "Wanderesque" themes of a general sense of discontentment, of a pervading personal restlessness and the urge to travel in an almost aimless fashion. Hence, it is quite appropriate that Wander be the final author to be discussed in this study, since his un-ease (*Unbehagen*, in the Freudian sense) is quite emblematic of his Austrian contemporaries.

Notes

1. Representative of these, among others, are Roy Pascal (1960) or, more recently, Oliver Sill (1991).
2. See the introduction and first chapter of Adorno (1989).
3. See Handke's essay, "Wenn ich schreibe" (1966, 467).
4. "Die Tragödie einer lächerlichen Frau," in the Web review of Karin Cerny, http://www.literaturhaus.at.
5. "Ein Reiseführer durch die Abgründe der Psyche Österreichs."
6. For philosophical variations on each of these positions, see both Hofstadter and Dennett (1981) and Deleuze and Guattari (1987).

Works Cited

Adorno, T. W. 1989. *Ästhetische Theorie* [9. Auflage]. Frankfurt am Main: Suhrkamp.
Borges, J. L. 1962. Borges and I. In *Labyrinths: Selected Stories and Other Writings*. Edited by Donald A. Yates and James E. Irby. New York: New Directions.

de Bruyn, Günter. 1995. *Das erzählte Ich. Über Wahrheit und Dichtung in der Autobiographie*. Frankfurt am Main: S. Fischer.

Deleuze, Giles and Félix Guattari. 1987. *A Thousand Plateaus: Capitalism and Schizophrenia*. Translation and foreword by Brian Massumi. Minneapolis: University of Minneapolis Press.

Frischmuth, Barbara. 1996. Ein Gespräch mit Barbara Frischmuth. Interview by Lori Ann Ingalsbe. *Modern Austrian Literature* Vol. 29, No. 1.

Handke, Peter. 1966. Wenn ich schreibe. *Akzente* Vol. 13, No. 5.

Hofstadter, Douglas R. and Daniel C. Dennett, editors. 1981. *The Mind's I: Fantasies and Reflections on Self and Soul*. New York: Basic Books.

Pascal, Roy. 1960. *Design and Truth in Autobiography*. Cambridge: Harvard University Press.

Sill, Oliver. 1991. *Zerbrochene Spiegel. Studien zur Theorie und Praxis modernen autobiographischen Erzählens*. Berlin: Walter de Gruyter.

Will the Real Barbara Frischmuth Please Stand Up? On Autobiography and Literary Creation

Gerald Chapple

From 1956 to 1978, a popular television quiz show, *To Tell the Truth*, used to have as its weekly guest a famous person accompanied by two imitators. All three would be seated with their faces hidden from view. Then the trio would be quizzed to see if people could figure out who was the real McCoy, until the emcee would ask, "Will the real X please stand up?" The masks would come off and the famous face would come to light. The show died in spite of a few attempts to revive it, but it bequeathed to the language the now legendary formula which suggested the title for my contribution to the present volume. I am interested in the portrait of the author as it emerges from that author's writings, either literary or nonliterary, as a clue, ultimately, to a better understanding, first of those written works, and second of the person who created them. My concern is not to discover a portrait of the author's "real" self as the citizen or private person who buys groceries and weeds gardens, but rather to piece together from those works the self-portrait(s) of the author as "persona(e)" which are hidden to varying degrees. The object of my study closely resembles what Hugo von Hofmannsthal came to call, after reading an author intensively, that author's "face"— more precisely, his "*geistiges Gesicht*"—a difficult phrase to translate because *geistig* can mean intellectual, spiritual, or mental, or all three at once.[1] The metaphor became his favorite one for trying to describe his overall understanding of the unique and essential quality of any writer's work and of the person(ality) who created it, for these were inseparably and equally "real" to Hofmannsthal in all the senses of *geistig* just listed.

At some level or other, autobiography is unavoidable for any writer. Turning life into literature is always the first stage of a hide-and-seek game; the author is in disguise, but present, so that each work of fiction—my object of study in this article—is in part an autobiographical document. For some reason we as readers find it difficult *not* to want to "seek" the "hidden" authors through, behind, or beyond their works. (To yield to this innate curiosity is more legitimate in some strands of critical theory than it is to follow the well-known heresy of going in the opposite direction and explaining the work *through* the author.) Perhaps we are fascinated by literary documents because by their very nature they are designed both to tell and to hide truth, or maybe even different truths, at one and the same time.[2] By the mere act of creating literature, a writer turns biography into art to some degree, and it is precisely the mixture of "fictionality" and "factuality" that can generate both the reader's attraction and the critic's questions.[3]

Thomas Mann was once forced to deal in public with the issue of using real models without disguising them sufficiently after one of his relatives found that Mann's first novel, *The Buddenbrooks* (1901), contained too much "reality" because it seemed to him that the family was too transparently portrayed. For some in his family, art had too closely imitated life. Years later, Mann rethought the issue in a piece for a Munich newspaper, which is worth reading in the context of transposing either life into literature, or the "real" world into the reality of fiction. *Bilse and Me*—other reasons for the article's origins need not concern us here—defined and defended the writer's necessary use of (auto)biographical material (Mann 1984, 17–28). To use older rhetorical terms: he avoided picking one of the alternatives, *imitatio* or *inventio*, and ended up with a *transmutatio*, arguing that the writer was not a recorder of objective, external realities but a processor of them. Literary creation was subjective, always about the author; writing was a "subjective deepening or intensification [*Vertiefung*] of reality" (22).

The question of the author's real presence and actual visibility in the work was famously epitomized by the ambiguous title of Goethe's memoirs, *Dichtung und Wahrheit*—"Poetry and Truth," but not "Poetry *or* Truth," leaving the question open as to whether the two are complementary or mutually exclusive. This has long been a moot point, of course, even before the Romantics' concern with the self in fiction, which grew out of Rousseau's "confessional" literature and fed on Goethe's later and oft-quoted statement that his own works were nothing but "fragments of a grand confession." The issue is as persistent as it is vexatious, and I turn to Barbara Frischmuth as an example of a contemporary writer who provides a case study on the matter of turning biography into a piece of fiction. What follows are some thoughts on the problem of using a particular approach for studying the question. Surveying some central themes should demonstrate why and how Frischmuth's oeuvre seems to me to be worthy of a more thorough study along lines similar to those I will suggest.[4]

To avoid misunderstanding: the genre of autobiography per se is not relevant here by virtue of the simple fact that Barbara Frischmuth has not written one as yet. There are some questions arising from the fact that every work of literature is to some extent a self-portrait of the artist. If it is a given that autobiographical elements are a part of every fiction, then how can the student of an author's complete works bring that writer's "face" into focus in order to make use of this knowledge for the ultimate twin goals of understanding the work *and* the writer without having to write a full-blown biography?

Stating the same problem in another way, Frischmuth herself once spoke on the relationship between what the writer finds in the real world (*Vorgefundenes*) and what the writer invents for himself (*Erfundenes*):

> In my case, I can never sever the connection between invented things and those I find around me. It's a separation I hardly ever make because it's often not really important in practice to go back and see where I got something from. It has to fit the context I need it for, has to fit and sit right, whether I've made it up or simply found it.... It's always just a question of composition, of connecting up, of a new context for the things you

find or invent. So I don't think it's very important to make any distinction here. (Frischmuth 1989, 91)

Frischmuth downplays the difference between things you make up and what is really there before your very eyes. For her, the age-old controversy in literary creation of *imitatio* vs. *inventio* is of little importance.

A theoretical approach I find attractive for my purposes is the stimulating one that Jacques Catteau adopted in 1978 for his *La Création littéraire chez Dostoïevski*, which the bibliographic article on Dostoevsky in the *Encyclopedia Britannica* has called "outstanding." Let me briefly outline what is appealing about his method.

Catteau's theoretical framework allows him to connect Dostoevsky to his themes, figures, and works, while avoiding the pitfalls of pure biographism on the one hand and of pure formalism on the other. It is a psychological approach, not a psychoanalytical one; the holistic, synthesizing method examines the formative factors in his subject's life and person to see how they shaped a particular literary imagination. He divides the "creative environment" into two types: the real, physical one composed of what a traditional positivist would have called external influences, and the mental one that an author has in part created because of his psychological make-up, his reading, and so on. Catteau's primary goal is challenging: to isolate "deep structures" by tracing how personality, the unconscious, and the literary mind, together with formative life experiences, determine artistic decisions. Catteau disengages the psychological constants, showing how they ultimately surface in actual poetic works. In so doing he can often account for *why* an author (not just Dostoevsky) writes *what* he writes and *when* and *how* he writes it—and also, interestingly enough, why an author's obsessions may lead to bad artistic decisions and cause a work to fail. In the interpretive process, everything Dostoevsky wrote receives equal hermeneutic weight: the successes and failures among the published works, as well as the drafts, notes, plans, letters, articles, and his collections of newspaper clippings.

This may sound like a mere offshoot of psychological positivism, or like a variation of the genre of the "inner biography," but that might well be because a short descriptive summary cannot do justice to the subtlety and excitement of Catteau's argument and its implementation. For myself, I find his technique valuable because it can shed new light on key works, upgrade minor or overlooked ones, and lend new significance to fragments, drafts, notes, essays, and articles, which literary critics often underplay or ignore completely if they choose to focus on a canon of major publications.

I think this approach can be fruitfully applied to Frischmuth, even though she is, admittedly, no Austrian Dostoevsky, and although there are no letters or large collections of notes and drafts to consult. After more than thirty years as a practicing author and translator, she has created a body of published work substantial enough to bear this kind of critical scrutiny, with more than four hundred primary texts (including reprintings) listed in the most recent bibliography of her work.[5] Fortunately, there are more than two dozen personal interviews as well, and Renhardt's bibliography lists an astonishing number of essays and speeches that contain much material about Frischmuth herself. And of course there is a bonus: the author is there to be questioned, which Catteau could not do.

My proposal, then, is to weigh Catteau's method to find out whether it can help with at least part of the hermeneutic task of discovering some deep structures in Frischmuth. This would be done primarily by interpreting the connections between her literary figures and themes and the person who created them. The crux is this: How can we integrate the two Barbaras ("persona" and "person") to arrive at the desired in-depth image of the author, to have her "stand up" and let us see her "spiritual face," in Hofmannsthal's sense? With Catteau in mind I examine Frischmuth's writing in two stages, first by isolating seven readily identifiable themes and concerns from works that seem suitable for Catteau's type of analysis, without prejudging or putting the theoretical cart before the horse. The second step is to examine how certain themes reappear, change, or disappear, in two periods of her creative work. Because space is limited and her thirty-year oeuvre is vast, I restrict the second part to two periods, one at the beginning of her career and the other in the 1990s. More specifically, the first time span covers 1968 to 1974 (the self-portrait in her best-known work, *The Convent School* [*Die*

Klosterschule, 1968], is crucial here) and the second time period is the decade beginning in 1988 (where the semi-autobiographical figure of Vevi Schwarz in the 1990 novel *Einander Kind* is the most recent partial self-portrait in her fiction).[6] This means omitting the years from 1974 to 1987, including her first trilogy of novels, but there is enough material here to try out Catteau's model and its possible relevance for understanding all of Frischmuth's works, their creator, and her process of literary creation. We should keep in mind Frischmuth's own cautious and sensible caveat about using a writer's biography as an interpretive aid: "The simple fact of your own biography brings you into contact with particular problems, or even makes you aware of certain issues in the first place. But there is a lot of leeway between your life story and whatever it is that's supposed to turn into a book. I think people very often make the mistake of pursuing autobiography too energetically—it's at best an initial cause—and of reducing far too much down to it."[7]

As I have said above, Frischmuth has yet to write that autobiography, and it so happens that biographical material on her has been slow in becoming available.[8] But there are tantalizing fragments *in loco autobiographiae*, as it were, in particular an extensive one titled *Years* (*Jahre*), which presents her childhood in a nontraditional narrative mode (Frischmuth 1971). Rather than writing a linear, continuous piece of prose, Frischmuth composed several dozen pages of randomly ordered "memory bytes" from her early childhood—that is, sharply recalled and straightforwardly described incidents. It is left up to the reader to "compose" the work and reshape the pieces of autobiographical information into some sort of continuous narrative. Twenty years later, in *Aquarii/Water Sprites* (*Wassermänner*), she included a few informative pages about herself—"Me on Myself" ("Ich über mich")—and reprinted the brief autobiographical sketch, "I Was Born beside a Lake" ("Ich bin an einem See geboren worden"), first published in 1982.[9] Putting these together with her nonfiction, interviews, essays, and speeches, where she speaks her mind and speaks out, we can sketch a portrait of a thoughtful, direct, and lively person who is committed to, and articulate about, her art and its purpose.[10]

The earliest determining biographical factors that she herself has repeatedly acknowledged are three: her childhood in her native village of Altaussee, the overpowering attraction of language, and then literature, which is not surprising in the case of so verbal an author. Let us look at these briefly, because they point to some concerns that lie more deeply than others, and so they inform her fiction to different degrees throughout her career.

Altaussee, a mountain village forty kilometers east of Salzburg, was "father and mother to me" (Serke 1982, 184). Growing up beside a lake made a powerful initial impact on the young Barbara: "I was already writing when I was ten; my first and favorite topics were corpses of drowned people. We lived right on the lake, and a body would turn up every now and then."[11] Frischmuth's fascination with water obviously was strong right from the beginning and is a fine example of those deep, psychological, and sensual responses that Catteau finds so revealing: an unconscious/conscious feeling, a "deep structure" of the mind that can, when creating literature, surface as an obsessive artistic theme. Lively and repeated responses like this one are a part of Frischmuth's make-up; not unexpectedly, they have frequently determined her choice of powerful literary subjects that have become her favorite themes. This feature of her work needs closer study, but for now it is enough to point to Georg Pichler's 1992 analysis, which tied her love of water to a deep-seated urge to travel; in her life, this meant going on study trips abroad beginning from the age of nineteen.[12] While examining the impact of this motivation on her fiction, he interpreted her 1981 short story that takes place underwater, "Journey to the End of the World" ("Reise ans Ende der Welt"), as a key instance where travel and the submarine experience are fused with an existential theme in a creative work.

As far as her talent for languages is concerned, her choice of a subject of formal study was dictated in part by the enclosed environment of her native valley, where she developed "something like an enormous longing for exotic things" (Frischmuth 1989, 90). While still in her late teens she studied Hungarian and Turkish in Graz, and then Near Eastern languages in Vienna, so that not only was language a theme in her writing from the beginning, but her linguistic aptitude also helped make her an accomplished translator from Hungarian, Turkish, and English. There are as yet no critical assessments of her translations into English, neither of the nonsense verse of Edward Lear nor, more importantly, of her adaptation of Salman Rushdie's *Haroun and the Sea of Stories* as a six-part series for German and Austrian radio in 1995 (a cursory review shows her to be very skilled indeed, but the texts await closer examination). Her study of Near Eastern languages was prompted by the reading of her first (and still much-loved) major work of world literature, *The Arabian Nights*, which had the secondary effect of establishing her attraction to the literature of Islam (von Matt 1991, 41). She has also been forthright about other predilections and formative influences, for example her delight in the literature of the fantastic and bizarre by—to name but a few—E. T. A. Hoffmann, Orlando-Herzmanofsky, and Vonnegut, and her admiration for experimental language jugglers like Arno Schmidt and Lewis Carroll, one of her enduring heroes. It is not so much a question of "influence" here; these names simply give an idea of the authors who can help us get closer to her own literary imagination.

To these three "conditioning" factors, which have become recurring themes in her writings, we may add three others. The first is a concern for children, both as subject and as audience. Riki Winter has made an eloquent plea for giving Frischmuth's literature for children and young adults equal consideration when assessing her creative work.[13] The second area develops logically from this: the portrayal and analysis of women's roles. From 1973 on, mothers, wives, and divorcées populate Frischmuth's works—all of them social roles she herself had assumed by then. Without being an "emancipating" feminist, she has presented a whole series of portraits of women and explored their problems (reviewers and critics have pointed out that her female characters are almost always better realized than the male ones). Beginning in the 1980s these portrayals and problems took on wider dimensions as Frischmuth started integrating her more recent understanding of history and myth into her fiction. Third, the study of foreign languages and literatures was bound to lead to study and travel abroad, and she spent a number of years in Hungary, Turkey, Iran, Egypt, and the United States, mainly in the 1960s and 1970s. Pichler was the first to put his finger on an all-important geographical and cultural factor, the alternating pull toward her homeland and toward foreign lands. He located a definite leaning toward the "Other" when Frischmuth embarked on her career as a student, which overtook the earlier attachment to her Styrian birthplace that had frequently functioned in all kinds of her writing as a setting or a motif. Pichler argued that, after her stays abroad, she turned again to focus on things Austrian rather than more exotic subjects. Pichler finished his article before 1992, but as we shall see below, this last claim was quickly out of date.

Finally, a seventh recurring topic in her work and thought is the dream world. I have pointed out the absence of a formal autobiography in Frischmuth's voluminous work. What we have instead is a remarkable surrogate: a series of six lectures on poetics that she gave in Munich in November 1990, *The Dream of Literature—The Literature of Dream* (*Traum der Literatur—Literatur des Traums*). The reader who knows German can do no better than to turn to this rich and engaging eighty-page volume as a gateway to Barbara Frischmuth's mind and work. Not only does it contain a thoughtful and informed discussion of women's literature and of myth, among other topics, but it is also a gold mine of information on her fascination with dreams and how they interact with her creative imagination to produce literary texts, and not just her own. Here the critic has his work cut out for him. *The Dream of Literature* is an eminent text for understanding Frischmuth's powerful fascination with the world of the unconscious, and for understanding her own, especially in the face of that absent autobiography. And a practitioner of Jacques Catteau's method who wants to delve into the connections between Frischmuth's mind and art will obviously find the volume a fertile field.

The themes outlined above—her Austrian childhood, the appeal of language and of literature, her concern for children and women, her openness to other cultures, and her exploration of the dream world—are central to Frischmuth's large and varied oeuvre. If her whole career cannot be reviewed here—it is indeed a task for a monographic study—at least a sketch of the topography of two important phases of her creative life can indicate how her key themes are articulated in her work, sometimes intertwined, at significant stages in her life and career. I focus first on the beginning of her literary career, and then turn to the last decade or so, which marks a significant shift in her literary and nonliterary interests and writing. This selective review of some of her works will give a sense of the author's development over a thirty-year span.

The period 1968–1974 opened when she was 27 with the sensational debut in 1968 of *The Convent School*, a prose work that a perceptive critic later called "a parable of adolescence" (Brunelli 1986). Initially it was seen in some quarters as a scandalous attack on the ideology and practice of education in a Roman Catholic convent. Having attended a convent school herself between the ages of eleven and fourteen, Frischmuth had to fend off charges that the book was either too directly autobiographical or an anticlerical tract slyly disguised in a modest volume written from the convent girls' point of view. Not so: her own stated purpose was linguistic, not religious, a defense articulated in an interview sixteen years later: "For me it was a book in which I tried to unmask a closed system by means of its language. Because I knew the Catholic system best, it's the one I chose.... For me the Catholic Church was a social system, a very closed one, and by using it I was able to demonstrate precisely what I wanted to show about systems like it" (Kuschel 1984, 113). Although the narrated experience may lean heavily on actual experience, it is coolly narrated in the first and third person, not as autobiography but as (often comic) fiction, as fourteen brief prose "chapters," structured so that they do *not* add up to a conventional novel or novella. Although the subject matter is something she knew inside out, her objectifying techniques temporize the autobiographical element, and these often ironic distancing effects were to remain a central part of her narrative arsenal. A dozen years later she pointed out the autobiographical parallels of using story-telling as a coping strategy during her stay at the convent school: "I evaded the pressure from above by my intellectual curiosity and delight in learning and sidestepped the pressure from my classmates by telling them stories every evening in the dorm or the infirmary (where I often sought asylum so I could read in peace). That way I was merely squished but not ground down."[14] Her fascination with language, her innate sense of humor, and her fledgling narrative gifts acted as counterweights to the oppressive regimen of convent life.

After *The Convent School* she composed her first pieces of children's literature along with an unusual work for adults about children, *Amoral Children's Rattle* (*Amoralische Kinderklapper*). The title is subversive, an inversion of a popular, eighteenth-century, edifying book titled *Moral Children's Rattle*. Her unexpected purpose here was to make children a fit subject for *adult* readers: "I've tried in some of my books, those that are not books for children, to emancipate the child as subject-matter for literature. To emancipate the child from its purely autobiographical role ... and by treating children as persons of equal rank in literature" (Frischmuth 1990).

The second part of *Days and Years* (1971), as was noted above, records with precision memories of her childhood; they are also technically interesting as five-finger exercises in pointillism. This was to pay stylistic dividends a few years later when she crafted her first novel and a group of four stories. The novel, *The Shadow Disappears in the Sun* (*Das Verschwinden des Schattens in der Sonne*, 1973), was part of the fallout from her studies of Islamic mysticism, which had taken her to Turkey when she was twenty. At first glance, autobiographical content seems to dictate the novel's premise, as it did in *The Convent School*. The heroine is carrying out research for a dissertation on exactly the same topic that Frischmuth chose for *her* dissertation. Whether or not the novel is more autobiography than fiction is a moot point. In a later essay, Frischmuth denies that it was the former—the novel "is not *my* story"—while admitting that *The Shadow Disappears* was what her "unwritten dissertation" had ultimately turned into.[15] I would prefer to regard it as her *re*-written dissertation, because the historical research material comes alive thanks to its being embedded in an extensive fictional narrative about a young Austrian student's first encounter with a Muslim country.

Frischmuth reserved her patently autobiographical reportage on her Turkish adventure for some prose sketches that appeared in the same year as the novel. In these four brief pieces, labeled collectively "The Better Life" ("Das bessere Leben"), the fictitious "I" is less veiled but nonetheless fictionalized in a style more personal, anecdotal, and experimental than the novel's.[16]

Turkey again provides the setting for impressionistic sketches centering around love and politics, with the former more graphically described, as it was in the novel as well. The title alludes to the idealism behind the entangling web of experiences in the politically unstable Turkey of the 1960s. Anonymously narrated, the texts are mostly written in the third person, with a cool delivery that might have had a flattening effect but for the passion smoldering beneath many of her responses to the people, situations, and scenery she describes.

After returning to Austria and entering into married life, Frischmuth's fictional world in the early 1970s was enriched by four long stories about problems that women have with others and themselves, *Chasing after the Wind: Four Stories* (*Haschen nach Wind: Erzählungen*).[17] Written while she was pregnant (although the last story was written after her son's birth), the book presents detailed psychological studies of women in dangerous or deteriorating relationships. It is told in the third person with what was to become her own particular blend of objectivity and intensity; her artistic versatility was already being acknowledged as another hallmark of her literary achievement.

The most striking feature of the latest decade in Frischmuth's career—the second phase of her life under examination—is the sheer volume of her productivity, an explosion unmatched in her substantial output. My survey of the period is restricted to elucidating how three important themes from the early part of her career are modified and complicated. First, she consolidates her earlier writings about Altaussee and her attachment to it; second, she starts to write works for children and young adults again; and third, she moves her cultural concerns ahead in a new direction: rather than keeping to the narrower compass of recounting her first-hand experiences in foreign cultures, she now speaks out as a citizen about the realities of contemporary interculturalism, which means the European-Islamic cultural interface in particular. A brief evaluation of her important relevant writings in this latest phase of her literary output—and her *non*-literary works are crucial here—will orient the reader to significant continuities and changes as they throw light on the relationship of biography to fiction.

The year 1990 had brought with it a new stage in her life. As she entered her fiftieth year she took on the task of summing up. She began to gather together what she had to say about her formative experiences in Austria, collecting some important statements and much of her miscellaneous prose and early poetry in *Aquarii/Water Sprites* in 1991. Perhaps she was spurred on by writing her "Heimat" novel about Altaussee, *Einander Kind* (1990). One of its main characters, Genoveva (Vevi) Schwarz, stands head and shoulders above her most recent fictional figures, who are readily recognizable as avatars of their creator. Consider some of the resemblances between author and character: As a child Vevi was a tomboy, attended a convent school, and loved to spin captivating yarns. At the time the novel takes place she too is a public figure, a writer and performer bent upon raising the political consciousness of her nation during the fiftieth anniversary year of the Anschluss, which was also a central aim of Frischmuth's in writing the novel. Although Vevi lives in Vienna (as Frischmuth did until 1997), she returns in the novel's climactic chapter to her roots, to the family hotel on the lake in the mountains (clearly Altaussee, which has also been Frischmuth's year-round residence since 1997).[18]

It was one thing for her to choose the child as a title and major metaphor for a novel; it was quite another to reestablish herself as one of Austria's foremost writers for children and young adults. Frischmuth once stated that she doesn't always simply sit down with the express intention of writing a children's book: "I write what I have to write, can write, want to write—and it often turns out that it's for children" (Frischmuth 1990). The fact is, she had not published a book for children or young adults since 1985; suddenly, from 1991, there was a spate of them. All in the same year, a children's novel from 1972 was reissued and two new novels appeared, one of which was immediately made into a film for television. Three subsequent books can be added to Renhardt's bibliography. *A Good-Night Story for Maria Carolina* (*Gutenachtgeschichte für Maria Carolina*, 1994) and *About the Girl Who Walked on Water* (*Vom Mädchen, das übers Wasser ging*, 1996) were large-format illustrated books for children. The more complex genre of the child-centered novel is represented by *Never Mind* (*Machtnix*, 1993), a problematic work to be discussed below. Several stories in the collection, *Heart of a*

Witch: Stories (*Hexenherz: Erzählungen*, 1994), have children as the main characters.[19] With a nod toward one of her literary heroes, E. T. A. Hoffmann, she then published *Donna and Dario* (*Donna und Dario*, 1997), a delightful prize-winning novel set largely in the animal world, starring two cats, a raven, and an assortment of other animals.

The 1990s, then, have seen in part a consolidation of some early themes as indicative of a coming to terms with her place of origin. The decade has also witnessed a rekindling of her lifelong interest in children, both as fictitious characters and as audience. These are but two chapters in the story, for there is a third way in which Barbara Frischmuth has put new wine into old bottles: Her earlier multicultural and intercultural interests have re-emerged in literary form and nonliterary media, with the focus less on Austria and more on Islam, or on the interaction between Muslim cultures and Western Europe.

Signs of this new development had been apparent as early as the mid-1980s, in her 1987 novel, *On Relationships* (*Über die Verhältnisse*), where Turkey and Turkish characters reappeared after a thirteen-year absence. Furthermore, the novel was strongly "international" compared to the earlier *The Shadow Disappears in the Sun*, because its cast of characters and settings are shared between two countries. Vienna predominates at the outset, but the scene shifts more and more fatefully to Turkey. The East-West encounter is further emphasized by the symbolic Turkish-Austrian parentage of Ayhan, the suitor of the rebellious Viennese daughter of a protective, Demeter-like mother. Two short fictional works from the 1990s deal with East-West encounters of different kinds and in varying degrees. One is "The Dalai Lama's Laughter" ("Das Lachen des Dalai Lama"), the masterful story concluding her 1994 collection of short stories, *Heart of a Witch*. Probably her best short story to date, it is both violent—a woman is slowly dying in the Vienna subway after trying to stop some skinheads from beating up a Turkish teenager—and poignant, when the woman's last thoughts revolve around her memories of a picture of the Dalai Lama and of quotations from the *Tibetan Book of the Dead* (162–174). A heavily autobiographical sketch based on some of her Iranian acquaintances followed in 1996, "The Persian Dinner" ("Das persische

Abendessen," 1996, 59–72). That same year also marked the reissuing of her first novel, *The Shadow Disappears in the Sun* from 1973, which brought her now decades-old interest in matters Turkish and Islamic more firmly back into the spotlight. The work can now be reinterpreted from a new perspective and in the context of our current awareness of the issues illustrated by the heroine's experience, as Daniel Rothenbühler remarked in an insightful review (Rothenbühler 1996). Her novel is quite possibly even more relevant in today's multicultural world than it was twenty-five years ago because its present context has caught up with its message, so to speak, and it made very good sense to reissue it for today's readers.

Frischmuth's latest work of fiction is one of her longest novels and one of her three best. *The Script of the Friend* (*Die Schrift des Freundes*, 1998) brings Turks to Vienna instead of an Austrian student to Istanbul, as was the case a quarter of a century earlier. For the interweaving of its many themes alone, the novel must be considered a tour de force. It is at once a love story, a detective novel, an exploration of the difficulties facing Turks living in a foreign country, a description of an old internal conflict between a little-known Muslim sect and Islamic orthodoxy, and a noncompetitive juxtaposition of Western modes of (computer) languages and Eastern modes of writing and thought—in order to say by implication that the one should learn about and from the other. Thomas Rothschild, always one of Frischmuth's most perceptive reviewers, went so far as to call this aspect of the novel "Lessing's parable of the rings in modern form," and I would agree (Rothschild 1998, 11). The young heroine, however, looks very little like Frischmuth, which is symptomatic of a severe reduction in the overt biographical component of her longer works.

It would be wrong-headed to dismiss these recent works of fiction as the mere recyclings of a sensitive and intelligent author's long-lasting love of other languages and cultures. There is far more to it. She has found a niche in European letters she has long been qualified to fill, that of interpreter of East to West as a recognized spokesman for a variety of Islamic causes, writers, and problems. In a word, she has become decidedly engagée and is wholeheartedly committed to this new role. Evidence of her seriousness and energy is everywhere in her nonfictional prose, her several essays, speeches, and reviews of Muslim writers from many different countries. Two of the most important ones, when read side by side, give an accurate picture of her thinking and of the impetus behind much of her writing. They are "Looking over the Fence" ("Blick über den Zaun"; Lützeler 1995) and "The Europe *I* Mean" ("Das Europa, das ich meine"; Frischmuth 1996, 46–59). An idea of the breadth of her knowledge can be gleaned from the series of articles she wrote for two major Vienna newspapers, *Die Presse*, in early 1996, and a number of articles and reviews in *Der Standard* in 1997 and 1998. (This is not to forget her translating achievements, the most significant being the adaptation for radio of Rushdie's novel, *Haroun and the Sea of Stories*, in 1995.) In 1996 she served on the jury for the Neustadt Prize in the United States, choosing the writer Assia Djebar, the Algerian woman who was the eventual winner. Her guiding principles are transparently clear: tolerance, openness, and mutual respect are recurring concepts. Listen, for example, to her in a recent speech giving a reason for translating Rushdie, for whom she has great personal sympathy and who is the only Muslim author she has actually put into German:

> The intensifying conflict between Islamic and Western countries can never again leave me cold, for the very reason that it is not only the incongruities on both sides that keep aggressions alive (like the centuries-old neglect of the spirit of Islamic culture), but because it is really an issue of opposing sets of principles (e.g., community vs. individualism). And since a small part of me is always a participant in this conflict, I can do nothing less than promote the Islamic tradition of tolerance which today's Islamists and fundamentalists seem to have long forgotten. That was one reason why I translated ... Salman Rushdie.... Not in order to antagonize devout Muslims. (Lützeler 1995, 26)

The composite portrait of the author that emerges from her fiction and nonfiction in the current decade reveals a versatile woman who speaks to many audiences in several voices and modes on topics of serious international concern. She carries out her program with all due modesty and a clear sense that literature is not politics: "In no way do I see myself playing the role of the nation's conscience, of the moral avant-garde or whatever. I don't think it's literature's job. What literature *can* do is to open up a topic and pursue it into every nook and cranny. Anything that aims too concretely at the political situation has misappropriated the medium" (Kuschel 1984, 124–125).

It is difficult to point to any one reason for this marvelous five-year outpouring of geopolitical writings. It could be a delayed reaction caused by a necessarily protracted gestation period, as was the case with her latest radio play, *A Love Affair in Erzurum* (*Eine Liebe in Erzurum*, 1994): "I had no idea how much distance you need to become a convincing poacher in another culture. It took me all of thirty years before I was able to get the phenomenon of Erzurum into some sort of shape that was halfway plausible" (Lützeler 1995, 20). What *is* clear is that the route Frischmuth has followed as author and intercultural commentator throughout the 1990s leads us to think that Georg Pichler's 1992 assessment must be revised and updated, certainly where he concludes that "other cultures are of no great importance in Frischmuth's work." The situation has since changed radically regarding "Heimat" and "Fremde" (Pichler's useful polarity), given the recent veritable explosion of spirited speeches, essays, and articles on matters Islamic and European, let alone of novels and stories.

I want to return briefly to one feature of Jacques Catteau's approach. We recall that he showed how necessary it is to consider failures along with an author's achievements, and sure enough, there is one dissonant voice in the chorus of Barbara Frischmuth's successes: the critical, and perhaps artistic, failure of the novel *Never Mind*, which had consequences for other works that Frischmuth was writing around the same time.

First, the sequence of events. Some time in 1991, the year after her best-seller *Einander Kind* came out, Frischmuth began work on the novel that was eventually to become *The Script of the Friend*. During these preliminaries she became fascinated by an idea for a novel about children, the end of the world, and computers, so she abandoned the Austrian-Turkish novel for the single-minded pursuit of this new artistic vision. *Never Mind* is hard to categorize as to genre: it is a hybrid, a sort of cross between *Alice in Wonderland* and science fiction. Now although Frischmuth has been adept at creating mixed genres, this time the result was a critical disaster. It is a puzzle why, after a string of critical successes, the author put aside a promising work-in-progress on a favorite theme and strayed off in a completely different direction, and with such dire results. Of course, you don't win them all, as the saying goes, but—to keep with the question of genre—why did she feel compelled to create a cross between allegory and futuristic fairy tale rather than keeping with the form of the realist novel, as she had been doing for several years? Was it maybe because the lure of fantastic literature just wouldn't leave her alone? Did yet another scenario constructed around the computer world, as both works were, send her usually reliable instinct down a garden path? It is a difficult problem to solve at this stage, but one result is apparent: after being sidetracked for years, her new "bicultural" novel, arguably her best work to date, did not see the light of day until early in 1998, many years after it would have under normal circumstances.

It appears to me, in the end, that Catteau's integrative approach of delving into the process of literary creation would indeed be profitable for a comprehensive study of Barbara Frischmuth and her works. Even though her "middle period" was omitted, I have tried to demonstrate that hers is a substantial, varied, and fascinating body of work, the product of a literate and versatile imagination—rich material that will be rewarded by further study along Catteau's lines. Just sifting through her fiction and nonfiction has already raised some intriguing questions. For instance, why has Hungary been relatively underplayed over the last twenty-five years?[20] Why does she by and large avoid tragedy, but not death or violence? How exactly does her love of "ironic subversiveness," especially of the female variety, play out in her works or constitute a major structural element?[21] What is the psychology behind her persistent attraction to water, and what are the poetic implications of this? Why the sudden return to writing fiction for young people? And since she is, after all, a *literary* artist, what about the formal and stylistic implications I have hardly touched upon, especially the choice of genres for the realization of the seven themes outlined earlier? These and other "Whys" call out for further investigation, as do the "Hows" or "How comes." For now, I have tried to make a start by simply mapping parts of the "What," "Where," and "When."

As we saw at the beginning of this article, Hofmannsthal's constant search for a writer's "spiritual face" was a synthesizing metaphor for an author as portrayed in the sum total of his works. Because no study of Frischmuth's entire literary career exists, I think an analysis of her works that mainly follows Catteau's approach will arrive at a larger, finer-grained, synthesized, "real" portrait of the artist—one, I would hope, that could "stand up" in both senses of the word.

Thomas Mann felt that a true poet (*Dichter*) "is working on himself when he works," in the full knowledge that in fiction, the "self," the "I," is always a fiction, always a mask (Mann 1984, 24). This was part of his argument against the all-too-common, naive belief that the "real-life" model is identical with the fictitious character, and that the author is one with his literary creations. Barbara Frischmuth too creates literary truth out of biographical truth, revealing "herself" while hiding her "self."[22]

Notes

1. Some typical examples from two volumes of Herbert Steiner's edition, Hugo von Hofmannsthal, *Gesammelte Werke in Einzelausgaben* (Frankfurt am Main: Fischer, 1950): Hofmannsthal uses the phrase when referring to Tolstoy and Kierkegaard (*Prosa III*, 1952, pp. 490, 351) and Molière (*Prosa IV*, 1955, p. 86; further general references on pp. 55, 132).

2. See Roy Pascal's (1960) valuable study with the telling title, *Design and Truth in Autobiography*.

3. For a discussion of these two terms see Elbaz (1987, pp. 9–13).

4. My contribution to the present volume is less an interpretive scholarly article than it is an essay serving as prolegomena to a longer study that will for the first time survey the whole range of Barbara Frischmuth's work. The projected book, which will not be a biography, has as its working title *Interpreting Barbara Frischmuth*, with a deliberately double meaning; it refers to both the author and her work, but my aim will be to explore the connection between the two in order to understand the work. The following considerations, although they spring from the larger concern, are germane in the immediate context.

5. Compiled by Maria Renhardt, it appears in Bartsch (1992, 163–201). An invaluable instrument for Frischmuth studies, the volume was

produced at the Franz Nabl Institute for Literary Research in Graz, which houses Frischmuth's manuscripts and a fine collection of her written works of all kinds.

6. *Einander Kind*—a title that so defies translation that I refer to the book only by its German title. An approximation: "You Be the Child for Now and I'll Be the Mother."

7. Interview with Bernhard Wieser, "Keine neue Mauern!" *das MEGAPHON* [Graz] 22, July 1997, 7.

8. The best sources in English are Donald G. Daviau's (1987, 185–206) article, "Barbara Frischmuth," and the up-to-date collection of essays edited by Renate S. Posthofen (1998), *Barbara Frischmuth in Contemporary Context*.

9. The title of *Wassermänner* is ambiguous, as my translation indicates. The articles appeared on pages 200–202 and 202–207 respectively.

10. Of the more than two dozen interviews in print, Gisela Roethke's interview in Posthofen's volume is the only one in English. See Daviau (1987) and Posthofen (1998).

11. "Ich über mich," *Wassermänner*, p. 200. The following stage in her life was the only one she did not write in: "I was already writing as a child, but during puberty I did not write at all" (Frischmuth 1985, p. 43).

12. Georg Pichler, "'Seltsam, daß es mir so wenig ausmacht, nicht anzukommen': Heimat und Fremde bei Barbara Frischmuth," in Bartsch (1992, 57–72). The story referred to in the next sentence first appeared in 1979 and is easily accessible in *Borderland of Dreams: Stories* (*Traumgrenze: Erzählungen*), pp. 42–59.

13. "Zur Kinderliteratur von Barbara Frischmuth," in Bartsch (1992, 99–110). Winter also establishes relevant links between Frischmuth's works for young people and her love of nonsense literature. Further useful material on the subject of the author and children can be found in Gisela Ullrich's little volume (1981), *Barbara Frischmuth: "Jahre" "Zeit, Tschechow zu lesen" "Unzeit" "Bleiben lassen": Mit Materialien*.

14. "Me, about Myself," in *Wassermänner*, pp. 206–207; first published in 1982.

15. "Looking over the Fence" (Blick über den Zaun), originally in Lützeler (1995, p. 22). Since the translations are my own, I refer by title and page to the German version.

16. Published as part of the prose collection, *Return to a Provisionary Point of Departure* (*Rückkehr zum vorläufigen Ausgangspunkt* (Frischmuth 1973).

17. Further interpretation of the work is found in my "Afterword: 'The Vanity of Human Wishes': An Austrian Update," pp. 143–162.

18. For a fuller treatment of the novel's themes, see the author's comments in her Munich lectures, *The Dream of Literature—The Literature of Dream*. For an analysis of Frischmuth's new spin on the Demeter myth in this and two preceding works, see Paul Michael Lützeler, "Barbara Frischmuths Demeter-Trilogie: Mythologische Finde-Spiele in der postmodernen Literatur" (Bartsch 1992, pp. 73–97). See also two articles in English: Gerald Chapple (1996), "Demeter in Altaussee: Frischmuth's Response to Broch's 'Die Verzauberung,'" pp. 544–558; and Gisela Roethke (1998), "Barbara Frischmuth's Novel *Einander Kind* : Fifty Years after the Take-Over of the Nazis in Austria."

19. For a study of the whole book see Gerald Chapple, "The Art at the Heart of Barbara Frischmuth's *Hexenherz*," in Posthofen 1998 (forthcoming).

20. "Relatively," because it is true that two Hungarians play supporting roles in two recent novels. The female companion to the Demeter figure in *On Relationships* is the boisterous and bawdy Borisch, probably Frischmuth's best-realized comic character, whereas the brooding figure of Botond in *Einander Kind*, who murders his first wife and deserts his second, is more nebulous and less successfully realized.

21. Frischmuth used the term in an interview, "Im Land der Amaryllis Sternwieser" (von Matt 1991).

22. I would like to thank the Arts Research Board of McMaster University for their help in financing the researching and preparation of this article.

Works Cited

Bartsch, Kurt, Ed. 1992. *Barbara Frischmuth*. Graz: Droschl.

Brunelli, Maria. 1986. Il diavolo e l'educanda. *Il Giornale* (Rome), 25 May.

Catteau, Jacques. 1978. *La Création littéraire chez Dostoïevski*. Paris: Institut des études slaves. Translated by Audrey Littlewood (1989), *Dostoevsky and the Process of Literary Creation*. Cambridge: Cambridge University Press.

Chapple, Gerald. 1996. Demeter in Altaussee: Frischmuth's Response to Broch's 'Die Verzauberung.' In *Geschichte der österreichischen Literatur, Part 2*. Edited by Donald G. Daviau and Herbert Arlt. St. Ingbert: Röhrig.

Daviau, Donald G. 1987. Barbara Frischmuth. In *Major Figures of Contemporary Austrian Literature*. Edited by Donald Daviau. New York: Lang.

Elbaz, Robert. 1987. *The Changing Nature of the Self: A Critical Study of the Autobiographic Discourse*. Iowa City: University of Iowa Press.

Frischmuth, Barbara. 1968. *Die Klosterschule*. Suhrkamp, Frankfurt am Main. Translated by Gerald Chapple and James B. Lawson. *The Convent School*. 1993. Riverside: Ariadne.

Frischmuth, Barbara. 1969. *Amoral Children's Rattle (Amoralische Kinderklapper)*. Frankfurt am Main: Suhrkamp.

Frischmuth, Barbara. 1971. *Days and Years: Propositions Concerning the Situation (Tage und Jahre: Sätze zur Situation)*. Salzburg: Residenz.

Frischmuth, Barbara. 1973. *Das Verschwinden des Schattens in der Sonne*. Salzburg: Residenz (reissued in 1996). Translated by Nicholas J. Meyerhofer. 1998. *The Shadow Disappears in the Sun*. Riverside: Ariadne.

Frischmuth, Barbara. 1973. *Return to a Provisional Point of Departure (Rückkehr zum vorläufigen Ausgangspunkt*. Salzburg: Residenz.

Frischmuth, Barbara. 1974. *Haschen nach Wind: Erzählungen*. Salzburg: Residenz. Translated by Gerald Chapple and James B. Lawson. 1996. *Chasing after the Wind: Four Stories*. Riverside: Ariadne.

Frischmuth, Barbara. 1982. Die Macht neu verteilen, so daß sie keine Gefahr mehr für die Welt bedeutet! In Jürgen Serke, *Frauen schreiben: Ein neues Kapitel deutschsprachiger Literatur*. Frankfurt am Main: Fischer.

Frischmuth, Barbara. 1983. *Borderland of Dreams: Stories (Traumgrenze: Erzählungen)*. Salzburg: Residenz.

Frischmuth, Barbara. 1984. Vom Vergnügen, seine eigene Religion zu haben: Über Mystik, Märchen und Gnosis. In Karl-Josef Kuschel, *Weil wir uns auf dieser Erde nicht ganz zu Hause fühlen: 12 Schriftsteller über Religion und Literatur*. München: Piper.

Frischmuth, Barbara. 1985. Graz—the Key City (Graz—Schlüsselstadt). In *Graz from the Inside: An Anthology (Graz von Innen: Eine Anthologie)*. Graz: Droschl.

Frischmuth, Barbara. 1987. *On Relationships (Über die Verhältnisse)*. Salzburg: Residenz.

Frischmuth, Barbara. 1989. Distance, Restriction, Expanse (Ferne, Enge, Weite). *Autorenporträts*. Transcript of a leaflet accompanying a video. Klagenfurt: Zentrum für Schulversuche und Schulentwicklung des BMUK.

Frischmuth, Barbara. 1990 (December). Lieb ungstüm wie der Wind! *Die Welt*, No. 286, p. xiii.
Frischmuth, Barbara. 1991. *Wassermänner*. Salzburg: Residenz.
Frischmuth, Barbara. 1991. *The Dream of Literature—The Literature of Dream (Traum der Literatur—Literatur des Traums)*. Salzburg: Residenz.
Frischmuth, Barbara. 1993. *Never Mind (Machtnix,* 1993), Salzburg: Residenz.
Frischmuth, Barbara. 1994. *A Good-Night Story for Maria Carolina (Gutenachtgeschichte für Maria Carolina)*. Vienna: Dachs.
Frischmuth, Barbara. 1994. *Heart of a Witch: Stories (Hexenherz: Erzählungen)*. Salzburg: Residenz.
Frischmuth, Barbara. 1995. Blick über den Zaun. In P. M. Lützeler, Ed., *Schreiben zwischen den Kulturen: Beiträge zur deutschsprachigen Gegenwartsliteratur*. Frankfurt am Main: Fischer. p. 22. Translated by Elisabeth Hock. 1995 (Summer). *World Literature Today* 69 (3), 459–462.
Frischmuth, Barbara. 1996. *About the Girl Who Walked on Water (Vom Mädchen, das übers Wasser ging)*. Vienna: Dachs.
Frischmuth, Barbara. 1996 (July). *Literatur und Kritik*, 305–306.
Frischmuth, Barbara. 1996. (Nov-Dec). The Persian Dinner (Das persische Abendessen). *neue deutsche literatur* 43.
Frischmuth, Barbara. 1997. *Donna and Dario (Donna und Dario)*. Aarau: Sauerländer.
Frischmuth, Barbara. 1998. *The Script of the Friend (Die Schrift des Freundes)*. Salzburg: Residenz.
Mann, Thomas. 1984. Bilse und ich. In *Self-Justifications (Rede und Antwort)*, Frankfurt Edition. Frankfurt am Main: Fischer.
Pascal, Roy. 1960. *Design and Truth in Autobiography*. Cambridge, MA: Harvard University Press.
Posthofen, Renate S., Ed. 1998. *Barbara Frischmuth in Contemporary Context*. Riverside: Ariadne.
Roethke, Gisela. 1998. Barbara Frischmuth's Novel *Einander Kind*: Fifty Years after the Take-Over of the Nazis in Austria. In R. S. Posthofen, Ed., *Barbara Frischmuth in Contemporary Context*. Riverside: Ariadne.
Rothenbühler, Daniel. 1996. Die Suche nach dem Simurgh: Ein alter Roman von Barbara Frischmuth. *Tagesanzeiger*, 29 April.
Rothschild, Thomas. 1998. Gott im Internet: Kabinettstück *zeitgenössischer* Prosa. *Freitag: Die Ost-West-Wochenzeitung* (Berlin), 8 May.

Ullrich, Gisela. 1981. *Barbara Frischmuth: "Jahre" "Zeit, Tschechow zu lesen" "Unzeit" "Bleiben lassen" : Mit Materialien.* Stuttgart: Klett.

von Matt, Beatrice. 1991 (February). Im Land der Amaryllis Sternwieser: Ein Gespräch mit Barbara Frischmuth. *Neue Zürcher Zeitung* 8, p. 41.

Amy or the Metamorphosis as a Bildungsroman

Michael Ossar

At the end of the first novel of her trilogy, *The Mystification of Sophie Silber* (1976), Barbara Frischmuth has her fairies and spirits describe the metamorphosis that is later realized in *Amy or the Metamorphosis* (*Amy oder Die Metamorphose*):

> We can take on the form of their women and children and distribute the power in such a way that they are no longer a danger to the world. We can try to teach them, especially friendliness, affection, and pleasure in all beings and all things.

And when Amy Stern discusses with her new-found acquaintance, Hans Altmann, what she learns from observing life in the restaurant where she works as a waitress, she also uses the term "metamorphosis," this time to describe both a personal and a social transformation:

> The quantity of internalized modes of behavior is getting more and more oppressive to the degree that one tries to escape them. They avenge their neglect. And yet they are not strong enough to prevent the metamorphosis. They have failed so often and on such a scale that their slow disappearance is certain, and it will take generations until new, accepted modes of behavior will have arisen. (186)

It is the tension between these two meanings of metamorphosis, between Amy Stern's personal transformation and the transformation of society, that gives this novel its schizophrenic face.

> When Gregor Samsa one morning awakened from restless dreams he found himself in his bed transformed into a huge

bug ... "What's happened to me," he thought. It was not a dream. (Franz Kafka)

Unlike Gregor Samsa's metamorphosis in Kafka's story, which is the objective correlative of his own idiosyncratic psychological *condition* (and simultaneously a metaphor for his punishment), Amy Stern's metamorphosis is not a condition but a process that plays itself out before our eyes in the course of the book. Gregor's post-metamorphic fate is largely static, concerned with discovering the meaning of "what has happened to him." Amy Stern (who is always referred to by her full name throughout the novel, with the sole exception of the title) begins as a passive observer, a role that is emphasized in the first part of the novel and even remarked on by her interlocutors. Her function seems at first to be to serve as a fly on the wall in the service of the reader, a device for prompting the many women with whom she comes in contact in Die Windrose and in the laundermat to tell their stories, which inevitably revolve around the men in their lives and their struggles to fulfill themselves in the face of a patriarchal society and its demands on them. These men are mostly absent from the novel and are only seen filtered through the consciousnesses of the women. All of these relationships are unsatisfactory, but not because of the patriarchal behavioral models that Amy Stern sees as the root of the problem in her conversation over coffee with Altmann. On the contrary, it is because the men are individually all monsters or sexist boors of one kind or another: If they are not sexually abusing the women to the point of hospitalizing them, they come home from the bar in a drunken stupor and beat them, or they gamble away the household budget, or they allow their babies to die in their cribs because they can't stand missing a few moments of a television program, or they are adulterers, or even worse, they subject their wives to boring lectures on politics.

Now we all know that there are such men, but unfortunately verifying once again the existence of such individual monsters adds very little to the more fundamental theme that occupies the second half of the novel, the social structures that dominate society and the question of how these structures would have to be or can be changed. The recurring question that Amy Stern asks herself at key points in the story, "Who am I and what are my problems?" provides a sense of the reasons for the failure of this novel: These questions imply that what we are about to read will be a feminist *Bildungsroman*, a chronicle of Amy Stern's metamorphosis and development following her choice in *The Mystification of Sophie Silber* to forswear the fairy realm and become a mortal, to transform herself from Amaryllis Sternwieser into Amy Stern. In fact, however, Amy Stern's role as fly on the wall in the first part of the novel is not only passive, but is also largely static. For example, when Amy Stern, a dwarf named Willi, and Pola plan a vaudeville act, Pola says of Amy Stern, "She's supposed to take care of the verbal end. Lately she's been saying such funny things that we've all had to laugh whenever we see her." Willi replies, "but she says nothing at all" (152). Later on, Amy Stern defines her own role:

> I feel as if I were drawn from moment to moment deeper into a network of relationships that forces me to pay attention to my own consciousness. My curiosity is aimed more and more at myself. I discover things I had no inkling of. Or have I simply decided to start my search with myself? I envy you, Pola, even Miranda—all of you who do something in order to be able to express yourselves. Myself, I have 'til now only watched, listened, empathized. (161–162)

Amy Stern is told at one point that the members of the Jockey Club (a group of four women who gamble in Die Windrose so that Pia can discreetly give them the money she has inherited from her husband) regard her as a bystander, as a referee in their various disputes. It is only in the second part of the novel that Amy Stern's own development moves to the forefront. But when it does, it is a personal development inextricably linked with larger questions of social organization, seen not only in Amy Stern's first attempts at writing a fable about what a literature of dolphins would look like, but also by examining the roles of the five exceptional men who appear in the text.

We have noted that what Amy Stern learns from the women in the laundermat or in the Jockey Club tells us little about social organization for the reason that it is the *normal* man and not the pathological monsters described in these stories who exemplifies the system. This is the obvious function of Klemens, the son of the actress Sophie Silber and a man driven by his love for theater and his ambition to rise in the world of journalism as a theater critic. Klemens, as he appears in this novel (he reappears in *Kai und die Liebe zu den Modellen* [Kai and the Love for Models, 1979]), is a kind of pale figure; he occupies relatively little space in the novel and the reader gets very little sense of what he is like, one of the major weaknesses of the novel. But it is clear that he is no monster, nor is he intellectually inferior to Amy Stern as Frischmuth's husband was to her: "Women too must learn to accept a partner who is intellectually inferior," she tells an interviewer (Prillmann 1978). On the contrary, here Frischmuth has taken care that his flaws be connected with his function: to serve as the incarnation of a patriarchal society. Thus, with great self-discipline he works on his dissertation, refusing to subordinate his work to Amy Stern's emotional needs and to his putative love for her. When he is faced with the opportunity of a lifetime (to report on a theater festival in Greece), he immediately accepts without consulting Amy Stern or asking her to accompany him, assuming that she cannot give up the job with which she finances her desultory studies. Worst of all, in an important conversation with Sophie Silber, Amy Stern imagines the test that she will subject Klemens to: she will reveal that she is pregnant and observe his reaction:

> She tries to imagine all his reactions, his face, his features, his gestures and his words. She ought not to count his very first sentence. And yet, she knows already that she will be on edge. That she will forgive no part of his immediate reaction.
>
> It depends on the *how*, on *how* I tell Klemens. And she is already furious. Why on the *how*? The facts are the same. And if he's responsible, then it's not because of the *how* but because of the *what*. (282)

When the moment finally arrives, Klemens fails the test. His first words are "From me?" He fails a similar test in *Kai and the Love for Models* where Amy Stern thinks about how noisily he is reading his newspaper and how this racket (like that caused by her son Kai) is hindering her creativity, her attempts to concentrate on her writing. She wishes he would leave:

> If I for example continue to describe how I hear Klemens rustling his newspaper through the rather thin wall. Which causes my hope that he might go to the movies to recede but not en-

tirely disappear. As long as he is reading a paper and not a book, he can change his mind. Then I hear how he rolls over on the couch springs, yawns, and then—after all—lies down again. (10–11)

Now the problem with this technique is not so much that Klemens is not enough of a presence in the novel for us to tell whether he really loves Amy Stern or instead is, in the words of Dr. Lindenberg (a reincarnation of Drachenstein from *The Mystification of Sophie Silber*), merely a man whose lack of feeling is disguised by his charm. The more important problem from the reader's point of view is that one never really believes that Amy Stern loves him, for the weight and the value of all her decisions depend not on his feelings for her, but on hers for him: how much she is willing to give up for him; how much she expects him to give up for her; finally, and most importantly, whether she should bear their child. An index of the reason for this lack of conviction on the part of the reader can be gleaned from a glance at the organization of the novel. We experience Klemens directly in two somewhat perfunctory sex scenes and in one scene where he and Amy Stern are having breakfast, which is obviously intended to showcase his charm and the easy banter of two young people in love with one another. The problem is that such dialogue is not Frischmuth's strong suit, and it never really rings true. One short example (the German is equally awkward):

> Please, come right over here ... Klemens raises the blanket invitingly.
> I wouldn't think of letting myself be abused by you again in such a bestial fashion ...
> Even now, when the few hours of sleep have freed me from the impotence caused by stress?
> And what awakens first of all? Your compulsion to penetrate. Instead of thinking of the cuddling I deserve or helping me in the kitchen. (168)

It is not just the rather difficult task of portraying the love behind the jocularity that defeats Frischmuth; it is also clear from the failure of the scene where Amy Stern, Pola, and Willi plan their vaudeville act, the "Soft Eggs" (soft-boiled eggs). Here too the language rings false. After Pola has demonstrated a trick that will be part of their act, Willi remarks:

> Very good. I must admit, you've learned something in the meantime.
> That's by no means all, and already she is portraying Medea with an invisible dagger in her hand, not to kill Kreusa but to castrate Jason. Her lust for blood can only be quenched with an infusion of champagne. Whereupon, as Gretchen in labor she succeeds in scaring away two of the pairs of lovers on the neighboring park benches. (151)

The critic Franz Zalto (1978) deals similarly with the question of the dialogue in the laundermat scene, remarking, "Not what these women are talking about is embarrassing, but how the writer Barbara Frischmuth causes them to talk in a colloquial tone valiantly struggling to achieve authenticity that nevertheless comes across as false." Another critic, Gert Ueding (1978), characterizes these stories even more harshly:

> They are supposed to be typical female biographies in our time and our society, complementing her [Amy Stern's] own experiences, but they turn out to be only very wooden paraphrases of traditional modes of behavior which are lacking all experience and in which even the expression of suffering has ossified into a stereotype. For long stretches the impression arises that someone is sloppily relating a story he has read somewhere in the past. Since he has forgotten much of it and he no longer feels confident of the chronology, he takes refuge in expository circumlocutions and incomprehensible repetitions, stumbles from one forced comparison to the next stylistic excrescence, and tries at least to reveal the poetic brilliance of the source occasionally.

Or consider the language in the scene where a woman Amy Stern meets in the park describes the feelings engendered in her by her love for her son:

> I will have to walk with careful steps, so that the soles of my feet do not caress the ground too much. My whole body, my whole being has fallen victim to love. I don't know how I should behave in order not to dissolve between the blades of grass of this meadow. Just how have I ended up here? Maybe the light is to blame for everything. If the sun keeps on shining on my lap, I will have to perish. Help me. A trembling shakes the body of the young woman, who grasps Amy Stern's hand and presses her nails into it like a woman in labor, while she

throws her head back and breaks out into sighs of rapture. (182)

In general, the representation of sex is a problem in this novel, as it is in Frischmuth's other novels, where she often relies on mentioning body parts like Amy Stern's nipples or certain objects like flip-flops (*Mittelzehenriemen*) that have for some reason acquired a fetishistic significance for her but not necessarily for the reader, so that they cannot be counted on to produce the desired emotional effect.

Whereas Klemens is human, all too human, the other male "exceptions" noted above, Altmann, Herwater, and Dr. Lindenberg, are reincarnations from the fairy world where, for example, Altmann appeared as Alpinox. However, unlike the world of the dolphins described later on in the novel by Amy Stern in her first literary étude, which is characterized by a coherent social structure underpinned by traditional mythology, the fairy world of imagination and genuine feeling represented by these three men seems anything but coherent. On the contrary, Altmann and Herwater (the von Wasserthal of *The Mystification of Sophie Silber*) are presented as adversaries, advocates of competing social theories, which, surprisingly, seem to have more to do with ecology and our stewardship of the Earth than they do with the unfairnesses engendered by a patriarchal society. The latter seems to be a question confronted exclusively by women in this novel and one on which men, whether human or spirit, have no opinion.

In fact, however, it turns out that the ecological theme is not so irrelevant as it appears at first glance. The point at issue is Herwater's sense of an ecological crisis (akin to the alarm felt by the dolphins in Amy Stern's fables) that can only be dealt with by consciousness-raising and by a deliberate and revolutionary act of self-denial and change on the part of humankind. Humankind will have to learn to accommodate itself to nature, to the planet Earth with her limited resources, and will have to learn to deny itself the indulgence of all of its desires rather than selfishly continuing to rape the environment whenever it wishes (the sexual metaphor is one that Frischmuth herself suggests in her text). Altmann of course does not disagree with Herwater in his analysis of the crisis, but he cannot believe that humankind is capable of changing itself so radically. Amy Stern's role is at first glance that of a tennis ball, bouncing between the two men and apparently influenced by the one she has talked to last. But on closer examination, it becomes clear that Amy Stern is critically weighing these two ecological positions because in fact the resolution of the ecological argument proves to be crucial for the resolution of her own dilemma, her own problems.

"Who am I and what are my problems?" she asks. All of her problems crystallize at the end of the novel in the one decisive question of whether she should have her child: "Have the baby or have an abortion," as she puts it to herself. This phrase is shorthand for a lengthy discussion about the dilemma of a woman with literary ambitions faced with a society and a lover who will make it very difficult for her to realize those ambitions if she bears a child. The discussion—which is largely between Amy Stern and her friends Maya, the sculptress who has in her own life decided in favor of her career and against a child, the old woman who owns Die Windrose, and Sophie Silber (as indicated above, no man plays any role in this discussion, especially not Klemens)—turns on the question of whether men and thus society can be radically changed or changed only gradually through evolutionary means. Thus, the ecological discussion between Herwater and Altmann proves to be relevant after all to Amy Stern's development, albeit by indirection.

The phrase "Amy Stern's development" brings us to another fundamental aspect of this novel: the question of its genre as a feminist *Bildungsroman*. The reader may feel that in posing this question I am raising a straw person in order to knock it down, but in fact Frischmuth alludes to the archetypal *Bildungsroman*, Goethe's *Wilhelm Meisters Lehrjahre* (Wilhelm Meister's Apprenticeship Years), in a number of ways in *Amy oder Die Metamorphose*—just as the first novel in the trilogy, *The Mystification of Sophie Silber*, is a kind of *theatralische Sendung*, a theatrical mission like the original version of *Wilhelm Meisters Lehrjahre*. The old woman's offer to sell her business to Amy Stern to enable her to acquire a measure of independence (even though running Die Windrose is the last thing that Amy Stern wants to do) is akin to the plans that Werner and Wilhelm's father have for him for a career in business. In Book III, chapter 11 of *Wilhelm Meisters Lehrjahre*, Jarno offers Wilhelm an opportunity to travel:

> Don't give up your resolve to embark on an active life, and hurry to use well the good years granted you. If I can be helpful to you, I'll do it with all my heart. I haven't yet asked how you got mixed up with this troupe for which you seem neither destined nor suited by education. But I hope and believe I detect that you are longing to get out. I know nothing of your origins, of your parents; consider what you want to reveal to me. I can tell you this much: the days of war we are experiencing can bring with them rapid changes of fortune; if you would like to dedicate your energies and talents to our service and shun neither effort nor, if need be, danger, then I now have an opportunity to put you in a position you will not later on regret having occupied for a while ... Consider my suggestion, decide, give me in a few days your answer and trust me. I assure you, it has been a mystery to me so far, how you can have made common cause with such a band. I have often watched with disgust and dissatisfaction how you have given your heart, just in order to earn a living, to an itinerant ballad-monger and an insipid androgynous creature. (193)

Wilhelm reflects on Jarno's words and as he does, he realizes how much it pains him to hear Harfner and Mignon, for whom he has come to feel great affection, spoken of in this way. "Since this time," we are told, "he paid more attention to Jarno's actions, not all of which seemed to him worthy of praise" (194). He finally turns Jarno's offer down and in doing so, resists a temptation and passes a test, a further step in his *Bildung* and growth.

Similarly, after abducting Amy Stern on her way home from Die Windrose and spiriting her off to his castle, Altmann offers to make it possible for Amy Stern to travel anywhere in the world she wishes so that in her new career as an author she will have some experiences to write about:

> It would give me infinite pleasure to see how a female being like yourself acquires the world. I would give a lot to be a witness of how you transform reality, transform your surroundings. I have already thought of suggesting to you to go traveling with me. I know the world, Amy Stern, and I could show it to you where it is most interesting ... The price [i.e. "my recompense"] is the joy of a voyeur who is allowed to witness how a woman to whom all possibilities are made available, who cannot use as an excuse any kind of discrimination, want, or social pressure, becomes an artist. (226)

Amy Stern is advised to refuse by a number of people, including another refugee from the spirit world, Dr. Lindenberg, and after some hesitation she does so:

> We just wanted to know how you were, Dr. Lindenberg continued, after all that our good Altmann has put into your head.
>
> I didn't know that there were bets being made, laughs Amy Stern. But unless I change my mind at the last moment, you can rest easy. (258)

Just as Wilhelm Meister begins to see another, less praiseworthy aspect of Jarno, Amy Stern is shown by Lindenberg the problematic side of Altmann:

> I can imagine that our old friend Altmann has nothing more in mind for you than to show you all the things he could make out of you if you were to trust him, which means to make yourself his, deliver yourself into his hands. (219)

Indeed, Wilhelm has the increasing sense as he progresses on his path that a force has been guiding his life and his development, as in his ultimate encounter with Lothario and the Abbé and his initiation into the mysteries of the Gesellschaft vom Turm. The reader and Amy Stern also have this sense that people whom she apparently meets in chance encounters are somehow intimately involved in her life and her decisions. Sophie Silber, Altmann, Dr. Lindenberg, Wolfgang, Maya, and Mares all flit in and out of her life, some of them mysteriously appearing for example at Altmann's party, like the two old women whom she has just served at Die Windrose a few hours before. At one point, she invites Altmann (who, as we have seen, is an echo of Jarno in *Wilhelm Meisters Lehrjahre*) on the spur of the moment to visit Sophie Silber in Altaussee and then hears from Sophie the next day that he has left for an appointment. Amy Stern thinks: "So the excursion here wasn't spontaneous after all? Not her own idea after all?" She tries to remember if he had suggested it to her—perhaps when he said, "I'd suggest to you to take a trip somewhere with me" (274).

This crucial relationship between *Amy or the Metamorphosis* and *Wilhelm Meisters Lehrjahre* and the problem of genre brings us to the center of Frischmuth's novel and Amy Stern's self-definition. For with the major exception of his clandestine affair with Mariane, Wilhelm Meister begins his career almost as passively as Amy Stern does. Yet, as he matures he begins to change, to develop, to seize the initiative (for example in advising the troupe to choose the dangerous path that ultimately leads it to fall victim to the marauders and Wilhelm to encounter the woman he calls his *Amazone*). Very early on in the novel, in his conversation in Book I with the stranger about the painting of the sick prince, Wilhelm is given a hint of the Turmgesellschaft's program and guiding philosophy:

> The fabric of this world is woven of necessity and chance; man's reason mediates between these and is able to control them; it treats necessity as the basis of its existence; it guides the incidental, directs and makes use of it and only when it remains steadfast does man deserve to be said to approach the divine. Woe to him who from his youth is accustomed to finding in necessity something arbitrary, who wants to ascribe to the incidental a kind of reason. (71)

The Turmgesellschaft has indeed been watching over his life and guiding him, just as Altmann tells Amy Stern "I'll be keeping an eye on you," but it has allowed him to make his own mistakes (281). When finally he is initiated into the Saal der Vergangenheit and allowed his "*Parzival-Frage*," he asks about his son Felix. This is the right question, and as a consequence of asking it Wilhelm's apprenticeship is nearing its end. Like Parzival, Wilhelm's question shows that he has learned that to live in society it is necessary to live for others as well as for oneself, that if one truly cares about other people, then in a process of compromise and mutual accommodation to each other's needs, each partner will be able to renounce certain desires for the sake of the person he or she loves. Thus Wilhelm's development is a path toward self-realization and self-knowledge, but one aspect of this self-knowledge is that he is willing to relinquish the fulfillment of certain desires to integrate himself into society, albeit in a way far different from that foreseen by his father and Werner.

It is this balance that is the crux of Amy Stern's problem. In her desire to realize her ambitions, ambitions every bit as strong as Klemens's, she is presented with five offers of help: the old woman's daughter, a gynecologist, offers to help her abort the child; Altmann offers to place unlimited means at her disposal so that she can travel anywhere in the world she wishes; the old woman offers to make it possible for her to buy Die Windrose so that she can be financially independent of men; Pia, the patron of the Jockey Club, offers to let her join the group, in effect promising to support her financially so that she can pursue her writing career; and finally, Sophie Silber (who has abandoned her own son Klemens so that she can pursue her acting career, just as Mares has abandoned her daughter) offers to help care for her child both personally and financially. The one solution that would allow her true independence of any other person and a chance to devote herself completely to her writing, the one suggested by the old woman and by Maya—an abortion—she rejects. Maya's advice is, *mutatis mutandis*, that of the *schöne Seele* (beautiful soul) in Book VI of *Wilhem Meisters Lehrjahre*: to opt out of the world of activity and to devote herself completely to her inner life. As Maya puts it for her, "There is only one solution: to keep oneself free. To keep oneself free as much as one can and as far as possible. It's better to pay in the hard currency of solitude than to be in debt to all of those unresolved relationships. You can't have everything, Amy Stern, and certainly not everything at once" (292).

Amy Stern rejects each of these five offers. Like the old woman, she decides: "Then I swore to myself never again. Never again be dependent on another person" (260). Each promises one kind of independence, but each would presuppose another kind of dependence (even if benevolent), and this is a concession that Amy Stern is unwilling to make. But the consequence of this uncompromising, absolutist position is that Amy Stern on the last page of the novel decides to give birth to Kai, thus making herself dependent in a different way, not on the old woman or Pia or Altmann, but on her son and on tying herself to another human being. However, if one reads the last few pages of this novel, where Amy Stern (who has never been shown yearning for a child elsewhere in the book, who has not planned to have this baby) makes this fateful decision, one gets the strong feeling that its basis is more a desire to show Klemens that she has the courage that he himself lacks than a desire for a child: "I accept the challenge," she says defiantly (296). The results for her and for her son are clear in *Kai and the Love for Models*, where Amy

Stern attempts to steal a few moments to write in the face of demands by Kai so importunate that the reader sometimes wants to spank him, as Otto F. Beer (1979) suggests: "And so the boy around whom everything revolves, the adored Kai, is by no means the angel he was doubtless meant to be. His mother fulfills his every wish as a matter of principle ... It's clear that he not only keeps his mother on the go, but also eventually begins to get on the reader's nerves" (132).

At this point in our analysis the fateful consequences of Frischmuth's failure to portray a convincing love affair become especially clear. It is perhaps not so hard to understand Amy Stern's decision to live and work as a single mother and renounce the charms of Klemens, because we feel viscerally that she never really did love him in the first place, despite her assertions to the contrary. A truer novelistic test, however, would have been to portray a deeply caring relationship between the two. One has the feeling that the failure to depict such a relationship is not so much a lack of skill on Frischmuth's part as it is a psychological unwillingness on the part of Amy Stern to cede to a male partner any claims whatever on her emotional life. This makes the work interesting as a feminist statement, but more difficult for the reader, whether male or female, to become emotionally engaged.

Works Cited

Beer, Otto F. 1979. Die Fee ohne Blütenstaub. *Stuttgarter Zeitung* (October 9). Reprinted in *Barbara Frischmuth* (n.d.). Edited by Kurt Bartsch. Graz: Literaturverlag Droschl.

Frischmuth, Barbara. 1976. *Die Mystifikationen der Sophie Silber*. Munich: dtv.

Prillmann, Hilke. 1978. Eine handfeste Fee. *Berliner Morgenpost* (March 19).

Ueding, Gert. 1978. Als Fee überall dabei: Barbara Frischmuth's Roman *Amy oder Die Metamorphose*. *Frankfurter Allegemeine Zeitung* (May 19).

Zalto, Franz. 1978. Marionetten: Barbara Frischmuth's papierene Welt. *Wochenpresse* (April 12).

Autofiction: Peter Handke's Trilogy of Try-Outs

Ingeborg Hoesterey

In recent years the conventional difference between fiction and nonfiction has tended to be blurred in Peter Handke's texts, with fictional elements appearing merely as strands of indeterminate genre. Such is the nature of the three prose pieces collected in English under the title *The Jukebox and Other Essays on Storytelling* (1994), which the author had separately published as *Versuch über die Müdigkeit* (1989), *Versuch über die Jukebox* (1990), and *Versuch über den geglückten Tag* (1991). It is important to note these original titles because the translators decided on a distinct generic classification—the essay—for texts that actually waver between autobiography, essay, fictional narrative, prose poem, aphorism, and philosophical reflection. By naming each of the three pieces "Versuch" (attempt, try-out), Handke conspicuously avoids the genre designation of "essay." The use of the term *Versuch* reactivates the notion of writing as a tentative search into uncharted intellectual and emotional territory, which Michel de Montaigne's *Essais* and his "que sais je?" (what do I know?) exemplified at the beginning of modernity. Although the experimental, tentative tenor, indebted to Montaigne's example, became an important aspect of the Western essay tradition, the essay of twentieth-century German cultural discourse with its mandate of witty and ironic diction, as well as polished, rounded-off form, differs sharply from Handke's textuality.

Rather the *Versuch* trilogy embraces Robert Musil's "essayism" and the self-mandate of his *Man without Qualities* (1995)—to live hypothetically (*hypothetisch leben*).

Nonfictional autobiography—the memoir of a life—is characterized by a truth claim, whereas the notions of truth and authenticity by definition do not apply to fiction or to fictional autobiography. To be sure, recent research has problematized this opposition and has revealed the tendency of historical selves toward "fictions" in their retrospective narratives (Eakin 1985). Conversely, postmodern poetic practices have produced hybrid styles of fiction in which, for example, the author figures under his real name as a character in the story. It is a device that prompts reflection upon the fictionality of a novel, but it is not typical of Peter Handke's prose. His toss-up of fictional and nonfictional codes is more elusive because poetic language and literariness cover fragments of authenticity relating to biographical fact. We will call this hybrid mode "autofiction," a category coined by the French author Serge Doubrovsky for his novel *Fils* (1977) that aimed at rewriting the parameters of the autobiographical genre, as would so many postmodern authors in the next two decades.

Handke's autofiction in the shape of these three short prose texts conflates the autobiographical voice with an almost lyrical tautness. In German the *Versuche* exist in three slim volumes with an aesthetic typographical layout on artist's paper and cover art that reproduces the first pages of each manuscript. Despite their insidious mélange of literary and nonliterary codes, these verbo-visual pages make for a strong poetic presence. It is a presence that positions itself emphatically vis-à-vis the inflationary discourses of our *Lebenswelt* that flood the mind's attention and electronically escalate from day to day. One is tempted to look at the voluminous *Mein Jahr in der Niemandsbucht: Ein Märchen aus den neuen Zeiten* (1994) as the author's most excessive project so far to combat the information age. The book of 1067 pages, which continues the narrative indeterminacy of *The Afternoon of a Writer* and the *Essays*, arrogantly asks the reader to treat it like the Bible, book of books, and savor only a passage at a time. Paradoxically, in the midst of an electronic usurpation of print media, Handke's tome claims a new importance: a book may enable one to go from a mundane daily routine to something truly "other," the poetic text.

Such resistance to the aporias of our digital modernity works from a base of relative artistic autonomy that today breeds an ambivalent sensibility of "suffering and triumph" (Ribbat 1994, 177). Yet it is precisely this much-dismissed distance that empowers the author to take up the challenge once more to perform difference in a progressively homogenized high-tech society.

One could assume that the essay of expository prose might be more suited to Handke's project for a mankind more in touch with itself than to the virtual realities that its Faustian drives have produced. The autobiographical mode, however, fits the discourse of the "basic need" that prevails in the essays and, more importantly, fits Handke's post-Lacanian way of living as he writes and writing as he lives. Jacques Lacan conceived of human desire as the attempt of the "transcendental subject" to make a mark in the world of signification, all the while cherishing the illusion that this "I" could find a stable identity in the symbolic system (Rosemann 1993, 5). By making the complexity of this search undertaken by a subject, of the essay as try-out, the very stuff of his narrative, Handke situates his writer-narrator in a space of reflection beyond the trap of self-deception as described by Lacan. To be sure, the nomadic movement of the *Essays* leaves no illusion concerning the fractured status of the self that Rilke had thematized early, and Lacan later in his rewriting of Freud.[1]

In his previous works Handke often and in an unmarked manner drew upon French phenomenology (Wesche 1985). The *Essays* show an affinity to Maurice Merleau-Ponty's *The Prose of the World* (1973) where prose is defined as the "art of capturing a meaning which until then had never been objectified and of rendering it accessible to everyone who speaks the same language" (xiii).

The central themes of the three textual try-outs are indeed of a type not represented by earlier literary discourse in German in more than a peripheral fashion. To be sure, philosophers have thematized happiness through the centuries (e.g., Emerson's "Pursuit of Happiness"). In contrast to the conceptualizing operations of most philosophical inquiry, Handke offers almost pure *An-schauung* (reflective gaze), naturally in the secularized mode of post-Husserlian phenomenology. He is not looking for an Husserlian *eidos*, as essentialist as his textuality may appear at times. The literary author writes about insistent psychic structures at work in our emotional household, like fatigue or worry about the success of a day. The quasi-phenomenology of basic human experiential patterns is, however, only one level of significance in these complexly layered texts. Other meanings come about through the many instances of open or veiled intertextual reference that recall aspects of the literary and cultural archive in a flash-like manner: classical antiquity, Montaigne, Rousseau, Goethe, Lichtenberg's *Sudelbücher* (Scrap Books), *décadence*, sensibility, Benjamin, Heidegger, and more.

The *Essay on Tiredness* begins by hearking back to a rare autobiographical form, the interior dialogue:

> In the past I knew tiredness only as something to be feared.
> When in the past?
> In my childhood, in my so-called student days, in the years of my first loves ... (3)

A subsequent question reveals that this is indeed an interior dialogue:

> Why must you always accuse yourself? (4)

In *Je est un autre* (I am an Other), Philippe Lejeune (1980), borrowing Rimbaud's formula, points to the double character of the addressee: "If I talk to myself saying 'you,' I give this enunciation at the same time to the listener or reader who assists in the discourse. The enunciation is theatricalized" (37). There are few models for the dialogical mode in the biographical tradition; one is Rousseau's self-examination titled *Rousseau Juge de Jean Jacques* (Rousseau Judges Jean-Jacques) written between 1772 and 1776. These three (sic!) dialogues give an objective bend to the reflections of the speaker named Rousseau through the introduction of a personalized fictional addressee, "un Francois."

Whether Rousseau, whom we know to be of importance for Handke, is a model here, is less interesting than the fact that the Austrian author uses the dramatic mode to diffuse and break up the traditional flow of autobiographical narrative.

Wasn't that sort of tiredness likely to degenerate into arrogance?
Yes, I'd often, in looking myself over, surprise a cold, misanthropic arrogance or, worse, a condescending pity for all the commonplace occupations that could never in all the world lead to a royal tiredness such as mine. (25)

A view of the self as a dialogical process rather than a unified entity emerges. The textual voice relentlessly exposes a fragmented psychic existence that the reader tends to experience as compelling because such fragmentation is hardly the exclusive property of an artistic consciousness. Moreover, the *Essay on Tiredness* ties into the postmodern predilection for narrative autoreflexivity and belongs as "autobiography of writing" (Meyer 1989) to a large group of contemporary hybrid texts. Conventional knowledge about artistic production, indebted to Enlightenment discourse, has tended to stress the alert mind as agent of the act of creation; the author-narrator of *Essay on Tiredness* proposes to see creative thinking as being facilitated by a relaxation of the forces of the *ratio* and the pragmatic drive. "So let's have a Pindaric ode, not to a victor but to a tired man" (41) which delicately twists its reference, as the Greek poet after all sang about *heroes* and their victories at Olympia. It is here that one of Handke's intertexts becomes visible, the segment "Idyl on Idleness" in Friedrich Schlegel's novel of reflection, *Lucinde* (1799). In this influential model for the evolution of anti-realist fiction, the Romantic critic proposes to make the practice of indolence into an art, even a religion, while ironically suggesting that this would lead to a divine life of pure vegetation.

Moreover, Handke's concept of fatigue can be seen in a relationship of intertextuality to Sten Nadolny's novel of 1983, *Die Entdeckung der Langsamkeit* (The Discovery of Slowness) as well as to the slim volume by Milan Kundera, published in French shortly after Handke's *Essays* in 1993, *La Lenteur* (*Slowness*). All three studies in *fin de siècle* perception point back, with their implicit critique of teleological modernity, to Adorno/Horkheimer's *Dialectic of Enlightenment* of the forties. What these stylistically different texts have in common is that they critically revive the artist's distance to a proliferating industrialization and rising mass culture as practiced by the engineers of aesthetic modernism in the nineteenth century (Ribbat 1994, 177).

Against the all-encompassing rule of the secondary, the banal, "tiredness" denotes a productive absence away from the self-proliferating systems in the global village. The last notion launched by the text is the image of a "cosmic tiredness" for humanity that importantly extends a neighboring phrase: "Tiredness is greater than the self" (41, 43). The sensibility projected in these utterances pleads for a relaxation of the hubris-driven technologies of the modern self and for a new communal orientation of the self in the future. This unusual fatigue would bring about a self-possession, a tranquillity befitting a consciousness aware of the end of certain epochal utopias. To a degree, *Essay on Tiredness* may be read as an allegory of the concept of *posthistoire*, without, however, the apocalyptic tone of much German discourse on postmodernism (derived more from Jean Baudrillard than Arnold Gehlen, who coined the term). Instead, Handke's metaphor of fatigue calls for a new song, a poetics of life that would arise from the need to hear birds sing (44). Tranquillity is rewritten as a medium of rebirth by one exemplary subject, desiring to facilitate a change of pace for others.

That the three texts are of one, however loosely textured, weave is signaled in a number of subtle ways, most visibly on the last page of *Essay on Tiredness* when the writing of the second piece, *The Jukebox*, is projected in a conversation with an unnamed addressee. In his curious search for the fanciful aggregate of a forgotten mode of musical entertainment, the author-narrator tells himself (and his readers): "and here he wanted to essay the unworldly topic of the jukebox, suitable for 'refugees of the world,' as he told himself now; a mere plaything, according to the literature" (58). Epithets such as unworldly (*weltfremd*) and play (*Spiel*) describe the realm of the aesthetic and may purposely address their negative application by a certain faction of Handke criticism. Perhaps as a response the author comes forth with a contemporary variant of Mörike's homage to the aesthetic object, "Auf eine Lampe" (To a Lamp), a poem that ends with the line "Yet what is beautiful seems blissful within itself," a line that has been perceived as a notorious icon of *l'art pour l'art* discourse in German literary studies.[2] The jukebox is a cipher for the deconstruction of the "autonomous" work of art and not only because it is drawn from the realm of the so-called trivial. A work of art nevertheless, it exudes a strange presence that effects in those exposed to it "a sort of heightened awareness such as otherwise occurs only with a book that stimulates reflection" (99). In the space of a few sentences, the author-narrator ingeniously links high and low culture and dismantles traditional aesthetic hierarchies. In the postmodern toss-up of high and low, the pop object of the jukebox is the central motif of the text and the agent of its self-reflexive move. Indeed, like the effects ascribed to the magic of the jukebox in Linares, the poetic immediacy of the *Essay on the Jukebox* affects our consciousness and stops the flow of routine mental activities.[3]

In the first part of the *Essay on Tiredness* the autobiographical signs—first-person reference, interior dialogue—structure the essayistic and aphoristic quality of the text as they do in many examples of the essay genre following Montaigne. The *Jukebox* piece varies the narratological category of person; it is autobiography in the third person, a narratological variant already practiced by Caesar in *De bello Gallico* and, to name a considerably more recent example, in *Roland Barthes par Roland Barthes* of 1975.

Today the manipulation of the grammatical person in autobiographical narrative, moving it closer to fiction, shows an author's awareness of the constructedness of artistic self-representation and the problem of authentic self-representation. The *Jukebox* is doubtless a writerly text in Barthes's sense; it challenges the reader to contemplate the conflation of narrated character, narrator, and author into a hybrid narrative voice that tells of the attempt to write *The Jukebox*. Turning to paratextual evidence, the name and title on the book cover, the general reader will, with conventional wisdom, assume that the character is indeed the author, objectified by third-person reference. Jonathan Wilson ascribes the "naked self-referentiality" involved in the above operation as a prominent tendency in American autobiographical fiction in the 1980s and associates it with the deconstructionist project. Self-reference is rendered completely unreliable in works by Joan Didion or Philip Roth, which "make the reader aware that characters in novels, names on title pages, and photographs on jacket covers are equidistant from a reality that is itself unstable" (Wilson 1988, 391).

Handke's cluster of texts occupies a space beyond the play of the author posing as character in his/her creation, a distancing effect conspicuously practiced by Uwe Johnson in the first volume of his tetralogy *Jahrestage* (1970–1983). The *Essays* try to construct a textuality that would keep all prose forms in suspension (*in der Schwebe*): autobiographical fragment, historic fact, poetic interlude, quasi-scholarly inquiry, essayistic reflection. The jukebox is the central allegory of the authorial project for a polyphonic, nonhierarchical text:

> He did not like a jukebox's program to embody any plan, no matter how noble, any connoisseurship, any secret knowledge, any harmony; he wanted it to represent confusion. (101)

A mishmash of the different writing styles present in the selection area of the music boxes is highly desirable, as is the intersection of different genres of writing for the new type of text imagined by the narrator. The "epos" on tiredness had pleaded for such a "mess" and had dismissed the notion of an orderly progression by steps. In *The Jukebox* we read:

> and the "essay" hovered before him as an un-connected composite of many different forms of writing, corresponding to the—what should he call it—uneven? arhythmic? ways in which he had experienced a jukebox. (80)

Friedrich Schlegel's proposal to dissolve genre boundaries comes to mind as well as poststructuralist subversions of genre. In the lengthy and complex reflection on writing that follows in Handke's *Jukebox* piece, the act of narration itself emerges as the potential for a new textual identity of both author and product. *Ecriture*, the thought process and production of writing, is inextricably implicated in the existence of the writer for whom the real and the imaginary are interchangeably present most of the time.

The writing in *Jukebox* has a lucidity as deceptive as poetry, a lyrical appeal that commentary cannot reproduce. What can be described, however, is the motif of the author-narrator as traveler, as a Rousseauian *promeneur solitaire*. Solitary walking and moving from place to place are recurrent motifs in Handke's work, and this movement only bears a superficial resemblance to Walter Benjamin's flaneur or Franz Hessel's city walker of 1920s Berlin. Handke's fascination with the peripatetic mode of creative thinking is heightened by the congenial act of reading that accompanies the search for the jukebox: the narrator delves into the *Characters* of Theophrastus. It is noteworthy that the Greek philosopher (372–287) who was Aristotle's pupil and successor as head of the Peripatetic School wrote mostly fragments, a minor genre that has been elevated to the nonteleological text *par excellence*. (Not incidentally, the readings in Theophrastus led more or less directly into another act of writing that came to fruition in the play without words, *The Hour We Knew Nothing of Each Other*, performed and published in 1992.)[4]

The third part of the trilogy, *Essay on the Successful Day*, is subtitled "A Winter Day's Dream," thus relativizing any claim to a straightforward autobiography from the outset. Even though there are long passages without any personal pronoun and others with third-person reference, the text is visibly a type of autobiographical account long before the first "I" shows up on page 39. Here, as in *Essay on Tiredness*, we find frequent use of the "narrative you" as pronominal mode for the interior dialogue occurring in the narrator's mind and as an address to another, possibly the reader. The diffusion of the autobiographical voice by means of negation or hybridization serves the discourse of reflection and of living "hypothetically."

The basic human desideratum of a happy, successful day, the central theme, is explored throughout with urgency and sensitivity regarding the most minute sensations provoked by the banality of everyday living. Later the covert autobiography of a persona resembling the author Peter Handke goes into a looping motion when he produces its most authentic moment: the idea of the successful, happy day develops from a "life idea" into a "writing idea" (151). Seemingly trivial occurrences, the chance encounter, the gesture of a passer-by, become epiphanies that generate the creative impulse and resolve the earlier tension.

> So your idea of writing an essay about a successful day was itself a successful day? (153)

The question arises of how this happy-end in the day of a writer, how the most autobiographical moment of this text, can carry the generality of appeal typical for literature of merit. Literariness is clearly implicated in Handke's text, despite genre contamination and fiction–nonfiction ambiguities. Earlier in the book, reference was made to "mein, dein, unser Tag" (29) that the English translation shortens to "such a day, yours or mine" (132). Moreover, the essayistic mode, though interspersed with signs of the personal, offers the reader a more general, quasi-anthropological perspective on happiness as a cultural construct on whose ideological bindings the citizens of the West and other world regions depend.

It is important to keep in mind that Handke's central concept in the third Versuch is happiness (*Glück*), not success (*Erfolg*) as the English translation suggests. The obsessive probing into emotional registers hitherto unexplored in literature, which characterizes *Essay on the Successful Day*, may have a downright therapeutic effect on readers. A poetic voice undertakes to describe astutely a phenomenon, the desire to be happy, that holds most contemporaries hostage most of the time and offers an ingenious solution to the problem: forego the desire for a solution. The reflection upon the volatile object of desire called *Glück* is a more authentic feeling than the obsessive search for what can only be momentary satisfaction. The third essay can be seen as the literary variant of Robert Spaemann's (1989) philosophical formulation of the "antinomies of happiness" (11). The author of a study on happiness and benevolence, an essay on ethics, holds that "happiness as fulfillment pulls the subject onto an infinite path that under the conditions of finality is inseparable from the pain of dissatisfaction."

Conventional autobiography, both nonfictional and fictional memoirs, is an invitation to the reader to identify with the narrating subject who, equipped with a certain stability of psychological makeup, moves through stations in life in search of fulfillment. By contrast, the new autobiography as autofiction exhibits the illusionary nature of this process. Lacan interprets human desire as the attempt by the transcendental subject to acquire form in the world of signification. Handke's text describes the search for fulfillment in its function as the threshold for the subject's emancipation from a cultural dominant, the concept of happiness.

William Hogarth. The Painter and his Pug, 1745. Oil on canvas. Tate Gallery, London/Art Resource, New York.

Essay on the Successful Day opens with a short, evocative description of a version of the famous self-portrait by the English eighteenth-century artist William Hogarth in London's Tate Gallery. The inscription on his palette "The Line of Beauty and Grace" is called upon throughout the text. The picture gives allegorical expression to those currents in the *Essays* that function as the constructive element amidst what we have treated in many ways as a deconstructive enterprise. The line, the *figura serpentinata*, connotes a playful aspect of Renaissance art, especially Botticelli's flowing curves. (It should not be likened to the intricate ornamental symmetry of the arabesque.)[5]

The association of the motto of classical beauty inscribed on the tool of an artist energizes the sociopolitical scene of the day of the genre painter and dismisses the conventional notion that art and artist reside in an autonomous aesthetic realm. Similarly, Stifter's concept of art in *Indian Summer* (1857) rewrites classical beauty as inconspicuous (*unscheinbar*), slowly inscribing its ethical thrust on the beholder. Hogarth's and Handke's "line of beauty and grace" implies a simultaneously modest and intense involvement with art, one that defends aesthetic consciousness as a natural state, intimately bound up with ways of worldmaking. And although Handke's *Essays* may have arisen from the extensive archive of cultural pessimism written in German, they dismiss this tradition by energizing an image of humanity framed in the engraving by Hogarth: the trinity of human, animal, and art.

Notes

1. Handke developed this view of the self in his remake of Rainer Maria Rilke's *The Notebooks of Malte Laurids Brigge* (1910), the diary novel *The Weight of the World* (1977).

2. "Was aber schön ist, selig scheint es in ihm selbst." It is the subject of a 1951 dialogue between Emil Staiger, Martin Heidegger, and Leo Spitzer presented in translation in *PMLA* 105: 3 (May 1990).

3. For a sophisticated critique of Handke's poetic use of popular culture, see Koepenick 1996.

4. The gaze is the drama, and the text for it exists entirely in the shape of poeticized stage directions.

5. Uwe C. Steiner's important philosophical and systems-theoretical treatment of the second and third *Essay* (Steiner 1996) has one blindspot: the *figura serpentinata* should not be likened to the intricate ornamental symmetry of the arabesque.

Works Cited

Doubrovsky, Serge. 1977. *Fils*. Paris: Galilée.
Eakin, Paul John. 1985. *Fictions in Autobiography: Studies in the Art of Self-Invention*. Princeton, NJ: Princeton University Press.
Handke, Peter. 1989. *The Afternoon of a Writer*. New York: Farrar, Straus and Giroux.
Handke, Peter. 1994. *The Jukebox and Other Essays on Storytelling*. New York: Farrar, Straus and Giroux.
Handke, Peter. 1994. *Mein Jahr in der Niemandsbucht: Ein Märchen aus den neuen Zeiten*. Frankfurt am Main: Suhrkamp.
Handke, Peter. 1996. *Voyage to the Sonorous Land, or the Art of Asking* and *The Hour We Knew Nothing of Each Other*. New York: Farrar, Straus and Giroux.
Koepenick, Lutz. 1996. Negotiating Popular Culture: Wenders, Handke, and the Topographies of Cultural Studies. *The German Quarterly* 69: 4.
Kundera, Milan. 1996. *Slowness*. New York: Harper Collins.
Lejeune, Philippe. 1980. *Je est un autre*. Paris: Seuil.
Merleau-Ponty, Maurice. 1973. *The Prose of the World*. Evanston: Northwestern University Press.
Meyer, Eva. 1989. *Die Autobiographie der Schrift*. Basel: Stroemfeld/Roter Stern.
Musil, Robert. 1995. *The Man without Qualities*. Translated from the German by Sophie Wilkins; editorial consultant Burton Pike. New York: Knopf.
Nadolny, Sten. 1983. *Die Entdeckung der Langsamkeit*. Munich: Piper.
Ribbat, Ernst. 1994. Peter Handke's *Versuche*: Schreiben von Zeit und Geschichte. In *Sein und Schein—Traum und Wirklichkeit*. Edited by Herbert Arlt and Manfred Diersch. Frankfurt am Main: Peter Lang.
Rosemann, Philipp W. 1993. Die verpatzte Therapie. Philosophische Motive in der Psychoanalyse Jacques Lacans. *Frankfurter Allgemeine Zeitung* 136 (June 16).
Rousseau, Jean-Jacques. 1959. *Oeuvres completes*, Vol. 1. Paris: Gallimard.
Spaemann, Robert. 1989. *Glück und Wohlwollen: Versuch über Ethik*. Stuttgart: Klett-Cotta.

Steiner, Uwe C. 1996 (June). Das Glück der Schrift: Das graphisch -graphematische Gedächtnis in Peter Handkes Texten. In *Deutsche Vierteljahrsschrift für Literaturwissenschaft und Geistesgeschichte:* 2.

Wesche, Ulrich. 1985 (May). Peter Handke und Frankreich. *German Studies Review*.

Wilson, Jonathan. 1988. Counterlives: On Autobiographical Fiction in the 1980s. *The Literary Review* 31: 4.

Identity as Schizophrenia: The Autobiography of Peter Henisch

Linda C. DeMeritt

Peter Henisch's entire oeuvre can be read as one continuous text with returning figures and motifs drawn more or less directly from the author's own life. Such continuity accounts for the frequent revisions of individual works, the recurrence of specific names, people, and even titles within them, the verbatim repetition of quotes from one work to the next, and the incorporation of texts both past and future into current writing. The reader is left with the impression that Swoboda, Paul Grünzweig, or Franz Kreisler—even Hamlet and the Baronkarl—share common characteristics and, what is more, that they are all variations on the author himself. In a television interview from 1975, Henisch confirms that for him narration derives from subjective reality; he rejects an "invented literature" in favor of a "literature of experience" (Ulmer 1986, 57). In an interview more than ten years later, Henisch claims that while he now feels freer to explore other worlds, his own personal experiences remain the basis— the "springboard"—for his writing. Even the works that appear to break the parameters of autobiography nonetheless play with possibilities and choices once considered by the author himself (Roscher 1987, 75).

Henisch's autobiographical impulse can be placed in the context of the literary direction that has since come to be known as New Subjectivity. Sandra Frieden (1983) investigates the reasons for the "individualization of political perspective" (47) that occurred during the seventies. More than a mere reaction against the politicized literature preceding it, the autobiographical trend grew from two tendencies already apparent in the previous decade: documentary literature with its search for authenticity, and New Realism, which declared the private to be political. Authors of the New Subjectivity grew suspicious of a supposedly true and objective viewpoint as espoused by contemporary theories and ideologies and reacted with an outpouring of accounts of reality limited to the authority and authenticity of the author alone. At the same time, however, the privileging of the authorial perspective was itself to be questioned. Identity, previously determined by political groupings, now splintered. Autobiography of the seventies is characterized by "an extreme disjuncture of identity which asserts itself both in form and content of the literary works" (52).

For Henisch, too, the personal possesses political import and ramifications. In an essay from 1972 titled "Literature of the Future/The Future of Literature—Or What?" he defines literary engagement as critical examination of societal structures as reflected in the experience of the individual (144). Upon acceptance in 1977 of the Anton Wildgans Prize, he stresses that he presents the reader no objective truth, no solutions, but instead imparts his own life as a concrete example for others: "I have subjective experiences [to offer] as well as resultant insights which may be of interest to others" (1982, 187). Truth lies no more in the personal than in the political, and Henisch confronts his reader not with answers, but with "unsolved problems and unsolved contradictions." The critic Eva Schobel (1983) labels the author's combination of the experiential with political relevance "personal realism," defined as the expression and attempt to come to terms with subjective as well as objective crises (359).

The central crisis depicted in Henisch's works is a rupture within the assumed naturalness and wholeness of identity; it is a split of personality manifest on the individual as well as societal level. The author terms the split schizophrenia and characterizes it as follows in an early piece (1972) titled "Mixed Profiles":

> Schizophrenia is the state of consciousness which, in my opinion, corresponds most fully to our societal existence. With one

half of our personality still in the interrelations that we want to leave, we find ourselves standing with the other half in new and unaccustomed ones. Due to this crisis, something archaic can invade a civilization with all of its normative patterns. To bear and sustain this in the Hegelian sense is, I believe, the central problem of our time. (64)

Schizophrenia assumes form in Henisch's works in a narrator writing about another person who serves simultaneously both as an identity figure for the narrator and as his opposite. There exists a tension between objective norms versus subjective fulfillment, a conformist versus an outsider position, and passive acceptance versus active resistance. The vagabond inhabits the pages of Henisch's prose as a potential incarnation of self-determined identity, but at the same time this perspective is broken; it is not related directly, but is mediated or reflected through eyes still caught within the structures of conformity as imposed by society. The process of writing is a self-conscious one, reflecting and thematizing the personality split.

The title—Mixed Profiles—depicts the schizophrenic condition. It implies the partial blending of the side (third person) and frontal (first person) views of the human head, thereby indicating the presence of two perspectives within one consciousness. In an essay titled "Why I Don't Want Austria to Go Under" (1988a), Henisch declares his "preference for the periphery" and delineates this position as "not only an outer, but also an inner cityscape, landscape, an area of opposition, of contradiction" (91). It is not possible to abandon norms and roles entirely, but on the other hand it is dangerous to live in oblivious and unconditional harmony with them. To reiterate the author's words from above, our responsibility is to resist the temptation of consonance and unanimity, to endure contention and ambiguity. Henisch's novels portray the frightening prospect of doubting supposedly objective categories of identity, but also the disastrous consequences of failing to do so.[1]

Nowhere are these consequences more ominous and devastating than in the emergence and persistence of fascism within the biography of the author and the history of Austria. Born in 1943, Henisch challenges the versions of personal and national identity transmitted through the family and state. His scrutiny results on both levels in resistance, in the writing of a dissenting story. In his "Austria" essay (1988a), the author asks: "How and why to such an extent did this home of 'great sons' fall prey to a barbarism which was by no means mere occupation and which unfortunately does not yet belong to a past over and done with?" (82–83). Henisch's question decries the "Austrian lie of life" (Langbein 1987, 15), institutionalized through the Moscow Declaration of 1943, which denied collaboration with Nazism, pronouncing Austria instead the first victim of Hitler's aggression. The image of innocence has allowed Austrians to avoid their historical guilt and culpability for many years, right into the present, and it is a myth that threatens the future: "Coming to terms with the past, and by that I mean the most recent past, is very important for the sake of our present and, even more so, for the sake of our future" (Roscher 1987, 74).[2]

Henisch is not alone in exposing Austrian complicity with Nazism, but is one of a growing number of authors to reexamine the victim status, thereby embarking on a process of critical self-examination initiated previously in West Germany.[3] Although isolated works had appeared earlier, this literary impulse gained momentum in the seventies and was fueled further by political events in the mid-eighties, most notably the official handshake welcoming convicted war criminal Walter Reder home and Kurt Waldheim's successful presidential campaign.[4] Such incidents were lent even sharper and more disturbing contours within the context of the fifty-year anniversary of annexation in 1988, for the coincidence of fascist behavior past and present underscored its ubiquitous constancy. Many of the works are autobiographical, depicting fascism as it lurks within and controls the family. This "personalizing of fascism" (Kecht 1991, 315), or "everyday fascism" (Koppensteiner 1992, 54), rests on the belief that fascism is a hierarchical structure of domination, authority, and conformity reflected in and perpetrated through societal institutions, above all the family. The personal is the political; the search for self-identity is simultaneously a questioning of national identity.

For Henisch, questions of identity center on the absence or suppression of a Jewish heritage—within his family the denial of its Jewish ancestry and for Austria silence concerning the atrocities committed against its once-thriving Jewish community. The

"Austrian compromise" (Dürr 1990, 9) prolongs the systematic eradication of Jews within Austrian society beyond the conclusion of World War II. In a recent study, Helga Embacher (1995) details how Austria, in order to preserve its image, has simply denied the fact of anti-Semitism, both past and present. Thus "just-Jews," as opposed to those persecuted, for example, due to political reasons, had no right to compensation or other forms of support after the war (139–140). Furthermore, Austria has made no attempt—not even through a verbal invitation—to bring back Jews who survived the war in exile; in fact, it has obstructed repatriation efforts repeatedly (114). Even as late as 1995, a broadcast commemorating the fiftieth anniversary of the liberation of Auschwitz cited the murder of Austrian politicians, journalists, and artists, among others, but did not once utter the word "Jew" or "Jewish" (111). Such policies have guaranteed the continuing absence of Jews in contemporary Austria, both physically and in the collective memory. According to Richard Mitten (1992), there exists in Austria today "an anti-Semitism without Jews and without (acknowledged) anti-Semites" (7). The political scientist Anton Pelinka (1990) states that the "great Austrian taboo" has led to "an underlying structural problem with their national identity" (64).

In two novels in particular—*Negatives of My Father* and *Stein's Paranoia*—Henisch gives voice to the silence surrounding the missing Jews in his personal story and his country's history. In portraying the identity crisis within his own autobiography, Henisch exposes Austria's crisis of identity. On both levels something is missing, and to acknowledge that something requires the ability to sustain the contradiction of the schizophrenic perspective.

Negatives of My Father was first published in 1975, then was revised in 1980 and again in 1987.[5] The fact that Henisch twice returned to the text suggests the significance and weight that it holds for him. It is his most personal work, employing family names and places and events from lived reality. The first-person narrator, identified as Peter Henisch, relates his attempt to understand the role that his father, Walter Henisch, played in the war as a highly successful and decorated war photographer responsible for propaganda and accountable to Goebbels. As such it is an example of "father literature" which, according to Craig Decker (1991), emerged as a literary genre in both Austria and (West) Germany by the mid-eighties (148). The generation of children born during or immediately after the war began to question the role of their parents, in particular of their fathers, under Hitler. Eveline L. Kanes (1983) defines "father literature" as the attempt to divest the child's picture of romanticism, to pare down the childhood image in order to get to the core (4), which may well be deemed rotten.

But *Negatives of My Father* thematizes more than the collaboration of Austria during the war. The confrontation here between father and son, the attempt to understand, is rendered all the more difficult by the fact that Walter Henisch is part Jewish—his mother is a Jew—and the family survived the war only by denying this fact. In the Roscher interview, Henisch states that as soon as he understood what it meant for his father, in spite of his Jewish heritage, to work as a war correspondent for the Nazis, it became a problem for him, one that he had to work through, and what is more, one that pertains to a broader audience: "This is not just his and my problem" (74).

The novel portrays the obliteration of Jews on two interdependent levels, the political and the personal, on the one hand by the Nazi murder machine and on the other by the author's own father. Furthermore, denial of the Henisch Jewish ancestry persists into the present. When, after the war, the young Peter asks what the words Jew and Nazi mean, his inquiry provokes silence and evasion (131–132). Later still, his paternal grandmother, herself a Jew, complains that the beard he grows makes him look like a Polish Jew (12), and she offers him his "nice big Proof of Aryan Descent" with words of praise for the good that Hitler did (47). Concomitant with repression of the family's Jewish background, then, is the uninterrupted approbation of Hitler and Nazism. While his father's past actions are disturbing, it is the pride with which he still recounts those completed deeds, the admiration he continues to express for the efficiency of Hitler's war machine that are incomprehensible. Both grandmother and father acquired and preserve identity by becoming Austrian, which has meant shedding their Jewishness. Austrian and Jewish were and have remained mutually exclusive concepts.

The opening scene of Henisch's novel vividly paints the lack of a Jewish presence in the personal and political biography of Austria. The deputy mayor of Vienna bestows the golden badge of honor upon Walter Henisch. In her speech detailing his accomplishments, she conveniently deletes any mention of his participation in World War II, an omission noted by the son with the words: "Whew! That went fast! I say to myself" (1). The grandmother imagines placing this medal in the same box containing Walter Henisch's Iron Crosses earned during the war, thereby seamlessly uniting past and present. The biographical hole, however, remains as a bubble beneath the surface that must either be filled or burst. Identity is determined by absence, or lack, and the search for self undergone within the pages of the novel is the attempt to acknowledge and confront that omission. It is the task of the son to fill in the gaps of his father's biography, which again, on the political level, means that Austria must recognize the deletions within its own history.

The author approaches this task as a self-appointed detective in pursuit of clues and evidence. The analogy is appropriate, for we do indeed know the end of the story, the crime, and must now reconstruct the obscured how, why, and who of its occurrence. The bits of missing evidence uncovered by the author include tape recordings of his father's war stories, the son's own taped response to those stories, his father's war letters, testimony by the grandmother and mother, the son's childhood memories, various official letters, and of course his father's war pictures. The narrator, Peter Henisch, strives to combine these fragments into a coherent whole, a unified picture, a story with beginning and end.

As such the son's writing process resembles the father's photography, a similarity the son gradually and reluctantly concedes. Just as Peter begins to photograph during the course of the novel, Walter starts to write. Both father and son perceive the world from a distance, be it through the lens of a camera or the keys of a typewriter: "Everything that exists, I think is good, to the extent that it provides *material*. What you turn into a photo, Papa, I make into text" (69–70). Both approach life as motifs to be framed into neat scenes that are selectively remembered, manipulated, prettified. The position of father and son as distanced observers of a mediated reality finds expression in the metaphor of the tightrope walker, central to the novel. They are involved in a balancing act above the fray of life, with their camera/typewriter serving as balancing pole. From this perspective they look down upon others with dispassionate coldness, called "brutal curiosity."

The difference between father and son, and this is a crucial difference, is that the younger man loses his balance. Two dreams depict his fall. In the first the narrator realizes during the very act of crossing that the wooden planks of the bridge he traverses are "temporary," that they are laid across "damaged piers," and that the boards are "rotten." They cannot hold the weight of him and his "as-yet-unborn child" (142). In the second, the son follows his father across the tightrope, but suddenly realizes he has no balancing pole and falls (172). In other words, for the narrator Peter Henisch the unity of the story, its seamlessness, becomes a problem. The "magic" of the father figure for the young boy (149), created through his stories and photographs, is revealed as an illusion, and the son must now rectify this picture through opposing pictures, through his own negatives of his father. The (cleverly) translated title of the novel encapsulates the split of perspective: on the one hand it refers to the father's photographs, on the other to the subversive lens of the son. The subjectivity of the son's story undermines the imputed veracity of officially transmitted pictures of history.[6] Thus Henisch's novel at one and the same time relates a story and reflects upon it. The narrator simultaneously constructs and deconstructs sanctioned discourse concerning identity.

Formally, the schizophrenic perspective assumes shape in contrasts and contradiction. The narrative switches back and forth without warning between past and present, father and son, and fact and fiction. Dreams, memory, and reality merge. The supposed objectivity of narration is questioned throughout the novel by means of capitalized words, which indicate subjective emphasis, skepticism, or irony. There is no single narrative strand or voice, but rather a multiplicity of viewpoints and versions positioned side by side, lacking an overarching and ordered hierarchy. Quotation marks are omitted, thereby creating confusion concerning the speaker. Although the story recounts Walter Henisch's biography, constant interruptions confound a sequential chronology. As the narrative progresses it increasingly fragments, relating less and less about the father and more and more about the son, and eventually Peter Henisch is unable to write at all. He turns to his childhood camera as an alternate method to generate meaning, but his first attempt produces totally black images. The son cannot bring his story to a close; the pictures previously used to order and capture the world have become invalid. He realizes that they manipulate and falsify reality by rendering it linear, coherent, and closed.

Peter Henisch ultimately concludes his novel by recording his father's final words, and these words suggest that the father figure—as reader of this text—has undergone a process of change similar to, though less radical than, that of his son. He describes two, not one, pictures of a balloon ascent, and these pictures contrast. In the second "happy" story his assignment is to cover Children's Day. However, seeing that the children are exploited for political purposes, he rebels against the very opportunism he previously applauded. He rejects the politician as "magician," as someone who turns every negative into a positive, just as his son earlier had rejected his own acts of magic, and refuses to participate any longer in the whitewashing of reality (181–182).

For both father and son, alienation from the official line effectuates a redefinition of identity. Walter Henisch starts to spout Yiddish jokes and at one point affirms his Jewishness, although it remains tentative, punctuated with a question mark as opposed to a period: "You know, [my father said], a Jew always has two possibilities. But why a Jew: I asked. Well, he said, why not?" (177–178). For Peter Henisch, long-suppressed memories increasingly erupt into the present and culminate in an affirmation of his Jewish heritage:

> At that point something strange happened in me.
> I wanted to repeat: I'm no Jew.
> But oddly enough, the answer turned around.
> Yes, I said, you're right—you've seen right through me. (168)

The schizophrenic process of questioning and doubt, however threatening it may be, contains a positive potential for resistance and change.

The narrator cannot provide an alternate story—recall Henisch's words that he has no solution to offer his readers. What he can and does accomplish, however, is to interrupt and thereby undermine the seemingly natural flow of the officially sanctioned story. Jürgen Koppensteiner (1992) is correct in stating that Henisch, in contrast to many of his contemporaries, writes with the assumption that literature possesses the possibility for instruction and illumination (46–47). The text's questions, comments, insertions, variations, and alternatives subvert claims to unequivocal truth and propel the reader out onto the periphery along with the narrator. From this position, burdened with the schizophrenic perspective, the reader may perhaps undergo a similar process of acknowledgment of Jews in Austrian society.

Stein's Paranoia, published in 1988, is not as overtly autobiographical as *Negatives of My Father*. The protagonist, Max Stein, is born two years later than Henisch and his place of birth is Canada. However, these discrepant life statistics function only to magnify an experience that is intensely autobiographical for the author. Stein's date of birth—April 27, 1945—is the day when, eleven days before the end of the war in Europe, the 1938 *Anschluß* was declared null and void and Austria was "liberated" by the Allied powers. Canada is the country of immigration for Stein's Jewish parents, from which he returns at age five with his father. Despite his obviously fictitious status then, as a Viennese Jew growing up amid the silence imposed by the Austrian lie of life, Stein serves the author as an "identity figure":

> [He] is approximately as old as I, although, for reasons that we have considered passé until just recently, he was born in Quebec, Canada. This Stein wants nothing but to be a good Austrian; however, one day in our present past he begins to notice that he can no longer be so without further ado. But on the other hand, he also is not able simply to shed this skin. (90)

Stein functions to illustrate the author's own experiences, and here as in the earlier novel the central experience is the choice he is forced to make between being Austrian or being Jewish. Again these identities are mutually exclusive, and to acknowledge one's Jewishness necessitates a split personality, the schizophrenic perspective that permeates this novel in both its content and form.

As a "good Austrian," Stein marries the gentile Brigitte and gets along with her Nazi father. He forgets the traditions of his Jewish ancestry and wants to hear nothing of his family's persecution or of Austria's part in it. "That's all just part of the past" (17); it's "*your* past," he tells his father. Stein, like Walter Henisch, is at one with his identity as an Austrian, which means effacement of the Jew past and present.

But then one day he overhears what is presumably an anti-Semitic remark in a newspaper kiosk, and this sentence precipitates a loss of balance similar to that suffered by the narrator in *Negatives of My Father*. Echoing Henisch's words from above, Stein no longer feels comfortable in his Austrian skin, but he cannot step out of it either (55). His unity of identity fragments. His position before the mirror—turned half toward and half away from his image—manifests his split personality, and he asks: "Where are you? There I am! Am I identical with myself?" (28–29). Similarly, he mistrusts the identity lent to him through his Austrian passport—eye color, height, and in particular the imputed lack of distinguishing marks, that is, the omission of the fact that he is a Jew (54). It becomes increasingly apparent to Stein that his Jewish and his Austrian identities are incompatible, and his experiences after the sentence in the kiosk alternate between scenes where Austrians denigrate Jews and other minorities and scenes where Stein rediscovers the Jewish presence in both his personal biography and the city around him.

Stein encounters numerous examples of "good Austrians." There is the racist taxi driver, symptomatic of the everyday working man, who draws a clear line between "the likes of us" and "the likes of them"—"all those other peoples: they're worthless after all" (89). There is the young man in the streetcar reading Hitler's *Mein Kampf* (*My Struggle*), the gang of soccer players yelling "We want no Jews!", the group of boys torturing a helpless frog to death, and there is the swastika painted on the very spot designated for Stein's plaque commemorating a destroyed synagogue. Such overt anti-Semitism is but the outward manifestation of the general Austrian disinclination to see and remember. The professor treating Stein's case personifies this blindness. He doubts the veracity of everything Stein experiences (see for example pp. 31 and 60), thereby exonerating himself and society from culpability. His diagnosis of paranoia not only neatly categorizes and therefore dismisses Stein's fears, as Jennifer E. Michaels notes (1984, 118–119), but in essence deflects responsibility and blame from society to Stein. The professor demonstrates the same victimized mentality, albeit in more subtle form, as the taxi driver, who states: "This *Judas-race* has already betrayed us *twice*" (57).

Here Stein's personal story intersects directly with national history, and past merges with present. The underlying continuity is that Jews are made responsible for their own persecution; it is the myth of innocence as propagated through Austria's postwar status as the first victim of Hitler. Stein sees the national basis for identity as the lie it is:

> What is truth? Can our politicians even begin to conceive of what this concept means?
>
> Truth is, on the contrary, that the Austrian way can no longer be that which it never in reality was.
>
> In the beginning there was the Austrian lie of life (the lie of survival; 63).[7]

The first Jewish "betrayal" was any insinuation of Austrian complicity in the Holocaust; the second is the tarnished reputation Austria suffered in the wake of the Waldheim election. In both instances the accusation explicitly perverts the perpetrator/victim constellation.

Such scenes of denial are juxtaposed with scenes of remembrance; Austrian silence meets Jewish voices. The basic premise of the novel is brilliantly simple: Stein, and he exemplifies all Austrians, must either admit or disregard the actuality of the anti-Semitic sentence. The Austrians clearly choose indifference and ignorance. Stein, too, would like to disclaim it—he wonders if he really heard it; he belittles its import by imputing drunkenness to the man. But more and more he must concede its existence, and with this recognition comes a rediscovery of Jewishness. He exposes the deletions in his personal and national history in a manner reminiscent of the narrator in the earlier novel. The detective work accomplished there parallels Stein's task as archaeologist here as he "digs" into history to determine where, when, and how the anti-Semitism all began (38–39).

Stein's choice marginalizes him in a society that has chosen the opposite. There is no room for him within the Austrian concept of identity, and he finds himself in a state of exile. He loses his home, family, job, and all of his possessions and becomes increasingly isolated from the world around him. His path retraces that of his ancestors, and at one point Stein also decides to emigrate to North America. However, during a stopover in London he dreams that a man asks him his intended direction. When he cannot reply, the man, an Austrian Jew who fled fifty years ago, says, "Go back where you belong!" (98). For Stein this means back to the kiosk, where he stands watch night and day hoping to rectify his prior omission: "Yes, Stein thought. I should have done that. Resist the beginnings. In my way. At my time, on my spot" (27). His act embodies resistance, for the German term *Widerstand* means literally "a stance or standing against."

Stein's original failure to counter the sentence propels him on a search for a *Gegensatz* (12), which translates as opposition. The success of the search, the effectiveness of his resistance, remains a matter for debate. On the one hand, his actions result in collapse and internment. At the conclusion of the novel, he is "cured" from his paranoia and refuses to see a spray-painted swastika, thereby apparently conforming to societal blindness and reticence. On the other hand, there are signs of hope throughout the novel such as the young people holding vigil for members of the Austrian resistance and the dream in which Stein's daughter shows him how to swim against the current.[8] These are examples of Austrians who resemble Stein by resisting their way at their time on their spot (78). Two other central figures—his grandfather and the American Jew Clarissa—repudiate the official myth; both personify remembrance in the midst of collective memory loss. They are counter-examples, and their perspective "enlightens" (hence the name Clarissa) Stein through shattering the naturalness and unity of his previous perspective, which at one and the same time jeopardizes his security and enables change. Hope lies in the very existence of contradiction in the face of a monolithic societal mindset.

This mindset is reflected and perpetuated in the seemingly immutable logic of tautology as epitomized in the sentences of a young Austrian: "What's over is over. And what's done is done. And the past is past. The past must be past. And an order is an order" (82). The name "Stein" (stone) evokes the immobility and petrification inherent in such language; Henisch's character is named for the Austrian refusal to budge from their assertion of innocence. However, Stein himself transcends the name. His search for a *Gegensatz* means, when literally translated, a counter-sentence; that is, he seeks a language to undermine the closure and uniformity of official discourse. Stein resists through sentences such as: "I just did not do my duty" (27). Recognition of his omission allows Stein to see through Austrian self-justification. By reversing the general tendency to forget, Stein also reverses the standard excuse, thereby authorizing a contradictory truth: It was the Austrians' duty not to just do their duty.

Stein's loss of a unified sense of self, his inability to identify any longer with the Austrian image, finds formal expression throughout the novel in a broken narrative perspective that vacillates between a first and third person narrator. Here, as in the earlier novel, the "I" perspective reflects upon the story being told. And here, as before, this self-reflexivity deconstructs both private and public history; it validates opposition and ambiguity. The subjectivity of a narrating consciousness marks Henisch's text on every level. It breaks and fragments the story with asides, associations, dreams, and memories. As a reflection of Stein's schizophrenia, it is incapable of imposing clarity or order upon its experiences and increasingly jumps from one isolated perception to the next, without commentary, explanation, or context, chronology determined only through the passage of time: "in the morning ... in the afternoon ... in the evening" (85–87). The narrative voice uses italicized words, question marks, parentheses, dashes, ellipses, the subjunctive mood, and colons, thereby relativizing or negating what was just affirmed. The slash, the single most characteristic and unique formal feature of the text, encapsulates in miniature the unity of opposites, that is, the existence side by side of the mutually exclusive or seemingly irreconcilable. It is used most consistently with the grammatical tenses of present, simple past, and past perfect to underline the interdependence of past and present (29). The broken narrative perspective destroys the assumption of objectivity necessary to silence doubt; it subverts the "logic" or unity of official discourse.

Thus the novel itself represents a whole series of counter-sentences that oppose the tautologies and inflexibility of the "good Austrian's" language, and as such it parallels Stein's attempt to resist from the beginning. The first-person narrator commences his novel with the same words Stein utters later (27):

> Beginnings —: It's a matter of finding a beginning.
> Yes, beginnings —: It's a matter of resisting beginnings.
> Resistance —: Resistance against writing on such a topic.
> But it's a matter of affording resistance—not too late this time.
> I think / *he* thinks. What could his name be?

The narrator's account of Stein's story—the novel before the reader—must be read as an act of resistance. The German word *Schreibwiderstand* from the aforementioned quote translates both as resistance against writing about this topic, and writing as resistance. The author offers no easy solution for Stein, but hope for change lies with the reader.

Henisch's novel does not end with Stein's capitulation. The novel's final, short paragraph—uniformly ignored by critics—negates his putative cure:

> But Stein's fingers felt for the matches. The commemorative plaque will have been mounted in the meantime. Its text will be shorter than that composed by Stein. I enter the house where I still reside, I close the apartment door behind me, the roof vis-à-vis reflects the dusk.

The first-person narrator—and the subversive, schizophrenic potential he represents—has the last word. Ambiguity and contradiction, signaled clearly in the first word ("but"), permeate the passage. The associations are multiple and at times obscure, but they circle and recall the central themes of the novel. The "matches" refer to the diagnosis of "slight pyromania" by the professor when Stein repeats his grandfather's words about "splinters of light" (109). Both phrases also refer to *Kristallnacht* when the synagogue was burned, as does the reflection from the roof. Now green, its light was originally red, "almost like a chimney" (33), and therefore unbearable to someone who finally remembers and sees not only the fires of that night but the crematoria of fascism. Stein may be going home, but the narrator heads back to his apartment to continue writing.

At the center of Henisch's autobiographical texts stands a

character no longer in unquestioned agreement with his societal identity. The protagonist loses balance and finds himself on the periphery, cognizant of a perspective secure within established norms and expectations as well as one imperiled by otherwise unvoiced doubts and questions. This split in consciousness, termed schizophrenia, characterizes every aspect of Henisch's work, both in content and form. His novels present a construction of personal and political biography and, simultaneously, a deconstruction of this same story or picture. The narrator's extreme self-consciousness or self-reflexivity destroys the coherence of the story he narrates, thereby compelling the reader to navigate a similarly contradictory path. We are subjected to unsolved problems and unresolved questions, but for Henisch the potential for change lies precisely in the ability to resist the temptation of closure, to walk the periphery. It is the struggle to withstand tension, the loss of one's balance to plunge into the risk of question, which is most important, for it demands a willingness to see the other position, to acknowledge the interdependence of seeming opposites, and to confront the absence, the silence, and one's own culpability in preserving it. The schizophrenic state fractures our seamless accounts of identity, and from this breach can emerge the missing element of the postwar Austrian image as well as of Henisch's own autobiography—the Jew.

Notes

1. Let us turn to two specific works as examples. In a novel from 1981 titled *Bali or Swoboda Drops Out* (*Bali oder Swoboda steigt aus*), Henisch frees his protagonist, Swoboda, which means "freedom," from the stultifying norms and expectations of society dictated through the school system and to a lesser degree the institution of marriage. Similarly, Swoboda, who shares many autobiographical details with Henisch, including his profession as a writer, sends his protagonist Franz off to fulfill his dreams by finally journeying to Bali. Swoboda rejects reified societal values to which he had previously conformed in an attempt to experience a more personally satisfying reality. His belief in traditional precepts gone and no substitutes in place, Swoboda loses balance and falls (80). He feels light and heavy simultaneously, as if he could—but for the force of gravity—float above the sidewalk (81). Swoboda strives to endure or live this contradictory state through writing

about Franz, just as Henisch plays out possibilities in an attempt to sustain contradiction through writing about Swoboda.

In *May is Passé* (*Der Mai ist vorbei*) from 1978, the first-person narrator (identified as Peter) writes a retrospective novel about the year 1968 (presumably the novel before us), while the protagonist Paul Grünzweig attempts an article on the same topic. Both narrative levels problematize the tension between the personal and political through the characters' interrelationships. They see marriage as one example of closed societal systems and decide to challenge its constraints by forming a commune. This alternative living experiment ultimately fails because its members form adversarial coalitions, spouting either psychoanalytical truisms (the personal) or Marxist theory (the political). For all their supposed difference, the feuding parties are really very similar: they cannot withstand contradiction; they cannot live outside the security of their conceptual system.

The danger of such a stance is illustrated in various scenes where Paul hears racial slurs or witnesses brutality against foreigners, but does not intervene. Henisch links generations and evinces parallels between present-day neutral Austria and historical fascist Austria. Paul/Peter contemplates the difference between the scene at Vienna's Heldenplatz in 1938 and Woodstock in 1968 and concludes that whereas one group yelled "yes," the other yelled "no" (153); whereas the older generation respected any uniform, their children rejected them all just as indiscriminately (46). Although critics have justifiably charged Henisch with oversimplification here (see, for example, Strelka 1980, 155), the author's point is that resistance depends on one's capacity to disagree with an assigned and natural-seeming role.

2. In his "Austria" essay (1988a) he reiterates: "But the present is the transition of the past into the future" (94).

3. Regina Kecht (1991) notes that this literary trend has dispelled the stubbornly held impression (whether justifiable or not) that Austrian literature was apolitical and reality-adverse (313–314). See also the article by Viktoria Hertling (1991).

4. Thomas Rothschild (1992) points out that the very silence veiling Waldheim's war record ultimately and ironically precipitated the ensuing "noisy" airing of responsibility (667).

5. The original version was published by Fischer, the 1980 revision by Langen-Müller, and the 1987 one by Residenz Verlag. My citations refer to the translation by Anne C. Ulmer (1986), which is based on the 1987 version. For a discussion of the differences between revisions, see Ulmer's afterword, especially 187.

6. Craig Decker (1991) identifies the reflections of the narrator as the third major narrative of the novel and correctly points out that this strand consists of an implicit discourse on modes of representation.

7. Henisch echoes Hermann Langbein, who also terms the deception the Austrian "lie of life" (*Lebenslüge*; 15).

8. See Michaels (1994) for a more detailed discussion of the signs of resistance and change in the novel (120–121).

Works Cited

Decker, Craig. 1991. Photographic Eye, Narrative I: Peter Henisch's *Die kleine Figur meines Vaters*. *Monatshefte* 83, No. 2, 147–160.

Dürr, Volker. 1990. Introduction. In *Coping with the Past: Germany and Austria after 1945*. Edited by Kathy Harms, Lutz R. Reuter, and Volker Dürr. Madison: University of Wisconsin Press.

Embacher, Helga. 1995. *Neubeginn ohne Illusionen: Juden in Österreich nach 1945*. Vienna: Picus.

Frieden, Sandra. 1983. *Autobiography: Self Into Form: German-Language Autobiographical Writings of the 1970's*. Frankfurt am Main, New York: Peter Lang.

Henisch, Peter. 1972. Gemischte profile. *Vom Baronkarl. Peripheriegeschichen und andere Prosa*. Frankfurt am Main: Fischer.

Henisch, Peter. 1972. Literatur der Zukunft/Zukunft der Literatur—oder was. *Literatur und Kritik* 63.

Henisch, Peter. 1978. *Der Mai ist vorbei*. Frankfurt am Main: Fischer.

Henisch, Peter. 1981. *Bali oder Swoboda steigt aus*. Munich, Vienna: Langen Müller.

Henisch, Peter. 1982. *Zwischen allen Sesseln: Geschichten Gedichte Entwürfe Notizen Statements 1965–1982*. Vienna: Hannibal.

Henisch, Peter. 1988a. Warum ich nicht will, daß Österreich untergeht. In *Reden an Österreich: Schriftsteller ergreifen das Wort*. Edited by Jochen Jung. Salzburg: Residenz.

Henisch, Peter. 1988b. *Steins Paranoia*. Salzburg: Residenz.

Henisch, Peter. 1990. *Negatives of My Father*. Translated by Anne Close Ulmer. Riverside, CA: Ariadne.

Hertling, Viktoria. 1991. Bereitschaft zur Betroffenheit: Neueste österreichische Prosa über die Jahre 1938 bis 1945. *German Studies Review* 14.2 (May).

Kanes, Eveline L. 1983. In Search of Fathers. *Denver Quarterly* 18, No. 1.

Kecht, Regina. 1991. Faschistische Familienidyllen—Schatten der Vergangenheit in Henisch, Schwaiger und Reichart. In *Austrian Writers and the Anschluss: Understanding the Past—Overcoming the Past*. Edited by Donald G. Daviau. Riverside, CA: Ariadne.

Koppensteiner, Jürgen. 1992. Zwischen Anpassung und Widerstand: Bemerkungen zu zeitkritischen Prosawerken von Peter Henisch, Elisabeth Reichart und Gerald Szyszkowitz. *Modern Austrian Literature* 25, No. 1.

Langbein, Hermann. 1987. Darf man vergessen? In *Das grosse Tabu: Österreichs Umgang mit seiner Vergangenheit*. Edited by Anton Pelinka and Erika Weinzierl. Vienna: Verlag der Österreichischen Staatsdruckerei.

Michaels, Jennifer E. 1994. Is Stein Paranoid? Peter Henisch's Reflections on the Jewish Experience in Austria after the Presidential Election of 1986 in his Novel *Steins Paranoia*. *Modern Austrian Literature* 27, No. 3/4.

Mitten, Richard. 1992. *The Politics of Antisemitic Prejudice: The Waldheim Phenomenon in Austria*. Boulder: Westview Press.

Pelinka, Anton. 1990. The Great Austrian Taboo: The Repression of the Civil War. In *Coping with the Past: Germany and Austria after 1945*. Edited by Kathy Harms, Lutz R. Reuter, and Volker Dürr. Madison: University of Wisconsin Press.

Rothschild, Thomas. 1992. Österreichische Literatur. In *Hansers Sozialgeschichte der deutschen Literatur: Gegenwartsliteratur seit 1968*. Vol. 12. Edited by Klaus Briegleb and Sigrid Weigel. Munich: Carl Hanser.

Roscher, Achim. 1987. Peter Henisch im Gespräch. *Neue deutsche Literatur* 35, No. 9.

Schobel, Eva. 1983. Henisch von Hamlet zu Hoffmann. *Literatur und Kritik* 177/178.

Strelka, Joseph P. 1980. Eine Phänomenologie des Mitmachens: Zur frühen, autobiographischen Erzählprosa von Peter Henisch. *Modern Austrian Literature* 13, No. 1.

Ulmer, Anne Close. 1986. The Son as Survivor: Peter Henisch's *Die kleine Figur meines Vaters*. *The Germanic Review* 61, No. 2.

An Experiment with Himself: Peter Henisch's Autobiographical Writing in *The Small Figure of My Father*, *May Is Gone*, and *Stein's Paranoia*

Jennifer Michaels

In his novel *May Is Gone* (1978), Henisch observes that writing is for him an experiment with himself (163). In most of his markedly autobiographical literary works, Henisch examines, often very critically, various aspects of his identity. Because he integrates his quest for identity into the history and concerns of his time, these works go beyond the private exploration of the self to address larger issues. This essay examines three of Henisch's novels that typify how he uses his private life in his works not only to gain insights into himself but also to address problems in his society. In *The Small Figure of My Father* (1975) Henisch investigates his father's complicity during the Nazi years in Austria. Through confronting his father's behavior during this time he seeks to understand himself. Beyond this personal search, the novel captures the painful struggle of Henisch's generation to come to terms with the past of its parents, especially its fathers. In *May Is Gone* Henisch looks critically at his marginal involvement in the student unrest of 1968 and his stance of being "an outsider out of passion" (Henisch 1982, 187), as well as at the failures of his own generation. In *Stein's Paranoia* (1988) Henisch not only explores his Jewish identity and his position in Austria as a writer with some Jewish ancestry, but also examines past and present anti-Semitism in Austria. In these and other works,

Henisch's private exploration of the self takes on wider relevance.

Henisch belongs to a generation of writers in Germany and Austria who were attracted to autobiographical forms (Ulmer 1986, 57). In keeping with this "autobiographical impulse" that was "the most characteristic literary phenomenon" of the seventies and early eighties (Frieden 1983, 42), Henisch insists on the close connections between his life and works (Schobel 1988, 1:5), and in his writing he is open about his personal life. Rather than inventing a story, he prefers to write about what he has experienced (2:345). In *The Small Figure of My Father*, for example, Henisch, who was also working on his Bali novel at this time (1981), notes that, compared to the real story of his father, the invented story of Bali suddenly seemed insignificant (Henisch 1987, 14). In a 1981 interview in which he talks about *The Small Figure of My Father*, Henisch explains that because a literary work deals with individual experiences, it can, in his opinion, approach a problem better from a subjective and psychological rather than analytical perspective: "This was the dimension I could grasp; the others I could have only quoted from" (Fischer 1989, 190). To explore his experiences Henisch uses a highly autobiographical style that he terms "personal realism."

The speech Henisch gave when he was awarded the Anton Wildgans Prize in 1978 yields insights into how he perceives his role as a writer. Henisch, who expresses here his discomfort with making theoretical statements and interpreting his own works, emphasizes that he is no literary critic. What he has to say, he remarks, is contained in his literary works. Henisch, who values critical distance and irony, points out that he has no objective truths to offer and thinks it presumptuous of people to expect that of him. He does, however, have subjective experiences and the insights that result from them, and these may, he observes, be interesting to others. By using himself as a model (not only as a good one, he notes) he hopes that his writing can go beyond private introspection to shed light on the problems that others face. Henisch does not pretend to have solutions, even to his own problems, and he doubts that writing about problems can help to solve them or indeed that they can be solved at all. He insists, however, that it is important to address such problems in his works because to keep silent about them would be dishonest (1982, 187).

Henisch's quest for his identity within the wider context of his generation's grappling with the Nazi past forms an important part of *The Small Figure of My Father*, one of his most successful and interesting novels and the work with which he established his reputation as a major author. Unlike much of the later "father literature" in Germany and Austria, Henisch wrote his novel while his father was still alive, although terminally ill at that time. Instead of having to rely only on memories of a dead father, Henisch could talk to him and ask him questions, and his father could read and react to his son's text. Henisch shares many of the concerns that preoccupied other writers of such works, especially their rejection of the legacy of the Hitler years, left to them by their parents, and their struggle to find a different historical identity. Through confronting their parents' pasts they hope not only to understand them better but also to avoid repeating their mistakes. Learning about the Nazi past and the role their parents played in it is therefore an essential first step, these authors believe, in understanding their society and defining their own identities (Kecht 1993, 245). Because for many years after the war discussion of their country's involvement in National Socialism was taboo, many recent Austrian writers sense that they lack a past (Langbein 1987, 9). Peter Turrini expresses this when he notes that he has grown up without a past because his parents, his teachers, and his whole environment remained silent about the Nazi years (Zeyringer 1992, 145). They have grown up, as Elisabeth Reichart remarks of her protagonist Ruth in the story *Come over the Lake* (1988), in a historical vacuum (Roscher 1987, 130). In the process of coming to terms with their parents' past they are forced to look critically at themselves and ask whether they would have behaved like their parents or whether they would have acted differently (Kanes 1983, 3). Henisch imagines, for example, his father asking him what he would have done in his father's situation in the Nazi period. Through writing these biographies these authors thus not only reconstruct their fathers' pasts but also try to find themselves. "In pursuit of another, one encounters oneself," Henisch observes in *The Small Figure of My Father* (e.g., 17, 106). This sentence also appears in the afterword to *Hamlet bleibt* (Hamlet Remains, 1971).

On one level *The Small Figure of My Father* is a biography of Henisch's father. To reconstruct this life Henisch tapes conversations with his father, talks to his mother and grandmother, and examines his father's letters and photographs from the Hitler years, which is the particular focus of the novel, although Walter Henisch also discusses his childhood and the post-World War II years in Vienna. Henisch stresses that his will be a subjective view of his father's life (9). He tries to understand why he wants to write this biography, an undertaking that also puzzles Walter Henisch, who remarks that his son had not previously been interested in his father's life. In one of the unmailed letters to his father included in the novel, Henisch writes that he is not sure why he suddenly became interested in his father's life. One reason is that he is now thirty. Elsewhere Henisch observes that at this age one gains a new ability, the ability to remember (Henisch 1982, 80). It is thus an age, in his opinion, that encourages a person to look back and take stock of his or her previous life. For Henisch, thirty is an age of uncertainty when one is no longer young but also not yet old. Until now, he writes, he had always been on the side of the sons in the generational conflict, but as he thinks of younger people's suspicion of anyone over thirty, he looks at himself in the mirror with growing mistrust (1987, 18–19). Because Henisch is soon to become a father himself, examining his own father helps him define how he intends to play this role. Yet another stimulus for Henisch to confront his father's past comes at the beginning of the novel at the awards ceremony to honor Walter Henisch for his work as a photographer. When the Deputy Mayor of Vienna presents Walter Henisch with the award, she sketches his accomplishments but is silent about what he did during the Nazi years. By writing the novel, Henisch tries to fill in this blank.

Henisch struggles to understand why his father contributed to Nazi propaganda through his photography. He wonders how his father could have supported a criminal regime that would have murdered him if it had known about his Jewish ancestry. Walter Henisch was no fanatical Nazi. He became involved by chance because his stepfather enrolled him in the German Gymnasts' Association from where he was promoted to the Hitler Youth. He later became an acclaimed war reporter, whose photographs Goebbels admired. Through his discussions with his father Henisch prods him to become aware of his complicity and to accept moral responsibility for what he did during the Nazi regime. In one of his unsent letters he asks his father why he and others went along and why they did nothing against it (145). As a child Henisch enjoyed hearing the war stories his father loved to tell on special occasions such as birthdays and holidays, but as he grew older, he found his father's behavior deeply disturbing. Henisch is critical of his father not just because he wore a Nazi uniform but because he wore it with pride. Despite his son's urging, Walter Henisch is reluctant to acknowledge that he did anything wrong. Even during interviews with his son in the seventies it is clear that instead of recognizing his guilt, he still admires the Nazi strength and organization. He was proud, he tells his son, of the small contribution he made to the campaign in France.

Throughout the war Walter Henisch used his camera with brutal curiosity to distance himself from events and without his camera he felt naked and imperiled (37). For him photographing was always of prime importance and everything else was secondary (55). His world consisted only of the small image he viewed through his camera lens and he saw the war as a series of pictures that provided him with motifs to satisfy his mania for documenting (37). Among his many photographs from the war are ones that capture what he calls a "beautiful" assault in France and a "classic" employment of a flame thrower (59). Another shows a man, turned into a living torch, trying to escape from the hatch of a tank. You wait for the highest point of his pain, he tells his son, and then press the shutter (77). In his view, he took his best pictures in Russia: from a human perspective, he recalls, the war there was a tragedy, but not from a photographic one (61). Walter Henisch also coldly photographed the execution of partisans in Yugoslavia. Particularly disturbing to Henisch is his father's refusal to be shocked by what he witnessed or to reflect in any way on what he was doing. Walter Henisch dismisses, for example, the atrocities carried out by the SS in the

East as the flip side of the organization he admired in France and he was not outraged by the brutal mistreatment of the Jews in the Warsaw ghetto when he visited there during the war. This visit did not lead him to question the war and the part he played in supporting it. After telling his son about his reactions to the Warsaw ghetto, for example, he immediately relates the adventure of how he won his Iron Cross. The brutal curiosity that pervades his personality and his art underscores his lack of ethical and moral principles and human compassion.

Through his depiction of his father, Henisch confronts all those who went along during the Nazi years and later refused to accept responsibility for their actions, and this subjective confrontation with his age is an essential part of the novel. Walter Henisch's personal life "assumes paradigmatic importance for the political life of Austria before, during, and after the Nazi regime" (Decker 1991, 154). In one of the unmailed letters to his father Henisch stresses the need to take responsibility. He wants his readers to keep a critical distance from his father and not identify with him or his humor. They should not admire his ability to survive or his personality (145–146). Some readers did, however, identify with his father, but others thought that Henisch's depiction of him was too forgiving. Because of this reception, Henisch revised the novel in 1980 to make his criticism of his father sharper. It was important for Henisch that his novel encourage his readers to come to grips with Austria's Nazi past.

The novel goes beyond the biography of Walter Henisch and Henisch's confrontation with his father's past, however, to become a confrontation with himself and his relationship with his father (cf. Aurenche 1993, 103). Early in the novel as he begins to write about Walter Henisch's life, he types twice by mistake that he wants his father "to tell me *my* life story" (9). This typing error makes Henisch realize at the outset that his purpose here is not only to examine his father's life but to explore his own. For Henisch it is essential to find out who his father is in order to become clear about who he is himself (9). Previously, he notes, it would not have occurred to him to connect the search for himself with the search for his father (17). Through this biography, Henisch wants to emancipate himself from his father. He has to write himself out of his father's story, he believes, order to find his own (108).

For many years Henisch tried to distance himself from his father. In one of the unsent letters, Henisch remarks that he understands his father but he does not want to become like him. He wants to escape from his father's path (106). Henisch's mother thought that her son looked like his father, especially around the chin and mouth. Henisch too notices how similar their features are in family photos and when he was twenty he grew a beard to hide the resemblance. Walter Henisch wanted his son to follow in his footsteps and become a photographer or a reporter, and as a result Henisch suffered from an allergy to cameras (Henisch 1988a, 89).

Despite such attempts to distance himself from his father, Henisch is forced as he explores his father's life to acknowledge the many similarities between them and the influence his father has had on him. In the fifth part of his endless interview he observes that he does not want to repeat the "nonsense" that his father had done. He stresses, however, that his father did not only do "nonsense" but also encouraged his son's creativity (Henisch 1982, 115). His grandmother, who is shocked that her grandson is writing about his father rather than choosing a more interesting topic, remarks that Henisch inherited the same family stubbornness as his father. In one of his unsent letters, Henisch asks himself whether he is perhaps using his father's story to distance himself from an important part of his own character. By capturing this part of his character in his depiction of his father's, he can pretend it is no longer his own (75). Henisch's growing awareness of their similarities enables him to get closer to his father and begin to understand him better. Despite his rejection of his father's past, he begins to love him (175).

Henisch realizes that because he shares his father's brutal curiosity, their art has similar roots. Like Walter Henisch's photography, Henisch sees that in his writing he, too, exploits human suffering as a motif. Through his photographs his father distanced himself from the agonies of war, even if he also used them to further his career. His son distances himself from his father's terminal illness by documenting it (Ulmer 1986, 60).

What becomes a photograph for his father becomes a text for the son (75). Through his brutal curiosity Henisch turns his father's illness into material. He describes the bloody sheets, the suffering his father endures, and his body that is wasting away. He watches the various stages of his father's illness and his despair and finds what he sees interesting. If his father were to fall dead, he confesses, it would provide him with a story (76). Henisch recalls that he first noticed this brutal curiosity in himself when he worked for a time at the Workers' Newspaper (*Arbeiterzeitung*). Told to obtain a photograph of a husband, wife, and small child who had been crippled in an accident, he went to the parents of the paralyzed and blinded woman and discovered that they did not yet know what had happened. Henisch, who had to tell them, was disturbed to notice in himself an interest in how the woman's parents reacted to the bad news. He observed, for example, how the young-looking woman became old in a few minutes (74–75). Henisch's examination of his father's past thus forces him to confront his own artistic identity and integrity.

Henisch uses the image of the tightrope walker, a central metaphor in the text, to express the connection between father and son. Henisch is a tightrope walker, just like he is, Walter Henisch tells his son early in the novel, and Henisch cannot forget those words with which his father offers him a clear if strange possibility for identification (14). When he arrives home after this talk with his father, he learns that his wife Sonja is pregnant. Subsequently Henisch dreams on several occasions that his father is carrying him on his shoulders. In one of these dreams Henisch is sitting on his father's shoulders while his father is balancing on a tightrope. This image then changes and Henisch becomes the father carrying his still unknown child on his shoulders (158). The dream refers back to an actual event in Walter Henisch's life. Eager to take sensational pictures, Walter Henisch persuaded a tightrope walker to carry him on his shoulders as he walked on a tightrope over the Danube canal. The police refused permission for this plan, and he narrowly escaped death; the tightrope walker and his daughter, who was sitting on her father's shoulders in place of Walter Henisch, plunged to their deaths. This recurring dream sheds light not only on the relationship between Henisch and his father but also on "the son's attempt to write about that relationship." The text for him is a balancing act in which he tries to strike a precarious balance between showing Walter Henisch as a father and showing him as a Nazi photographer (Decker 1991, 150). The dream also makes Henisch recognize the interconnectedness of the generations. Just as his father carried him on his shoulders, he will carry his still unborn child.

In his next novel, *May Is Gone*, Henisch turns from confronting his father's generation to criticizing his own. The novel is closely linked to the preceding one because of Henisch's critical exploration of himself, his portrayal of his generation's rejection of the legacy of the Nazi years, and its struggle to find a new historical identity. As Henisch observes, members of his generation did not want to live like their parents had lived (162). Through his depiction of the failed commune, however, he shows how difficult it is to live differently from them and he wonders how much of what his generation criticized in its parents still lives on in its members (107). In the novel, which he began in 1976, Henisch focuses in particular on the student movement in Vienna in 1968 and shows both its initial idealism and its later disillusionment. Throughout the novel he struggles to confront his own actions at that time as well as the failures of the student movement and the new left.

In this highly autobiographical novel Henisch draws extensively on his own experiences. The protagonist Paul Grünzweig, for example, edited a journal called *Bienenstich* (Bee Sting) while Henisch was copublisher of the journal *Wespennest* (Wasp's Nest). Henisch's wife is called Sonja and Paul's is called Silvi. Like Henisch, Paul was involved marginally in the student movement of 1968 and lived briefly in a commune. Paul's friends are closely modeled after people Henisch knew, such as Hermann Hakel, Brigitte Schwaiger, Helmut Zenker, Günther Nenning, and Wendelin Schmidt-Dengler (Strelka 1989, 153). Helmut and Christa Zenker become Willy and Bärbel Wüstenrot in the novel, and Schubert is a thinly disguised portrait of Friedemann Bayer. Because they could recognize people from the Viennese cultural scene, many readers treated the work as a *roman à clef* and tried to discover who was who in the novel, an endeavor that hindered an unprejudiced reading (Schobel 1988, 1:185).

Henisch splits himself here into two different people, Peter and Paul. Peter is writing about the writer and journalist Paul Grünzweig, who has been commissioned to write a ten-page article on the student unrest of 1968 in Vienna. Through his research for the article Paul relives his involvement in the student movement. He experiences in scarcely disguised form what Peter experienced himself (Strelka 1989, 153). Splitting the personality into two is an example of the schizophrenia that is a key concept in Henisch's works. He views schizophrenia not as a clinical but as an existential and political phenomenon (Schobel 1988, 1:28). In his view, it is a disease that is particularly prevalent nowadays because the present age causes the individual to feel divorced from his or her world and from a sense of identity. Paul, who suffers from this schizophrenic split, observes that it occurs when something old is passing and something new is coming, or when something new tries to come but the old still has too much force. This conflict between the two takes place not only around us, he believes, but also within ourselves (121–122). In the poem that introduces the fourth day in the novel Henisch calls schizophrenia an illness of the periphery because it is on the border between the old and the new. Through Peter and Paul, Henisch examines this split in consciousness and loss of identity. Paul is Henisch's fictive alter ego while Peter closely resembles Henisch himself. Paul, who is no positive role model, as Henisch notes, remains an isolated outsider whose marriage to Silvi has collapsed and who flees from reality at the end to join what seems to him to be an idyllic commune, though not for the ideological reasons that had drawn him to the earlier one that failed. Peter has managed more or less to adapt to reality and is still married to Sonja, although there are difficulties in the marriage.

At the beginning of the novel Peter tries to separate himself from Paul. He stresses, for example, that he is writing about Paul, not about himself (15). As the novel progresses and the two characters begin to merge, it becomes increasingly harder for Peter to differentiate himself from Paul. Peter writes that he often stays the night in his room in the Spengergasse while he is working on his novel. Or is it Paul, he asks, who is sitting in the room writing his article about the student unrest? Although Peter says he is not Paul, he confesses that he does not know whether that is still true (163). He begins to identify so closely with Paul that he thinks he should have signed the poems he recently wrote with the name Paul Grünzweig. Sonja tells Peter that he is hiding behind Paul (18), and Peter fears that he resembles Paul more than he would like (18).

Throughout the novel Peter struggles to understand not only Paul and thus himself but also why he writes in this particular way. He notes, for example: "I write, Paul wrote, first person present, third person imperfect" (70). It is difficult for him to write in the third person because although he is opposed to writing an imaginative novel, he feels that mere autobiography is also not enough (17–18). Perhaps, he reflects, one should not write as he does, always attempting to make life into literature and literature into life. When he is asked, "Why this Grünzweig? ... Why this pretense?" and "Why don't you write in the first person since your works are so subjective?" he responds that that would be a kind of unmasking and he is a little afraid to see himself without a mask (163–164). It would also mean writing without the critical distance and the irony he values.

A major focus of the novel is Henisch's ironical depiction of Paul's political engagement. Through Paul, Peter tries to analyze his own participation and discover what these events meant for him. Paul's growing disillusionment with the student movement and the new left reflects Peter's own. Like Paul, Henisch was scarcely involved in the student movement in Vienna (Henisch 1982, 185), a movement that was not as radical as those in Berlin, Frankfurt, and Paris. Paul thinks, in fact, of writing in his essay that in Vienna students observed what was happening as if through a window (22). Paul took part in a sit-in by chance. He did not want to become involved and did not even know what people were protesting against, but an acquaintance, Ferry Lampel, who liked to cite what Paul terms the usual Hegel, Marx, Mao, and Marcuse, persuaded him to stay. Although they did not wear uniforms, the demonstrators all looked alike to Paul with their long hair and their fantastic clothes. Theirs were different uniforms, he thought (44–45). Like Walter Henisch who went along with the mass psychosis of the Nazis, Paul goes along with the new left without really wanting to belong (Strelka 1989, 153), although he sympathizes with some of their goals.

But Paul is different from Walter Henisch because of his strong dislike of all forms of organization. He hates any kind of uniform. He does not want to become like his father, he says, who willingly put himself into a uniform that fitted him even better with time (46). Whenever people begin to shout slogans in the same rhythm it makes Paul break out in a cold sweat.

The short-lived commune in Willy and Bärbel Wüstenrot's apartment is an attempt to combat what its members view as bourgeois values and the bourgeois family. They hope to create a different way of living that will liberate them from the restrictions imposed on them by bourgeois society and marriage, foster political awareness, and have such practical benefits as making daily living easier and cheaper (196–197). As Henisch shows, their idealistic goals turn out to be difficult to put into practice, and he gives a sober, if also at times very funny, depiction of this doomed experiment in communal living. Willy's grandmother, hardly a radical person, lives in the commune and does some of the cleaning and cooking. A large part of the commune's subsequent failure stems from the personalities of the people involved. Willy Wüstenrot, who talks like a Marxist textbook (208), interprets everything ideologically. When Paul buys coffee, milk, eggs, and rolls for breakfast, Willy accuses him of being bourgeois. When Paul asks for napkins Willy declares them reactionary (196). Schubert plays the role of those exploited by capitalist society but is, in reality, a parasite. Other problems arise in the division of household chores. Willy turns out to be a male chauvinist who is content to let his wife iron diapers while he devotes himself to his writing. Despite his attack on bourgeois society, Willy still enjoys playing the part of the traditional husband. Such banal problems as wanting to sleep late but being woken up by the baby crying or having to wait in line to use the bathroom contribute to the commune's failure. Just by being themselves, they annoy each other. Their attempts at sexual emancipation are also an abject failure because of the resulting jealousies that arise. The failed commune makes both Paul and Peter realize that creating a new way of living is not as easy as they had thought.

Here Henisch clearly expresses his skepticism about all kinds of political involvement. Henisch, who defines himself as an outsider out of passion, likes to move freely and refuses to be imprisoned in closed systems or in the ready-made morals that belong to them and he dislikes any kind of uniform (Henisch 1982, 187). Throughout his works, Henisch reveals his distrust of mass movements: he views them as potentially fascistic because they incapacitate the individual (Schobel 1988, 1:17). He is suspicious of prophets and leaders who talk about resisting but who become themselves authoritarian. The pseudo-Marxist and pseudo-psychoanalytical gurus who sprouted like poisonous or at least inedible mushrooms in the years around 1968 and the gurus who came after them all use the same mean trick, he says. They promise their followers liberation from old dependencies while creating new ones (Henisch 1982, 219). Henisch is also critical of those like Paul who go along because people like Wüstenrot and the parasitic Schubert would not be possible without people like Grünzweig (Strelka 1989, 157).

Henisch sharply criticizes the new left and its failure to bring about and sustain a revolution in consciousness. In his estimation, the new left talked loudly about a new way of life but did not live it. He complains that the theory its members loved to expound disguised their lack of practice. According to Henisch such theory actually hindered rather than helped the practice. Theory, in his view, became the weapon of terror of the impotent (Henisch 1982, 138–139). Looking back from the perspective of 1976, both Peter and Paul realize that the new left of the student movement brought about neither an awakening of consciousness nor a new direction in society. Paul's friend, the writer Gabriele Stiller, asks him what was special about the year 1968. In her opinion, a few illusions were lost and that was all (122).

Despite Henisch's criticism of the new left, he was also sympathetic to some of their ideas. He is convinced, for example, that a revolution in consciousness is essential if people are not to fall into a new "Biedermeier" age in which the little people keep quiet so that the big ones can play their music. Think faster, he tells his comrades, the old is catching up with you (1982, 185). Although Henisch remains skeptical about political involvement, he also recognizes that the individual alone has little chance of effecting social change. Thus although he blames the new left for its failures, he also blames himself for his own lack of involvement and acknowledges that his preferred role of observer is ineffectual.

Another aspect of Henisch's grappling with his own identity occurs in his novel *Stein's Paranoia* in which he explores both his Austrian and his Jewish identities. Henisch stresses that in contrast to some of his colleagues, he always wanted to be an Austrian writer, not a German one (Henisch 1988a, 91). The entire historical development of Austria, particularly of the new Austria, he states, has played an important role in shaping his thinking and writing and he admires the Austrian language (Henisch 1982, 211). Henisch's Jewish ancestry is, however, also important to him, and he has addressed this part of his identity briefly in several works. His paternal grandmother Martha was Jewish, but his paternal grandfather was not. Unlike his grandmother and his father, Henisch is interested in his Jewish heritage and is critical of them for trying to hide theirs. In his poem "Heroes' Square" (*Heldenplatz*, 1972), for example, he mentions how, when he was a child, his grandmother evaded answering his question about what the word "Jew" means. In *The Small Figure of My Father*, Henisch's grandmother criticizes him for growing a beard because it makes him look like a Polish Jew instead of an assimilated Austrian, which has been her goal, and her comment gives Henisch great satisfaction. Despite her assimilation, Henisch suggests that his grandmother is not entirely at ease living in Austria. One time when he visits her, she gives him the certificate of Aryan ancestry that his family had procured for him when he was born. She insists that he take it, telling him that one never knows when it might be needed again. Henisch's assimilated father tries to ignore or deny his Jewish ancestry. He is, nevertheless, an expert at telling Jewish jokes, which Henisch admires for their ability to see the tragic from a comic perspective without, by so doing, making light of it (9). In *May Is Gone*, Henisch's alter ego Paul is attracted to anything associated with Judaism. He views the writer Kienast as a kind of father figure because, unlike his own father who had spent half his life trying to deny his Jewish ancestry, Kienast professes his Jewishness both proudly and sarcastically (63).

Henisch's sense of identity as an Austrian writer was disrupted during Kurt Waldheim's campaign and subsequent election to the presidency of Austria in 1986. The recurrence of Austrian anti-Semitism that surfaced during this time forced him to examine his own position in Austria as a writer with some Jewish ancestry and ask how he could fit in to a society in which anti-Semitic stereotypes and prejudices were still widespread. The fiftieth anniversary of the *Anschluß* in 1988 also encouraged Henisch and many of his fellow citizens to confront their country's past and to ask how Austria could have fallen into the barbarism of the Nazi period (Henisch 1988a, 83). In *Stein's Paranoia*, the novel that resulted from this crisis of identity, Henisch not only explores his own Jewish heritage but also addresses Austria's past.

Although this novel is less directly autobiographical than the two discussed previously, Henisch stresses nevertheless the close connection between himself and his protagonist Max Stein, through whom he explores his own Jewish identity. Stein is a figure of identification, Henisch emphasizes. In "Why I Don't Want Austria to Perish" (1988), he mentions that his new book will be called *Stein's Paranoia* and he links it with questions about his own Austrian identity. He has, he believes, always been more or less an outsider but one who was accepted in Austria. He wonders, however, whether an "accepted outsider" is a misnomer, whether one can, in fact, be an accepted outsider in Austria, and if so, for how long. Like Stein, Henisch felt comfortable until recently in his Austrian skin. Stein, Henisch writes, wants to be a good Austrian but suddenly sees that this is not possible at the present time (1988a, 90–92). At the beginning of the novel Henisch further points to his close connection to Stein. He writes: "I think, Stein thinks. I think that Stein should think" (Henisch 1988b, 6). Stein is about the same age as Henisch, is married to a gentile wife, and has a daughter Marion who is about the same age as Henisch's daughter.

Stein's main concern since his father returned to Vienna after the war has been to assimilate into Austrian society and to ignore his Jewishness, and in this he resembles at first Henisch's father and grandmother. He was born in Quebec where his parents had fled from the Nazis. For thirty-six years Stein has lived contentedly in Vienna and thinks of himself as Austrian. Like many of his fellow Austrians, Stein has not been interested in confronting the past. It is the past, he used to declare. He distances himself from the stories of persecution that his father related. It is your past, Stein once told his father (17). These frequently told stories of emigration and return used to annoy him, and he objected to what he perceived to be their lachrymose and reproachful tone (18). Stein has also distanced himself from his Jewish heritage and pays little attention to the customs and rituals of his remaining relatives (8). His marriage to the gentile Brigitte is an example of how divorced he is from his roots. This marriage led his father to declare that he no longer had a son, to which Stein had responded that he felt like an Austrian and would marry whomever he pleased. In his view, the past plays little or no role in shaping his present identity.

His sense of security vanishes when he overhears a remark when he is in a newspaper kiosk with his daughter. Although Henisch does not tell the reader what was said, the remark was clearly anti-Semitic. It makes Stein's comfortable world collapse and precipitates an identity crisis. He suddenly becomes aware of the anti-Semitism in his society and realizes that because of his Jewish ancestry some of his fellow citizens do not consider him the good Austrian he strives to be. Although he wants to remain in his Austrian skin, he sees that, given his society's attitudes, this will be difficult. Like several of Henisch's protagonists, Stein becomes an unwilling outsider. The man who made the remark was at least sixty, therefore old enough to have been shaped by the Hitler period, and was shaky on his legs. Stein tries to justify his lack of response by telling himself that the man was probably drunk and he should not have taken the remark seriously but he becomes obsessed that he did not try to defend himself. He becomes increasingly alienated from himself, his family, and his society, and his marriage deteriorates. At the end of the novel, he is taken to a psychiatric clinic where he is diagnosed as paranoid and then released.

Overhearing this remark leads Stein to an intensive confrontation with his Jewishness and what it means to be a Jew in Austrian society. Although at first he resembles Walter Henisch in his determination to deny his Jewishness and assimilate, the remark makes him aware that it is crucial for him to find his roots in the past in order to define his identity in the present.

Understanding the Nazi past becomes an important part of Stein's quest to understand himself as a Jew in Austria. Henisch believes that the present is the transition of the past into the future (Henisch 1988a, 94). Unless one confronts the past, as Stein comes to see, it lives on and continues to shape both the present and the future. With the help of the American student Clarissa, Stein begins to grapple with Austria's Nazi past and Austrian complicity during that time. On their walks through Vienna, she shows him places connected with the Nazi past, such as the building that housed the Gestapo. The Vienna she shows Stein is one that he has not previously noticed, one that contrasts sharply with the image the city wishes to project of itself of opera, Beethoven, Schönbrunn, the Hofburg, the Vienna Boys Choir, Strauss, and congeniality (39). Clarissa makes Stein aware that Austrian anti-Semitism did not first appear with the Nazis but has a long history in that country. She mentions, for example, the expulsion of the Jews from the Leopoldstadt in 1670 and the anti-Semitic former mayor of Vienna Karl Lueger. Where, she asks, can "people like us" be at home?

Because Stein sees that his society will not let him ignore his Jewish heritage, he begins to understand why his now dead father talked so much about the past. Thinking about what his father has said makes Stein reflect upon the burdens of being a Jew in Austria. His father, who represents the generation forced into exile by the Nazis, told him once that the family would have preferred to stay in Vienna where they had felt at home for generations rather than being forced into exile, but nobody consulted their wishes (17). On his return to Vienna after the war his father met with little sympathy. When he wanted his old apartment back he was told that if he had not left nobody would have moved in. Much like Henisch's grandmother, Stein's father is uneasy in Austrian society. He tells his son that "people like us" should always have a suitcase packed. At the beginning it is only a node, but when it metastasizes it is too late (29).

Stein's grandfather, who was murdered in a concentration camp, also plays an important role in Stein's confrontation with his Jewish identity. Stein imagines that his dead grandfather visits him, and in one of these encounters his grandfather sings about a calf tied to a cart on the way to the slaughterhouse. In the sky is a bird. The calf cries and the farmer says: "Who created you to be a calf? You could just as well have been a bird, a swallow for example." The song contains a cry of protest against God who created the calf to be killed. In it the calf is an image for all innocent and helpless victims, while the farmer represents the callousness of society. Stein's grandfather tells him that he should resist, not be a helpless victim like the calf (66).

Because of the anti-Semitic remark, Stein realizes that the past has spilled into the present. The sentence he heard is not an isolated incident but soon spreads into the print and electronic media. Stein becomes anxious about other indications of an unconfronted past. In the subway, for example, he sees a young man reading Hitler's *My Struggle* (*Mein Kampf*). He overhears a conversation in which a young man criticizes Jews for attacking Austria. In his opinion, the protests against Waldheim's candidacy from other countries are a Jewish conspiracy. This man, who is in his early twenties, regrets that Hitler did not win the war (82). Stein also hears a mob of young football fans shouting: "We don't want any Jews."

Is Stein really paranoid, as the doctor diagnoses? There are certainly occasions when he is oversensitive. When a worker tells him that his coffee is in front of his nose, he perceives this as a racial slur. Stein imagines that he was fired from his job because of being Jewish. Labeling him paranoid, however, makes it easy for society to dismiss his fears as pathological and thus avoid confronting the recurrence of anti-Semitism in Austria. Unlike Stein, those suffering from paranoia feel unjustifiably threatened. As Henisch suggests, however, there is justification for Stein's fears. That not just the older generation but also, as the novel shows, many young people continue to hold intolerant views demonstrates that the past has not been overcome. The taxi driver, the representative of the man on the street, who uses epithets to describe Italians that the Nazis had used for Jews, is a further example of the intolerance of Otherness in Austrian society.

The crisis that disrupts Stein's previously contented identity forces him out of his comfortable conformity into resisting. He becomes convinced that each individual needs to take some responsibility for the whole (Schobel 1988, 2:685). There must be a possibility to correct oneself and the society around us, he reflects (70), and he is guided in his new awareness by the quotation: "Whatever you do or refrain from doing today influences the condition of the world tomorrow" (21). Stein demonstrates civil courage when he protects a crippled beggar from being kicked and he stands in protest in front of the kiosk where he first heard the anti-Semitic remark. Although his protest is feeble, it indicates his determination to be vigilant to prevent history repeating itself and his refusal to accept the passive role of victim.

Stein's decision to write a memorial plaque for a synagogue that the Nazis destroyed during the *Kristallnacht* shows both his growing identification with his Jewish heritage and his decision to confront his country's complicity. Among the many points he makes, he addresses the painful topic of Catholic complicity when he notes that Cardinal Innitzer welcomed Hitler, expressed joy at the unification of Germany and Austria, and promised the cooperation of Austrian Catholics. Stein points out that Protestants also did not resist Hitler. He reminds people that 65,000 Austrian citizens of Jewish ancestry were murdered through the direct or indirect involvement of many of their fellow citizens (83–85).

Stein's identity crisis reflects not only Henisch's but also that of Jews, and by extension, of other minorities living in a country where some find it hard to accept people who are different from them. Henisch depicts a society that, in his view, still does not allow its Jewish citizens or its other minorities to feel comfortable and at home. In his view, the anxiety of Jews in Austria during and after the Waldheim campaign was not a paranoid but an understandable reaction. Because of the history of anti-Semitism in Austria, that country's treatment of its Jewish citizens during the Nazi years, and the increasing anti-Semitism that became evident during Waldheim's campaign, Henisch believes that it is not surprising that Stein and with him the small Austrian Jewish community should feel alarmed. Although Henisch does not suggest that history will repeat itself, Clarissa asks "Does it have to recur? Isn't it enough if it just looks similar?" (44).

As these three novels suggest, Henisch uses his writing "as a means of self-clarification or self-therapy, a way to explore possibilities and to reflect on the motivations for his decisions" (Fischer 1989, 191). For him literature is both an expression of and an attempt to surmount subjective and objective crises (Schobel 1988, 2:396). By using himself and his experiences as an example to make his readers aware of problems in their society, his literary works have a wider relevance than being only an experiment with himself. In them Henisch takes his readers on a journey not only into himself but also into their country's past and into the society that presently surrounds them.

Works Cited

Aurenche, Emmanuelle. 1993. *Die kleine Figur meines Vaters* de Peter Henisch: Un Exemple de Vaterbuch Autrichien. *Austriaca* 18, No. 36.

Decker, Craig. 1991. Photographic Eye, Narrative I: Peter Henisch's *Die kleine Figur meines Vaters*. *Monatshefte* 83, No. 2.

Fischer, Ludwig M. 1989. Peter Henisch. In *Austrian Fiction Writers after 1914*. Edited by James Hardin and Donald G. Daviau. Detroit: Gale.

Frieden, Sandra. 1983. *Autobiography: Self Into Form: German-Language Autobiographical Writings of the 1970s*. Frankfurt am Main: Peter Lang.

Henisch, Peter. 1971. *Hamlet bleibt*. Frankfurt am Main: Fischer.

Henisch, Peter. 1978. *Der Mai ist vorbei: Roman*. Frankfurt am Main: Fischer.

Henisch, Peter. 1981. *Bali oder Swoboda steigt aus: Roman*. Munich: Langen-Müller.

Henisch, Peter. 1982. Kurze Denkadresse des Autors (Trotz Entgegennahme des Anton Wildgans-Preises). In *Zwischen allen Sesseln: Geschichten, Gedichte, Entwürfe, Notizen, Statements 1965–1982*. Vienna: Hannibal.

Henisch, Peter. 1987. *Die kleine Figur meines Vaters*. Salzburg: Residenz.

Henisch, Peter. 1988a. Warum ich nicht will, daß Österreich untergeht. In *Reden an Österreich: Schriftsteller ergreifen das Wort*. Edited by Jochen Jung. Salzburg: Residenz.

Henisch, Peter. 1988b. *Steins Paranoia: Roman*. Salzburg: Residenz.

Kanes, Eveline L. 1983. In Search of Fathers. *Denver Quarterly* 18, No. 1.

Kecht, Maria-Regina. 1993. Resisting Silence: Brigitte Schwaiger and Elisabeth Reichart Attempt to Confront the Past. In *Gender, Patriarchy and Fascism in the Third Reich: The Response of Women Writers*. Edited by Elaine Martin. Detroit: Wayne State University Press.

Langbein, Hermann. 1987. Darf man vergessen? In *Das grosse Tabu: Österreichs Umgang mit seiner Vergangenheit*. Edited by Anton Pelinka and Erika Weinzierl. Vienna: Verlag der Österreichischen Staatsdruckerei.

Roscher, Achim. 1987. Elisabeth Reichart im Gespräch. *Neue deutsche Literatur* 35, No. 9.

Schobel, Eva. 1988. *Peter Henisch: Eine Monographie*. Vienna: VWGÖ.

Strelka, Joseph P. 1989. Eine Phänomenologie des Mitmachens: Zur frühen, autobiographischen Erzählprosa von Peter Henisch. *Modern Austrian Literature*, Sonderheft 13, No. 1.

Ulmer, Anne Close. 1986. The Son As Survivor: Peter Henisch's *Die kleine Figur meines Vaters*. *The Germanic Review* 61, No. 2.

Zeyringer, Klaus. 1992. *Innerlichkeit und Öffentlichkeit: Österreichische Literatur der achtziger Jahre*. Tübingen: Francke.

Autobiography and the Fiction of the I: Edgar Hilsenrath

Bianca Rosenthal

Edgar Hilsenrath holds a unique niche in contemporary German-language literature. Although he was born in Leipzig, in 1926, he fled as a child with his family to the Bukovina, the former most eastern outpost of the Austro-Hungarian empire. There he met the fate of other Jews who had been deported to the camps in Transnistria, the Romanian-occupied Ukraine. Like Günter Grass's Danzig novels, Hilsenrath's first largely autobiographical novels, *Night* (1966) and *The Nazi and the Barber* (1971), were conceived in exile, New York in this case. Both books are written from an ironic perspective that allows him to infuse horror with grotesque and absurd elements. His novel, *The Fairy Tale of the Last Thought* (1989), a work in which he depicts the genocide of the Armenians, brought him his long-awaited recognition with the 1989 award of the Alfred Döblin Prize. *Jossel Wassermann's Homecoming* (1993) deals with the life and death of Jews in the Bukovina. Hilsenrath goes back into the history of East European Jews within the Austro-Hungarian empire. He creates a glittering rainbow of episodes from the K.u.K. Danube monarchy, where a rich Jewish *shtetl* and city tradition flourished, before being destroyed in the course of recent history.

Hilsenrath's works are dominated by the unstated programmatic declaration "How did I become the person I am and who am I really?" The fact that he can appropriate it without problems perhaps most beautifully characterizes the man and his writing. In *Bronsky's Confession* (1980), he combines personal experiences of his almost twenty years in New York with strong criticism of the United States immigration policy during World War II and the American way of life in general. His latest novel, *The Adventures of Ruben Jablonski* (1997) is subtitled *An Autobiographical Novel*, yet the protagonist does not identify himself with the author's name.

Hilsenrath deserves to be characterized as one of the most important contemporary German-writing authors. As a survivor of the Holocaust, his is a unique voice that depicts unmeasurable horror with satire and black humor. This special style kept German publishers from printing his first two books, *Night* and *The Nazi and the Barber*, which were first introduced in the American version and became bestsellers. The Germans were supposedly afraid of a negative reaction from readers to the blunt depiction of Jews in the ghetto and concentration camps, given the so-called philosemitic tendencies of the sixties and seventies. As literary critic Peter Stenberg has stated: "Literary attempts in German to describe the Holocaust, dominated by feelings of guilt or moral outrage, have failed to make lasting impressions on the German public." In his article (1982), Stenberg attempted to show that the novels of Edgar Hilsenrath successfully break through into taboo areas by handling the Holocaust with black humor and savage irony (272–289).

Most literary descriptions of the Holocaust do not allow irony, satire, or humor, particularly not from the narrator, who is normally a survivor describing victims. Hilsenrath, however, shares the aforementioned biography. Born in Leipzig in 1926 to Jewish parents, he lived in Halle an der Saale with his family until 1938 when his father sent Edgar, his younger brother, and his mother to his grandparents in the Bukovina, the former Austrian province that in 1918 became part of Romania. His father later escaped to France. Together with most of the Jews of the Bukovina and Bessarabia, Hilsenrath was shipped to the ghettos and camps of Transnistria, the territory between the Bug and Dniestr rivers in the former Ukraine, which the Germans had ceded to their Romanian allies. In Transnistria the transported

Romanian Jews met a somewhat different fate than those in the German concentration camps. The bottom line was "survival of the fittest," a form of Social Darwinism. In his first novel, *Night*, Hilsenrath examined the misery, poverty, cruelty, and barbarism brought about by this ideology (Lorenz 1994, 214–223). Hilsenrath rejects some unspoken taboo against attempting to express the deaths of thousands of innocent people. Originally published in West Germany in 1964, the publisher Kindler refused to release more than a token edition. In addition, Hilsenrath was forced to provide an explanatory preface and epilogue, which he explains as follows: "The Kindler publishing house coerced me into writing this epilogue. *Nacht* is one hundred percent novel, not an autobiography. Of course, I did live in a ghetto. But this is not my story, it is an invented truth."[1] It took more than a decade before a small German publisher was willing in 1978 to follow the best-selling editions of American, French, and Italian publishing houses.

The Nazi and the Barber also appeared first in English translation. In this novel, Hilsenrath describes the exchange of identities of the fascist mass murderer Max Schulz, who after World War II becomes Izig Finkelstein, the friend from his youth whom he killed in a concentration camp, and how with his new stolen identity he manages to escape persecution and being brought to justice. Hilsenrath's convincing presentation of bleakness, pitilessness, and despair turns Transnistria into the epitome of an absurd world. Stenberg (1982) summarizes it as follows: "It is in this struggle between survival and an absurdly quixotic exterminator that Hilsenrath takes his first step towards the full-blown grotesque satire of *The Nazi and the Barber* (285).

Jossel Wassermann's Homecoming is a later novel about events scattered through Eastern and Central Europe, but for the greatest part in the Bukovina. Hilsenrath leads the reader through the culture he grew up in, which he describes so effectively. Paul Celan, the great German poet who was born in 1920 in the Bukovina metropolis Czernowitz, in his speech upon receiving the Bremen Literary Prize (1958), referred to the region as a "world that has lost its history."[2]

Let us sidestep into history to revive the fading contours of this region. Within the Austro-Hungarian monarchy, the Bukovina and its capital, Czernowitz, held a special place. The Jews amounted to one-third of the population and they were the bearers of the German language and culture. For this reason, the Austrian emperor made them full-fledged citizens, a situation that was unparalleled anywhere else in Eastern Europe. As a result, the Romanians felt disadvantaged compared to the Jewish population (Gelber 1958, 46). The year 1867 brought complete emancipation to the Jews; it turned the Bukovina in a short time into the "Jewish Eldorado of old Austria." Commerce and industry became their almost exclusive domains. They expanded into land ownership along with attaining political rights and social influence (Schamir 1975, 490–491). However, there remained great differences between the cultural center Czernowitz and the rural communities, especially the Jewish *shtetls*.

Jewish citizens became loyal fans of the Austro-Hungarian monarchy, to which they owed their civic rights. It was common knowledge that the Jews loved their emperor with devoted adoration, and the ruler let it be known sometimes that he was aware of this love. In 1918, the Bukovina came under Romanian sovereignty. The following years were full of anti-Semitic chicaneries for the Jews. World War II and the Nazi terror changed the situation even more drastically. The Czernowitz ghetto became the collection spot for the deportations into "work camps" in Transnistria. Only a small number survived the internment there (Steinberg 1958, 38). Despite the fact that war, expulsion, and the Holocaust have destroyed this German-Jewish cultural island, in the writings of the authors who originate there, the memory of it remains very much alive. Within this context, the importance of the author Hilsenrath in regard to the Bukovina is substantiated by the fact that the Bukovina as a topic runs like a red thread throughout Hilsenrath's oeuvre (Kraft 1996). First, one can detect an autobiographical streak. After fleeing Halle in 1938 to the small town of Sereth in the Bukovina, Hilsenrath was deported during the war and spent two and a half years in the ghetto of the Ukrainian city Moghilev-Podolsk, referred to as Prokow in his novel *Night*. After his liberation by the Soviets, he made his way to Palestine. In 1947 he moved to France, where he remained for a few years, reunited with his parents. There followed a long unhappy stay in the United States, and then in 1975 he returned to Germany, where he has been living in Berlin. Hilsenrath can be defined as existentially homeless; his novels describe essentially personal experiences in a disguised form. Thus, the camps and ghettos in Transnistria acquire a similar character as the *shtetls* in the Bukovina. Much that has been known for some time is being retold with a certain claim to originality. The "I" is peripherally present in relation to the topic being presented.

In his novel *Jossel Wassermann's Homecoming*, Hilsenrath takes us along with exuberant narrative joy to the vanished world of his childhood. It is the world of the Jewish *shtetls* in the frontier land between Romania and the Ukraine, where as a twelve-year-old he found refuge from the Nazis, along with his mother and brother. After World War II there hardly remained any Jews. Whoever did not get deported or killed left the place. The novel is not a nostalgic appeal to the reader's sympathy. By telling the story of Pohodna on the river Pruth, it also chronicles the annihilation of an entire world. The narrator, Jossel Wassermann, originally from Pohodna in the Bukovina and now living in Switzerland, awaits a peaceful death sometime in the near future. In the meantime, he sits in the Zürich office of his lawyer where he is composing his last will. He demands that he be buried not by lake Zürich but rather near the river Pruth in his hometown Pohodna. Since the actual date is September 1939, and war is imminent, execution of the will might become somewhat complicated. Therefore, Jossel Wassermann, the successful matzah manufacturer whose domicile is in Zürich, must ask himself why he is so powerfully drawn eastward. This question permits him to explain to his audience in the Zürich law office how the Jews lived and fared in former years on the most eastern frontier of the Habsburg empire. Pohodna remains an important name because it can be tied to events of great importance: When the emperor Franz Joseph got a salt herring stuck in his throat in a Jewish tavern there and it was successfully removed, he decided to bestow equal citizenship rights upon the Jews (Hilsenrath 1993, 124). According to Jossel Wassermann, Austria is very much indebted to the Jews. In 1866, for example, it was not completely overrun by the Prussians because although they would have loved to take over the Austrian territories, the land was full of too many Jews. Thus the Jews saved the land for Austria (151).

The place Pohodna appeared already in Hilsenrath's earliest and best-known novel *The Nazi and the Barber*. It is the place from which the family of the barber Finkelstein originates and whose identity the Nazi Max Schulz appropriates after the war while at the same time changing his perspective and way of thinking. Jossel Wassermann's problem, however, is that his earthly remains will not be able to be returned to his hometown after World War II takes its course. Therefore, he tells about the *shtetl*, and with a mixture of sad, bizarre, and outrageous anecdotes he paints the entire cultural history of East European Jewry. Through Jossel Wassermann, Hilsenrath provides a comprehensive overview of the attitudes toward old Austria and toward Judaism. The anecdotes are exemplary about the water carrier Jankl and his secret love for Rifke, the daughter of Katz the cobbler, the old scarecrow and the crucifixion on the road to Sniatyn, and of course the notorious salt herring episode. The prologue and epilogue provide the framework for the story. In it the train loaded with Jews headed for death somewhere in the East remains standing for eight days until everyone is dead. The following chapters describe the living conditions of the Jews in Habsburg, Austria, from the beginnings up into the twentieth century. The narrator attempts to stay positive and to minimize any confrontation between Jews and their society. The narrator can be credited for his efforts to illuminate some of the central issues in the lives of these people. He provides clarification of the historical conditions of a certain segment of Austrian Jewish life. He gives detailed analyses of Jewish neighborhoods with regard to the social background of the inhabitants and their employment, income, educational profiles, and love lives. The typicality of the historical experiences brought about inhuman consequences, among them loss of home, death, and indescribable suffering. The author's cautious approach constitutes an uncompromising quest for historical exactitude and plausible literary interpretations. Yet, his main intention is not to give a history of Austrian-German-Jewish relations in Eastern Europe. "We left behind forgetting, and what we took along is remembrance." This sentence, spoken by the Rabbi on the way to the death camp, is the leitmotiv for the writing of the author: Edgar Hilsenrath continues to write to defy forgetfulness. As the critic Ota Filip concluded (1993): "A story about Eastern Jews whose destruction not even the miracle Rabbi of Sadagura could prevent has now been miraculously revived thanks to Edgar Hilsenrath, by occupation a literary tango dancer, at home in Berlin."

His most recent novel, *The Adventures of Ruben Jablonski: An Autobiographical Novel* (1997), describes events with which many of Hilsenrath's fellow countrymen can identify. First, after fleeing Halle, came the beautiful adolescent years in an entirely Jewish provincial city like Sereth in the Bukovina and its close metropolis Czernowitz, which is referred to as Little Vienna. Thus the protagonist reminisces: "Those first months in Sereth, that is the late summer and fall of 1938, were the most beautiful of my whole childhood."[3] Born a German Jew, the Bukovina became the homeland of his choice and the Jewish township of Sereth his home. Despite the changes brought about by war and the alternating occupations by various powers, much of the Austrian ambiance remained. Sereth was only about forty kilometers from Czernowitz. "Rosenzweig's coffeehouse was famous for its genuine *Cremeschnitten* just like in the Emperor's time and real mocha with whipping cream. And other landmarks remained as well."[4]

And then there was the matter of language. Everybody in Sereth was used to a Balkan version of German, whereas the narrator's Saxon dialect continued to fascinate them. The majority of the people with even a small amount of education spoke a mixture of Yiddish and German. Despite all attempts by the Romanians to instill patriotic feelings, and to change the German street names, the Jewish population's allegiance remained to Austria. "We felt ourselves to be Austrians. The topmost ideal remained our Emperor Franz Joseph," continues Jablonski (38).

World War II brought about turmoil and changes—occupation by the Russians, Romanians, Germans, and again the Russians. The ghetto and deportation to Transnistria followed. After survival and then liberation by the Soviets came the return to Bucharest, then Palestine and the nascent state of Israel. Hilsenrath's realism of description is the overwhelming literary factor, making it almost a documentary. Everything is authentic, genuine, and one hundred percent realistic, from the names of places and people to the streets, houses, and landscapes. Even known personalities or public figures are included; for instance Itziu Herzig, a character in the book who is today Itzchak Arzi, a lawyer, former Knesset member,[5] and deputy mayor of Tel Aviv—at the time of the story a Zionist delegate in Bucharest.

From Bucharest, the protagonist Ruben Jablonski travels a circuitous route via Turkey and Syria to Palestine which at the time was under British mandate. He is eighteen years old; he tries his hand at living in a kibbutz, later as a dishwasher in a café in Haifa, as a construction worker in the arid countryside, and finally as a corpse bearer in a hospital. In true picaresque fashion he accomplishes everything playfully. While he is highly successful with older married women, the ability to write his first novel remains a dream that eludes him. He has not yet matured into a true writer. His immediate goal is to join his parents who in the meantime have settled in France. As the joyful raconteur of his sometimes outlandish experiences, he is blunt and nonchalant. Strange though that the author himself, the chief protagonist of the novel, has assumed another name—Ruben Jablonski. Two statements from the book provide possible explanations. In the preface, Hilsenrath himself states that: "I was reluctant to write this autobiographical novel, and I owe it to the convincing and gentle encouragement of my lector Uwe Heldt that the book was finally written" (4). The book itself, however, ends on a different note. In the final paragraph, Ruben Jablonski lets it be known that he intends to pursue a successful writing career in New York, one that will be worthy of mentioning in the *New York Times*. "'What is your name?' the lady asked. 'Ruben Jablonski,' I said. 'And you intend to publish under your own name?' 'Of course,' I said. 'Only shifty characters hide under a pseudonym'" (326). In referring to Melville, Frisch, and other writers, Franz Stanzel has shown that such uncertainty relating to the narrator's status and qualifications are symbolic of the modern I-novel. Typically it can already be found in the first sentence (Stanzel 1981, 35–37). Life, existence, and writing are recorded as a biography. The reader experiences along with the narrator the Bukovina, his youthful years, the time of his only and true *Zuhause*. The long journey of the man who in so many ways was robbed of his childhood leads back to an abode he calls home. Part of the narrator's strategy is not to shed any light on the dark circumstances that led to important decisions. Helpless exposure, forced isolation, denied beginnings, and failed departures are basic existential situations that he combines and manipulates in his texts. These are the experiential patterns of the universe and the emptiness of an I that has been marked and that keeps recurring in contemporary German and Austrian literature. The chapters in Hilsenrath's oeuvre represent segments and stations of life determined by outside forces. They could also be read as a loosely assembled Bildungsroman. Now and then, an auctorial voice intrudes into the I and personal narrative. This voice speaks in general terms; it reproduces the language of suffering of those affected, a technique that can be found in *Bronsky's Confession* in the letters to and by the American consul general, and in *Jossel Wassermann's Homecoming* in the touching references to the various voices that bear testimony to the annihilation of a people.

At times it can even become a more mundane voice. As Natascha, one of the characters in *The Adventures of Ruben Jablonski*, refers to the author Erich Maria Remarque and his book *All Quiet on the Wester Front* as the most popular book in her homeland Russia, the character Ruben has this to add: "I heard he was shunned by the critics. He was too forthright and simple for them. The German critics love complicated and bombastic literature." Natascha thought these were bad critics, to which Ruben replied: "The German critics are sitting on a high horse, but they exert disastrous power" (87). This statement most certainly mirrors Hilsenrath's experience in view of how he has been treated by critics and publishers.

Hilsenrath has presented his development as a writer and his biography in coded form in all his works. *The Adventures of Ruben Jablonski* emphasizes the literary quintessence of his life. At the start of his stay in Israel, when he lived in the kibbutz Tel Yitzhak, he began to write short novellas during his spare time in the evening. He knew that some day he would begin to write seriously his ghetto novel. He wrote a letter to Max Brod, Kafka's friend who at the time was living in Jerusalem, and informed him of his intention to become a writer and the difficulties he was experiencing. Brod's reply was rather ambiguous in his encouragement. At the same time, the narrator foreshadows his future ghetto novel *Night* by emphatically stating that he would write a novel and not a documentary (152–153).

From that moment on, no matter where he finds himself, he continues to take notes for his ghetto novel. While working as a dishwasher in the Café Hirsch in Haifa, he continues to write between shifts even though he often becomes discouraged: "You will never become a writer," he said to himself (175). But after his recovery from a serious illness and a new job that freed more hours, he was able to spend afternoons sitting in a café with a writing block and pencil. And with a trace of self-irony he is able to say: "I felt indeed like a famous writer," and referring to the café, "that's where he wrote his famous ghetto novel, the critics will say" (186). In a later segment, in a discussion with his young friend Joseph Lindberg who is also a writer, the two of them discount coffeehouse literature as being appropriate only for a city like Vienna, whereas a country like Israel demands stark realism. He also advises Ruben to wait for the time when the stuff he wants to say really pours out of him, as a more propitious time for his writing (215). Gradually, Ruben is becoming more upbeat about his writing endeavors. A certain degree of hubris almost overcomes him. "It is an intoxicating feeling to be working on a great novel. One has the sense of conquering the entire world." In his euphoria he even compares himself to Rilke or Zweig (259).

His father, whom he rejoined in France after having been separated for ten years, is vehemently opposed to his career as a writer. Instead, he makes arrangements for Ruben to start an apprenticeship with a furrier. This results in the failure of all his writing endeavors, three novels in all, on different subjects. At the same time this is accompanied by a failure in his sexual potency. The story ends, nevertheless, on an upbeat note. Just as his friend Lindberg had predicted, the words suddenly pour out of him and he fills the pages in rapid succession. By March 1951, he is on his way to America to join his brother in New York with the intent of publishing his book, provisionally to be called *Night* with the Doubleday publishing house, the latter of course wishful thinking on his part. Ruben Jablonski, his life and work, chronologically in inverse order, makes it the task of the reader to construct out of it some kind of organic continuity.

Bronsky's Confession (1980), although published much earlier, depicts events that are foreshadowed at the end of *The Adventures of Ruben Jablonski*. In the words of Thomas Kraft: "*Bronsky's Confession* is a heavily autobiographical novel, a work that completes the life history of the fictional I that began in the concentration camp of the earlier *Night*" (Kraft 1996, 119). The author himself clarifies the position of the fictional I in the preface in relation to the real I with the statement: "Even the supposedly disturbing scenes are part of this book, because they belong to my life, they are part of the environment that is being depicted here, part of all the frustration, the loneliness, despair and isolation that I have known" (1). The compulsion to self-revelation clashes with a contrary impulse to shame, concealment, and disguise. Jakob Bronsky, born as the son of a Jewish furniture dealer in Halle an der Saale, finally arrives in the early fifties as a displaced person in the United States. He remains in New York and attempts to write his first novel there to escape all those brutal memories. Hilsenrath writes at the beginning of the book that he consciously intended to mix fiction and truth; it remains nevertheless a novel while it is also autobiographical. He needed this mixture to overcome a certain hesitation that, given the nature of the subject, would have made it impossible to accomplish the task.

Hilsenrath is a committed challenger of the first person. His is a tedious way of saying I do not exist. Having many versions of the personal and not attempting to cohere them into one invariable person or, for that matter, one persona, while intellectually challenging, can be practically disorienting and can result in a somewhat tenuous sense of self. "This is my story, and even that which is fiction corresponds to the desire to enclose the truth in a different garment," he continues in the aforementioned statement (6).

The intrusion of this first person creates a scene of its own—a pose—loaded with negative connotations, with intimations of fraud and general dishonesty. The manifestations of the I can be seen as annoying and embarrassing narcissistic spectacles. They effectively call attention to misrepresentations, omissions, and differences that a general, impersonal discourse would ignore. Hilsenrath has repeatedly maintained that he had to create a voice for himself that didn't mimic somebody else and that expressed what he thought and felt. Therefore, it seems, he took systematic recourse to exemplary anecdotes as the sustaining design of his texts. They are all imbued with an ever-expanding plurality of personal and cultural narratives that give meaning and voice to a wide range of identities. According to Thomas Kraft (1996, 95), *The Fairy Tale of the Last Thought* assumes unexplored dimensions by methodically including deviations into the fantastic.

For many German-writing authors whose writing careers were suddenly interrupted when they left Germany after the Nazi takeover, autobiography remained the sole possible form of literary expression. It can be seen as an attempt to establish a communal identity but also to distinguish the author from everyone else. For Edgar Hilsenrath it is an exploration through Bronsky, Ruben Jablonski, Jossel Wassermann, and others of what it means to say, or to be I, the difficulty of saying I. His works constitute a fictional autobiographical journey to the near, hard-to-be-borne past, in which the one who saw and witnessed is hidden.

It is only natural that an impenetrable tangle of invention and biography results. In looking for the story of his experiences he defines his authenticity however he chooses. Often there is a temptation to use a complete disguise. From the beginning his deepest longing was to produce a masterpiece. "Writers are our memory," he claims in *The Fairy Tale of the Last Thought*. "In reality they are Gypsies, but they do not read the secret signs on forehead and hand, but the handwriting of the soul which they then change into word melodies" (460). Hilsenrath presents in his novels the sum of the experiences that were existentially imposed upon him. How wonderful it is when one succeeds in productively weaving the sum of events and facts that constitute one's life story into a glittering tapestry.

Aspects of autobiography predominate in Hilsenrath's

works. While he provides realistic, historically accurate details, he laces them with surrealist, grotesque elements. From this his *ars poetica* emerges. During a visit in California in 1987, he sought me out because of my personal connections to the Bukovina, and gave me a tape titled *Journey to the Bukovina*.[6] This was the transcript of the story *Why so cumbersome? or Woody Allen from Berlin*, a soliloquy and a text that had been presented in the radio series *Passagen* in Berlin in 1984 thanks to the initiative of Marianne Boehme-Reinecke. She was a radio reporter who had met Hilsenrath shortly after his arrival in Berlin in 1975 at the literary café Natubs, and who thought it was scandalous how Hilsenrath had been treated by the German publishers. In 1997 his latest novel, *The Adventures of Ruben Jablonski*, was published by the prominent publishing house Piper. Several chapters of the book first appeared word for word on the tape. This much remains to be said for creative material lying dormant and waiting to surface at the right moment.

The forces that have driven the writer Edgar Hilsenrath are interspersed in most of his books. In *Bronsky's Confession*, they appear repeatedly in conversations of the protagonist with various characters. Above all, there is the inner command to write: "You must write your novel, your novel that comes forth from your own experiences, experiences that you bring forth from the abyss, and then you can put them on paper in somewhat alienated form. You must write Jakob Bronsky ... A novel, not a figment of the imagination, it is sort of a factual novel, even though one has to alienate the facts at times in order to better understand them" (52, 57). The problems associated with writing when you are poor and unknown are well documented. They increase to the point of being unbearable when you are Jewish but writing in German in a country like the United States, a place that became a nightmare for Jakob Bronsky/Edgar Hilsenrath. "I remained there too long and constructed myself a prison made of books, since I have always had a love affair with the German language," Hilsenrath volunteers in an interview titled *Biographical Information About the Self: At Home Only in the German Language* (Kraft 1996, 18). This segment is part of a collection of essays, testimonies, and interviews about Hilsenrath recently published in honor of his seventieth birthday. He is singled out for having found a pictorial language to describe the horrendous crimes of this century, a language that mixes horror with laughter in a unique combination.

Notes

1. Peter Wapnewski, "Der neunte Autorscooter." Second Program, German Television, 1978. Hilsenrath described in detail in a letter to the author of the article and during the interview with Wapnewski the pressures and politics that forced him to agree to this preface.
2. My translation. "... von einer der Geschichtslosigkeit anheimgefallenen Welt." In Celan (1986), "Ansprache anläßlich der Entgegennahme des Literaturpreises der Freien Hansestadt Bremen" (185).
3. My translation. "Ich war zwar deutscher Jude, aber meine Wahlheimat war die Bukowina und das jüdische Städtchen Sereth. Das war mein Zuhause." In *Ruben Jablonski* (52).
4. My translation. "Rosenzweigs Kaffeehaus war berühmt für echte Cremeschnitten wie aus Kaisers Zeiten und echten Mokka mit Schlagsahne." In *Ruben Jablonski* (37).
5. Personal information of the author.
6. Tape, "Warum so umständlich? oder Woody Allen aus Berlin." In *Tonbandreihe Passagen*. Berlin, 1984.

Works Cited

Celan, Paul. 1986. Ansprache anläßlich der Entgegennahme des Literaturpreises der Freien Hansestadt Bremen. In *Gesammelte Werke 3*. Edited by Beda Alleman und Stefan Reichert. Frankfurt am Main: Suhrkamp.

Filip, Ota. 1993. Als die schwarzen Wolken über das Dorf zogen. In *Welt am Sonntag, Buchmagazin* 13 (March 28).

Gelber, N. M. 1958. Geschichte der Juden in der Bukowina. In *Geschichte der Juden in der Bukowina*. Edited by Hugo Gold. Tel Aviv: Olamenu.

Hilsenrath, Edgar. 1964. *Nacht*. München: Kindler Verlag; Köln: Literarischer Verlag Helmut Braun, 1978. Translated by Michael Roloff. 1966. New York: Doubleday.

Hilsenrath, Edgar. 1977. *Der Nazi und der Friseur*. Köln: Literarischer Verlag Helmut Braun. Translated by Andrew White. 1971. New York: Doubleday.

Hilsenrath, Edgar. 1980. *Bronskys Geständnis*. München-Wien: Langen-Müller.

Hilsenrath, Edgar. 1989. *Das Märchen vom letzten Gedanken*. München: R. Piper. Translated by Hugh Young. 1990. London: Scribners.

Hilsenrath, Edgar. 1993. *Jossel Wassermanns Heimkehr*. München: R. Piper.
Hilsenrath, Edgar. 1997. *Die Abenteuer des Ruben Jablonski*. München: R. Piper.
Kraft, Thomas. 1996. Hilsenraths Heimkehr. Die Bukowina als literarisches Motiv in den Romanen Edgar Hilsenraths. In *Edgar Hilsenrath. Das Unerzählbare erzählen*. Edited by Thomas Kraft. München: R. Piper.
Lorenz, Dagmar C. G. 1994. *Social Darwinism in Edgar Hilsenrath's Ghetto Novel "Nacht."* Detroit: Wayne State University Press.
Schamir, Haim. 1975. Die Jüdische Gemeinde von Czernowitz 1937 in deutscher Sicht. In *Jahrbuch des Instituts für deutsche Geschichte*. Edited by Walter Grab. Tel Aviv. (Publisher unlisted)
Stanzel, Franz K. 1981. *Typische Formen des Romans*. Göttingen.
Steinberg, Hermann. 1958. Zur Geschichte der Juden in Czernowitz. In *Jahrbuch des Instituts für deutsche Geschichte*. Edited by Walter Grab. Tel Aviv. (Publisher unlisted)
Stenberg, Peter. 1982. Memories of the Holocaust. Edgar Hilsenrath and the Fiction of Genocide. In *Deutsche Vierteljahresschrift für Literaturwissenschaft und Geistesgeschichte* 56.

The Trouble with Elfriede: Jelinek and Autobiography

Imke Meyer

> In Chinese legends, it is written that great masters have walked into their images and have disappeared. Woman is not a great master. That is why her disappearance will never be complete. She resurfaces, busy as she is with disappearing.

This statement by Eva Meyer is quoted by Elfriede Jelinek as a motto to her play *Sickness or Modern Women*.[1] Ironically enough, the same statement could well be used to describe the relation—or at least the perception of the relation—between the author Elfriede Jelinek and her literary creations: neither the media, nor the reading public, nor literary criticism will grant the persona of Elfriede Jelinek the opportunity to completely disappear in her oeuvre. Rather, Jelinek and her biography continue to resurface not only in interviews with the author and in feuilletonistic discussions of her literary texts, but also in the pages of academic monographs and journal articles focusing on her works. This continues to be the case in spite of the recent criticism that has been leveled against biographical readings of Jelinek's texts.[2]

A paradoxical situation has arisen: Jelinek's provocative texts have generated an interest that is at times superseded by an interest in the producer of these texts.[3] When looking at publications on Jelinek and her works, one cannot help but get the impression that a kind of reversal of not infrequently used critical methods has taken place: Instead of interviews with the author being screened for clues that could help with the interpretation of her literary texts—a procedure, to be sure, that itself should be subject to criticism[4]—critics began to screen Jelinek's literary texts, in light of the published interviews with the author, for clues about her biography. Ingeborg Hoesterey (1994, 151) describes this phenomenon as follows:

> A new type of positivism generated by the dialogicity of our media culture allowed the autobiographical presence of the author to structure the patterns of her works' reception.

In interviews, Jelinek herself likes to refer back to the above-mentioned quote by Eva Meyer.[5] While the public perception and critical reception of Jelinek and her works seem in large part to prove the point made in the quote by Meyer, it should also be stressed that Jelinek's own statements in interviews, for better or for worse, have often enabled conflations of the author and her work. A brief look at the critical as well as the media reaction to the publication of Jelinek's novel *The Piano Teacher* in 1983 can help to illustrate this point, since the tendency to screen Jelinek's literary works for clues about her biography became especially pronounced when this text appeared.

Jelinek's earlier prose works—such as *we are decoys baby!* (1970), *Michael. A Children's Book for the Infantile Society* (1972), and *Women as Lovers* (1975)—were stylistically and structurally experimental. They made use of radical alienation strategies and avoided providing the reader with figures that exhibited any kind of individual psychology or traditional character development. *The Piano Teacher*, in contrast, provided its readers with a protagonist, namely Erika Kohut, who seemed more like a psychological character[6] than any of the literary figures previously created by Jelinek. In short, *The Piano Teacher*, as Marlies Janz puts it, "seems to be more accommodating to conventional reading habits"[7] than any of Jelinek's other texts. To a large extent, this may explain the fact that Jelinek's *Piano Teacher* became a rather widely read text (see Janz 1971).

Erika Kohut, the piano teacher, works at the conservatory in Vienna and lives with her mother. Erika's father vegetates in a mental institution, and Erika has taken the place of the breadwinner in the family. Groomed by her mother for a piano soloist career that never materialized, Erika leads her frustrated and frustrating life under the constant supervision of her domineering mother. Erika spends her evenings watching TV with her mother, and she spends her nights in her father's old bed next to her mother. Erika rebels half-heartedly against the ties that bind her to her mother and alienate her from herself and her body: She secretly buys expensive clothes, watches porn movies in seedy suburban theaters, visits peep shows, and, through her father's old binoculars, observes couples fornicating in Vienna's Praterauen. Erika also tries to replicate the objectifying gaze of the male subject at women's bodies when she looks at her genitalia in her father's old shaving mirror. On one occasion, Erika uses a razor blade to mutilate her genitals while sitting in front of this mirror. Erika's attempt at establishing a sexual relationship with one of her students, Walter Klemmer, fails. In a letter, Erika asks Klemmer to sexually mistreat her in very specific ways. If Klemmer were willing to stick to the conditions stipulated in this kind of masochistic contract, Erika, by deciding how, specifically, she would like to be turned into an object, would retain power over her own objectification. Klemmer is not willing to give her this kind of power and does not enter into the offered contract. Instead, he later rapes Erika, making himself the master of her objectification and degradation.

In the feuilletons, interviews, and articles reacting to the publication of this novel, critics seized upon the seeming similarities between Erika Kohut's story and Elfriede Jelinek's biography. It was pointed out that Jelinek herself studied music at the conservatory and had a domineering mother who projected her own ambitions onto her daughter. Also, like Erika Kohut, Jelinek had a father who suffered from an unspecified mental illness and eventually had to be institutionalized; furthermore, Jelinek has allegedly been drawn to the commercialized worlds of television, fashion, and make-up.[8] It has been held that the construction of *Scheinparallelen*[9] between Erika Kohut's fictional story and Elfriede Jelinek's life story has not only been made possible, but has likewise been furthered by Jelinek's self-presentation to and self-representation in the media.[10] Not only does a voyeuristic public[11] constantly and eagerly wait to be fed new details about Jelinek's biography; not only does Jelinek's publisher, Rowohlt, have a stake in generating and keeping alive as much interest in

Jelinek and her texts as possible; but Jelinek herself seems rather willing to supply the media with detailed answers to their constant questions.

However, the statements Jelinek provides to the media about her biography have been so repeatedly made by her that they almost seem rehearsed. Likewise, even more than a decade after the first publication of *The Piano Teacher*, the particular *selection* of statements Jelinek makes in this regard continues to invite her readers to draw parallels between the fictional Kohut character and Jelinek herself.[12] Jelinek's biography, as presented by her to the media as well as to the academy, exhibits a quality of constructedness,[13] and it clearly possesses what Sabine Wilke calls an *Inszenierungsqualität* (Wilke 1993, 140). Since Jelinek appears to recycle her responses to interviewers, Juliane Vogel (1990) argues that the mythical totality attached to the author's self-portrait is in fact nothing but a configuration of stereotyped utterances assembled and made by Jelinek.[14]

These stereotyped, self-same utterances, according to Vogel, simultaneously stimulate and frustrate the voyeuristic tendencies of the audience (148–150). This voyeurism may thus be unmasked and made accessible to criticism. Jelinek, Vogel argues, cuts up her biography into quotable and requotable *Belegerzählungen*,[15] which are shaped according to the needs of different media and audience groups. The pattern-like, stylized quality that Jelinek's biography takes on in the process of its construction and subsequent narration leaves voyeuristic desires unsatisfied (Vogel 150). The constant reproduction of Jelinek's biography in and for the media results in an ironic doubling not just of Jelinek's image itself, but also of the culture industry's strategy of allowing for endless reproducibility by means of stereotypification. But since this irony, as Vogel points out, is often lost on the audience (147–148), Jelinek's strategy of dealing (and flirting) with the media—to the extent that it is a strategy[16]—may ultimately be self-defeating. Vogel notes that Jelinek's stereotyped statements about herself will, in all probability, be depicted by the media as utterances carrying the flair of a kind of "denunciatory authenticity."[17]

Academics have at times tried to bring up and discuss with Jelinek the image of her public persona. In an interview with

Jelinek in 1992, Sigrid Berka suggested that while Jelinek appears "not quite natural,"[18] her "posing," the "theatricality or masquerade" for the media seems like a "life in quotes."[19] Berka then concludes that Jelinek might be using this posing behavior as a protection mechanism.[20] Jelinek answers as follows:

> Yes, yes, sure. But that is precisely why I avoid journalists, because I don't want all that; basically, I do not have a tendency to pose at all, to the contrary, I am extremely shy and fearful; I am very afraid of people, and I hardly let anybody near me. If I am posing, then that is rather a kind of protective shield, but also the idea that I am not, that I do not exist or am nothing. An artificial protective cover. It is a strong phantasm of mine that I do not exist or do not exist outside of writing.[21]

Jelinek simultaneously disagrees and agrees with the interpretation of her behavior suggested by Berka. She claims that she is not given to posing, that she tries to avoid journalists as much as possible, but then admits that, to the extent that she ever poses at all, this posing does indeed serve as a protection mechanism. Ironically enough, of course, this protection mechanism ultimately seems to defeat itself: The more Jelinek poses for the media, presenting a rehearsed screen biography, the more eagerly the public hopes to see Jelinek "exist outside of writing."

In the interview, Berka interprets Jelinek's posing on the level of the personal, whereas Vogel interprets the posing and its implications within the larger socio-cultural framework within which it is performed. While these two interpretations of Jelinek's posing are by no means mutually exclusive, Jelinek's answer to Berka's question about the personal function of posing contains, in my view, a certain element of irony: Jelinek's response seems itself to be "not quite natural" and personal, but rather could be said to follow the patterns of stereotyped responses that Jelinek tends to give to personal questions, thus freezing into another pose—in numerous other interviews, Jelinek asserts repeatedly that she is afraid of people, that she seeks to avoid the spotlight, and that she uses writing as a strategy to avoid life; that is, she does not exist outside of writing.[22]

It seems to me that, since the media are interested in selling their products, they indeed have a better chance at achieving this end if they market Jelinek's statements about herself as unique, original utterances with a high degree of authenticity. One cannot completely avoid the impression, though, that Jelinek is implicated in this strategy of the media. After all, just as the media have an interest in selling their products, Jelinek and her publisher have an interest in selling her books.

In accordance with these interests, Jelinek's novel *Lust*, published in 1989, was marketed aggressively by Rowohlt, and a veritable media circus surrounded the appearance of the text.[23] Having variously been labeled as a woman's unsuccessful attempt to create pornography, as anti-pornography, and as pornography, the media controversies and the interviews with the author that followed (and in some instances preceded) the novel's publication helped to turn it into a bestseller.[24] Just the same, in an interview with Margarete Lamb-Faffelberger, conducted in 1990, Jelinek professed to have no idea as to why *Lust* turned into such a great commercial success:

> [The commercial success of *Lust*] is *inexplicable* to me. Maybe [it can be explained] by the title, which, after all, is not just irony, but sheer mockery. *Of course, a few interviews may have contributed to that. I cannot explain it to myself.* I can only explain to myself that people buy this book with wrong premises in mind and then don't finish reading it. Those people who do finish reading it are, in the end, the same ones that have always read me, people who are interested in aesthetic questions. That is, not the ones that are expecting a sensationalistic text. (Lamb-Faffelberger, 193, my emphasis.)[25]

Once again, as was the case with her reply to Berka's interview question, Jelinek's answer contains two assertions at once. On the one hand, the commercial success of *Lust* seems "inexplicable" to Jelinek, and on the other hand, she admits that interviews "may have contributed" to this success. After having made this admission, however, Jelinek backtracks and once again quickly emphasizes that she really "cannot explain" the book's popularity.

While, in my opinion, it might very likely be true that, as Jelinek ventures to guess, a lot of people purchased *Lust* in hopes of finding a pornographic text[26] between the book covers, it must also be said that Jelinek's statements to the press in the context of the novel's publication did not always help to stifle voyeuristic desires on the part of the reading public (see Vogel 1990). In addition, as pointed out earlier, ever since the publication of *The Piano Teacher* and the ensuing interest in Jelinek's biography—an interest that was at least in part furthered by Jelinek's self-presentation to the media—the reading public seems to have become eager to find out more about Jelinek as a person, and the abundance of biographical readings of *The Piano Teacher* made it all too easy to assume that certain other texts by Jelinek would yield further supposed insights into her private life. Thus, the commercial success of *Lust* does not seem all that inexplicable. It may not be possible to decide whether Jelinek really doesn't understand "the laws of the market" and whether these laws really "will always remain a riddle" to her,[27] or whether Jelinek consciously and deliberately plays on and manipulates particular kinds of market mechanisms. Suffice it to say that the way in which Jelinek has presented and continues to present herself to the press has greatly contributed to an interest in her literary production.

It can be said, then, that an interest in Jelinek's literary texts has led to an interest in Jelinek's personal life, and this interest in her personal life has led, in turn, to an increased interest in her literary texts. But this increased interest in Jelinek's texts, since it has been stimulated by a fascination with her biography, has not always resulted in readings that do greater justice to the aesthetic features of the texts. Not only has a constructed dialogue between Jelinek and her works become ubiquitous in the literature, but the interest in what is perceived to be Jelinek's persona often threatens to overshadow a critical concern for and appreciation of her texts. Even where this appreciation is clearly visible, the tendency to read Jelinek's works through the lens of what is known about her personal life can often be encountered. In addition, Jelinek's authorial intentions, voiced to and amplified by the media, are often treated as though their authority were greater than the authority of the literary texts Jelinek published. In this respect, the interest in the author Jelinek and in her life comes at the expense of a critical evaluation of her oeuvre.

To put it differently: unless literary texts are read with the express goal in mind to find out more about their author's biography, the tendencies described above seem problematic. Most readings of literary texts analyze a text's aesthetic features, seek to discuss a text's take on specific socio-historical issues, or are interested in a text's participation in particular discourses and discourse forms, and so forth. It is not methodologically sound, in the majority of instances, to ascribe, while concerned with the interpretation of literary texts, the same significance to the elements that comprise the texts as to the facts that comprise the author's life. Rather, a distinction between, for instance, a narrative voice created in prose fiction on the one hand and the voice of the author of that fictitious text on the other seems appropriate.

If such distinctions are not made, potential pitfalls occur. For instance, a creative intention that an author expresses in an interview might, without further question or investigation, be understood as having become fully realized in a given literary text. However, this need not necessarily be the case, and it seems, therefore, that if one wants to avoid potentially reductive readings of literary texts, one should not let one's analysis be guided by an author's expressed intentions.[28] Similarly, if a given literary character is understood to represent a fictionalized version of the author herself, an analysis of this character might become reductive; one might, for example, unwittingly exclude from one's reading of the text all aspects of this character that lie outside of the known parameters of the author's life. Reading literary texts through the prism of an author's life might lead to interpretations that fail to analyze literary elements which reside outside of the patterns constituted by an understanding of an author's biography. In addition, if too strong an emphasis is placed on the persona of the author of a given literary text, the dimensions and implications of certain discourse forms in this text—discourse forms that an author might participate in due to the fact that he or she lives under particular socio-historical and socio-cultural conditions—may become difficult if not impossible to grasp (see Foucault 1986, 138–148).

In her interview with Margarete Lamb-Faffelberger, Jelinek herself complained about the proliferation of autobiographical readings of her texts:

> I have to reproach myself for simply being too nice and for answering too many questions. Of course, this reached a special climax with my latest book, *Lust*; one has to add to this that

> the artistic production of women, much more so than that of men, is treated biographistically in the feuilletons. The biography of women—also their biological outside, their looks, the ways in which they dress—is much more strongly used for a judgment of their products than in the case of men. Then, with *The Piano Teacher*, which really is a bit more autobiographical—actually an exception from my other works—it was tried time and again to draw the biographical element, that is, my person, into my work and to stir everything together into a gooey mess, so that one ceased to know what was one thing and what was the other. I always tried to defend myself against that very much. But in my efforts to defend myself, I was sucked ever deeper into this.[29]

What Jelinek describes here, among other things, are the mechanisms encountered by female artists that Eva Meyer refers to in her quote cited at the beginning of this essay: The biographies of women writers, Jelinek claims, are referred to during discussions of their work much more often than the biographies of male writers. Women are not allowed to "disappear" in their artistic products—rather, they continue to "resurface."

Jelinek's assessment of the situation of women writers may well be accurate. The tendency to refer to the biography of women writers more frequently than to the biography of male writers could be explained by the fact that, until recently, the economic organization of Western societies, the division of labor, the structure of the bourgeois family, and the assignment of relatively fixed gender roles often made it difficult for women to take up writing as an artistic occupation. Therefore, much early feminist criticism concerned itself with a discussion of not just the socio-historic, but also the individual conditions under which artistic production was made either possible or difficult for particular women.[30] While this research was valuable and useful, it came at the expense of shifting the critical focus away from a given corpus of literary texts produced by a female author onto the biography and socio-historic conditions surrounding this author. Thus, the prejudice manifest in the traditional constitution of the literary canon and of literary history, namely that texts written by women do not constitute suitable objects for literary criticism, as they do not represent high art, was unwittingly and implicitly perpetuated.

The symptom diagnosed by Jelinek—the fact that the biography of women writers is more often drawn into critical evaluations of their texts than in the case of their male counterparts—may well have its historical roots in some of the issues discussed above. However, in addition to these wider historical issues, in the individual case of Jelinek, her own remarks in interviews surely exacerbate the problem she is addressing. Jelinek admits as much when she states that she is "simply too nice" and answers "too many questions." Some critics, as already pointed out, would hold that Jelinek by no means is that naive; that she isn't simply a nice person who answers too many questions too readily, but rather is a skillful manipulator of the media.[31] Be that as it may, one cannot but see a contradiction between Jelinek's professed efforts to defend her texts against autobiographical readings on the one hand and certain remarks she made in her interview with Adolf-Ernst Meyer.

This interview, in contrast to Jelinek's interview with Lamb-Faffelberger, did not primarily address an academic readership, but rather addressed a wider audience interested in Jelinek in particular and in women's issues in general.[32] The questions that Adolf-Ernst Meyer posed to Jelinek alternated between inquiries about her works and inquiries about her biography. During the first half of the interview, Jelinek stated the following:

> In general, I appear in my texts in a very enciphered manner. Except for in *The Piano Teacher*, I have the compulsion to encipher things to such a degree that I myself am unrecognizable. Of course, there are other authors who can always only write about themselves.[33]

This passage exhibits a certain ambivalence. On the one hand, Jelinek seems to want to discourage autobiographical readings of her texts. She is certainly right, by contrasting herself with other unnamed authors, in alluding to and reminding readers of the fact that issues are raised in her texts that have, in a direct sense, nothing to do with her personal life. One might think in this context of the aesthetic and political concerns manifest in Jelinek's texts. On the other hand, by stating that she herself is inscribed in her texts in a ciphered form, she may stimulate voyeuristic desires in some readers who might not believe that Jelinek, as a person, is really completely unrecognizable in her texts, and who might feel tempted to try to decipher Jelinek's texts in such a manner as to make visible the contours of the personal life of the author. Independently of the truth of Jelinek's statement, it might have a kind of teasing effect upon readers already inclined to interpret Jelinek's work biographically.

Later on in the interview, Jelinek, by either being "simply too nice" or by temporarily shelving her efforts to defend her texts against biographical readings, was indeed "sucked ever deeper" into a morass in which it became more and more difficult to make distinctions between her biography and her work. Jelinek's remarks furthered the already strong tendency to mix up her biography with her literary production.

For instance, when Meyer, a practicing psychoanalyst, discussed some of Jelinek's texts in order to interpret Jelinek's relationship to her parents,[34] she did not protest; neither did she attempt to steer Meyer's questions into a different direction. To be sure, Meyer is not a literary critic, and as a psychoanalyst, he is naturally more interested in, for example, what Jelinek's texts can reveal about her psychic economies than a literary critic would be. But since this interview, which reached a wider audience, was also read by academics and feuilleton writers, it did little to combat the tendency of confusing Jelinek's life and her work.

Not only did Jelinek willingly answer Meyer's questions, she also seemed to aid him in an autobiographical-psychoanalytic reading of her works. Jelinek did not merely agree that *The Piano Teacher* is her "most autobiographical book,"[35] but she herself even suggested a reading of a particular passage of the text that further conflates her own life and the fictional life story of Erika Kohut:

> For sure, *my* mother cast *me* in a phallic role, until today. That becomes clear in a passage that a psychiatrist has interpreted for me and that I myself would not have noticed, namely where the father is gotten rid of and where it reads: "The baton is passed on to the daughter." The baton is such an unambiguous image that it really can only have come from the subconscious. That becomes clear, that is like a relay race, the phallus is handed over to the daughter who now has to be the father. What also fits in with this, and what, to my knowledge, has not yet been discussed in the literature, is the lesbian rape scene of

the mother by the daughter in *The Piano Teacher*. This scene only works because the daughter occupies the phallic element. I don't know this in literature, even though it happened in reality, for instance with Unica Zürn. But she was raped by her mother. It obviously was such a horrible event that she later became schizophrenic. She obviously had to transfer this in a very complicated manner. In my case, it probably was possible in a more direct manner. (Adolf-Ernst Meyer, 51–52, my emphasis)[36]

In this passage of the interview, Jelinek herself, in addition to using a psychoanalytic-critical approach, actively chose an autobiographical-psychoanalytic approach to a reading of not just one of her own texts, but also the texts of Unica Zürn. Jelinek states here that transference took place in a more complicated manner for Zürn than it did for herself in her literary texts; the object of Jelinek's inquiry is not so much the corpus of Zürn's texts as it is Zürn's psychic life. As for her reading of her own text, at this particular moment, Jelinek did not seem interested in Erika Kohut so much as a literary figure whose aesthetic features have meaning and can be analyzed also independently of their author; rather, in the context of talking to a psychoanalyst, Jelinek looked at this fictional character as something that makes visible certain projections of her own unconscious.[37]

Jelinek is perfectly justified in taking this approach to the interpretation of her text—or, to put it differently, she is perfectly justified in using her own text as a tool to analyze herself. We as readers cannot expect Jelinek to conform to particular sets of expectations that we might have in this regard. As a matter of fact, we cannot even expect Jelinek to be consistent with respect to how she interprets her own texts. She is free to change her mind as to how she herself understands her writings. Likewise, it is understandable that Jelinek, in talking to different types of interviewers—journalists, academics, psychoanalysts, and so forth—would take into consideration the interviewer's background, interests, and agendas when answering his or her questions, at least partly shaping her responses according to the communicative context in which they are given.[38] One should not even necessarily fault Jelinek for her tendency to present, on the one hand, somewhat stereotyped, vignette-like, and rehearsed-sounding narratives of her life to interviewers while on the other hand approaching the interpretation of her own texts from changing angles.

In other words, while it is true that the media representations of Jelinek have furthered the tendency to read Jelinek's texts through the lens of her biography, and while it is true that Jelinek's responses to interviewers' questions, her own protestations notwithstanding, have not always discouraged this tendency, it is ultimately up to literary critics to clearly define their interpretive approach to Jelinek's literary works. It is their responsibility to emancipate their approach from the media's representation of Jelinek and her work, and it is, I believe, likewise their responsibility to emancipate their approach from Jelinek's own readings of her work—be those readings, as is sometimes the case, autobiographical or not. If it happens to be in a critic's interest to read Jelinek's work biographically, then this specific investigative goal should be clearly stated, and its implications and limitations should be reflected upon explicitly, just as any other critical interest should be stated clearly and reflected upon explicitly. The need for a reevaluation of the critical methods applied in reading Jelinek's texts seems particularly relevant at this point because, at present, a biographical approach to the interpretation of Jelinek's texts often makes itself felt implicitly rather than being stated explicitly. Approaching Jelinek's texts with *implicit* biographical tenets in mind, however, as mentioned above, can lead to, for instance, potentially reductive equations of the author's voice with narrative voices in her literary texts, of unreflected conflations of the author and the literary figures created by her, and so forth. Such pitfalls should be avoided if we want to give Jelinek's texts the full consideration as artistic productions they clearly deserve, and in my opinion, we cannot, as literary critics, ask Jelinek to avoid these pitfalls for us by never giving in to the public's voyeuristic desires for details about her personal life—voyeuristic desires that, to be sure, are the desires of an audience that we as literary critics are part of ourselves.

Just as literary critics can be faulted for not always steering clear of *implicitly* biographical and therefore potentially reductive approaches to Jelinek's work by reading Jelinek's life into her fictional texts, the media can be faulted for often engaging in the reverse procedure, namely the procedure of reading Jelinek's literary texts into her life. Journalists often seem to construct vague and illusory parallels between, for instance, sexual acts described in Jelinek's texts and aspects of her personal life—suggestive interview titles such as "I Would Probably Be a Sex Killer" (see Biron 1984, 47–48), "Men Take Me for a Great Domina" (see Lahann 1988), and "I Don't Like Men, But I Am Sexually Dependent Upon Them" (see Löffler 1989) abound. Even if the public's voyeuristic tendencies are thus stimulated, they are ultimately also frustrated, since in the interviews, the juicy details about the author's life are largely absent. Instead, as discussed above, the public is presented with Jelinek's rather stereotyped remarks about her personal life, remarks that Jelinek feeds to the machinery of the culture industry. The products of the culture industry are then eagerly consumed by the reading public.

Thus, various parties—academics, the media, the general reading public, and Jelinek herself—are implicated in the processes that help to bring about situations in which it becomes all too easy to sometimes engage in interpretive practices that threaten to foreclose an analysis of the *full* spectrum of critical questions that can be brought to bear upon Jelinek's rich and complex oeuvre. But especially academics—more so than the media, the general reading public, or Jelinek herself—are the ones who should practice disentangling themselves from the threads that weave these multilayered processes in order to arrive at the most reflected critical evaluations of Jelinek's literary texts possible. One need not discard the published interviews with Jelinek; one could rather view these interviews as a text corpus that is separate from Jelinek's literary production, a text corpus that is as multifaceted, complex, and at times, seemingly contradictory as the corpus of Jelinek's literary texts.

Jelinek herself, in the interview conducted by Sigrid Berka, stated that, as an author, one should not necessarily understand it to be one's calling to explain one's own texts (1993, 127). It seems to me that with this remark, Jelinek is not just cautioning herself against publicly voicing too many opinions on her own works, against feeding to interviewers too many narratives about her personal life—narratives that are then often used to interpret her fictional texts. Rather, Jelinek likewise seems to be cautioning her readers, urging them to come up with their own critical readings of her texts, readings based on the texts themselves, rather than on the interviews and feuilleton articles that surround these texts.[39]

Notes

1. See Jelinek (1992, 192). The German original reads as follows: "In chinesischen Legenden steht geschrieben, daß große Meister in ihre Bilder hineingingen und verschwunden sind. Die Frau ist kein großer Meister. Deshalb wird ihr Verschwinden nie vollkommen sein. Sie taucht wieder auf, beschäftigt wie sie ist, mit dem Verschwinden." All translations from the German are my own unless otherwise indicated.

2. Recent interviews with Jelinek continue to mingle questions about Jelinek's biography with questions about her literary texts. See, for instance, André Müller (1990, 55–56), "Ich lebe nicht: André Müller spricht mit der Schriftstellerin Elfriede Jelinek"; also "Elfriede Jelinek im Gespräch mit Adolf-Ernst Meyer" (Jelinek, Heinrich, and Meyer 1995, 7–74). In their collection of feuilleton responses to Jelinek's literary works, Kurt Bartsch and Günther Höfler (1991) make evident the media's tendency to produce biographical readings of Jelinek's texts. In this context, see also Margarete Lamb-Faffelberger (1992), *Valie Export und Elfriede Jelinek im Spiegel der Presse. Zur Rezeption der feministischen Avantgarde Österreichs*. In her study of Jelinek's early works, Elisabeth Spanlang is interested in highlighting certain connections between Jelinek's literary production and her biography; see Elisabeth Spanlang (1992), *Elfriede Jelinek: Studien zum Frühwerk*. Criticism of biographical readings of Jelinek's texts has also been voiced, though. See, for instance, *Gegen den schönen Schein: Texte zu Elfriede Jelinek*, edited by Christa Gürtler (1990); Sabine Wilke's (1993) "'Ich bin eine Frau mit einer männlichen Anmaßung': Eine Analyse des 'bösen Blicks' in Elfriede Jelineks *Die Klavierspielerin*"; Ingeborg Hoesterey (1994) in "A Feminist 'Theater of Cruelty': Surrealist and Mannerist Strategies in *Krankheit oder Moderne Frauen* and *Lust*." In her very useful and convincingly written monograph *Elfriede Jelinek* (1995), Marlies Janz steers clear of all biographical approaches to Jelinek's works.

3. Ingeborg Hoesterey has already described this phenomenon very succinctly: "For many commentators, as well as for general readers, the interviews Elfriede Jelinek gave in the eighties seemed to constitute far more impressive and engaging texts than the artistic production that usually provided their occasion" (Hoesterey 1994, 151).

4. It should be stated here that such a critical procedure of course, though used time and again, is itself methodologically questionable, since it often implicitly or explicitly posits that an author's intentions, expressed in interviews, autobiographical writings, or poetological texts, are actually mirrored in his or her literary production. This, however, need not necessarily be the case. To derive too many conclusions from an author's nonliterary statements about his or her literary ones is thus problematic. For instance, in her otherwise very useful monograph *Rewriting Reality: An Introduction to Elfriede Jelinek* (1994), Allyson Fiddler repeatedly refers to Jelinek's artistic intentions and has a tendency to equate these intentions with what can actually be found in Jelinek's literary texts. In keeping with this approach, Fiddler at times does not distinguish sharply between the author Elfriede Jelinek on the one hand and the narrative voices created by Jelinek in her prose texts on the other hand.

5. See, for instance, Sigrid Berka (1993), "Ein Gespräch mit Elfriede Jelinek." See also "Elfriede Jelinek im Gespräch mit Adolf-Ernst Meyer" (Jelinek, Heinrich, and Meyer 1995, 11).

6. This point is also made by Marlies Janz (see Janz 71).

7. See Janz 71. The German original reads as follows: "[In der *Klavierspielerin* findet sich] eine Schreibweise, die stärker als in allen anderen Texten Jelineks konventionellen Lesegewohnheiten entgegenzukommen scheint."

8. See, for instance, Neda Bei and Branka Wehowski (1984), "Die Klavierspielerin: Ein Gespräch mit Elfriede Jelinek," 3–9 and 40–46; Georg Biron (1984), "Wahrscheinlich wäre ich ein Lustmörder: Ein Gespräch mit der Schriftstellerin Elfriede Jelinek," 47–48; Sigrid Löffler (1985), "Der sensible Vampir," 32–37. See also the interview by Günter Kaufmann, "Mörderische Liebe," conducted in 1984 and quoted by Lamb-Faffelberger (1992, 66). Interviews published later, such as the one by A. Müller in 1990 in *Die Zeit* as well as the very extensive interview conducted by Adolf-Ernst Meyer, further elaborate on the supposed parallels between Erika Kohut's story and Jelinek's life. In her interview with Müller, Jelinek even claimed to have cut herself with a razor blade, just like her protagonist Erika Kohut does in *The Piano Teacher* (Müller, 55). Such statements are, of course, bound to increase even further the speculation about similarities between Jelinek and her fictional character Erika Kohut.

9. Wilke, 140. The term *Scheinparallelen* could be translated as "fake," "seeming," or "supposed parallels."

10. In this context, see, for instance, the very instructive essay by Juliane Vogel (1990), "Oh Bildnis, oh Schutz vor ihm" (142–156); see also

Wilke's (1993) article, esp. 115 and 139–141; see also Hoesterey (1994, 151), who speaks of Jelinek's "frankness and quasi-exhibitionist openness."

11. In this context, see especially Gabriele Riedle, "They call her Elfie" (1987, 5–9).

12. The already mentioned interview Adolf-Ernst Meyer conducted with Jelinek in 1995, 12 years after the publication of *The Piano Teacher*, can serve as evidence for this point. Similarly, when Sigrid Berka suggested in her 1992 interview that *The Piano Player* could be read autobiographically without many obstacles, Jelinek did not protest and thus at least did not actively discourage a biographical reading of her text (Berka, 148–149).

13. In this context, compare Wilke who speaks of Jelinek's "in mühsamer Kleinarbeit hergestellte Biographie," i.e., of a "tediously produced biography" (Wilke, 115).

14. The German original reads as follows: "Und so legt die Wiederkehr der immergleichen Repliken nahe, daß die dem Porträt mythisch untergeschobene Ganzheit eine Konfiguration stereotyper Selbstaussagen ist" (Vogel, 148).

15. Vogel, 149. The term could be translated as "demonstration narratives" or "proof narratives."

16. In her interview with Margarete Lamb-Faffelberger (1992, 192), Jelinek claims to be incapable of setting up and carrying out deliberate behavior strategies.

17. Vogel, 153. The German original reads "denunziatorische ... Authentizität."

18. Berka, 153. The German original reads: "Sie sind jetzt ganz natürlich."

19. Berka, 153. The German original reads: "Wie Sie sich manchmal in der Presse dargestellt oder in den Medien posiert haben, die Theatralität oder Maskerade, ... , das ist doch eher ein Leben in Zitaten, oder?"

20. Berka, 153. The German original reads: "Sie haben es auch als Schutz gemacht."

21. Berka, 153. The German original reads as follows: "Ja, ja, sicher. Aber deswegen gehe ich ja Journalisten aus dem Weg, weil ich das alles nicht will; im Grunde bin ich ja überhaupt nicht posierend, im Gegenteil, ich bin ja extrem schüchtern und ängstlich; ich habe ja wahnsinnige Angst vor Menschen, lasse auch kaum jemanden an mich heran. Wenn posierend, dann ist es eher so ein Schutzschild, aber auch das Bewußtsein, eben nicht zu sein oder nicht zu existieren oder nichts zu sein. Ein künstlicher Schutzmantel. Das ist ein starkes Phantasma von mir, nicht zu existieren oder außerhalb des Schreibens nicht zu existieren."

22. See, for instance, the interview with Adolf-Ernst Meyer, esp. 53–54 and 70–71; see also the interview with Lamb-Faffelberger, 192–193.

23. For an analysis of these strategies, see Vogel *in toto*.

24. See, for instance, Brigitte Lahann (1988, 76–85), "Männer sehen in mir die große Domina"; also B. Lahann (1989, 4–5), "Lust statt Pornograpie." For a more complete list of interviews with Jelinek regarding *Lust*, see Janz (1995), esp. 162–164.

25. The German original reads as follows: "Der [Verkaufserfolg des *Lust*-Romans] ist mir unerklärlich. Vielleicht [kann der Erfolg erklärt werden] mit dem Titel, der ja nicht nur Ironie, sondern eigentlich nackter Hohn ist. Natürlich wird dazu noch manches Interview beigetragen haben. Ich kann es mir nicht erklären. Ich kann mir nur erklären, daß die Leute unter falschen Voraussetzungen dieses Buch kaufen und dann nicht fertig lesen. Die Leute, die es fertig lesen, das sind dann eben letztlich doch die, die mich immer gelesen haben, Leute, die an ästhetischen Fragen interessiert sind. Also, nicht diejenigen, die einen Sensationstext erwarten."

26. It should be noted here that critics still debate whether Jelinek truly succeeded in writing an anti-pornographic text that frustrates voyeuristic desires by employing various stylistic alienation techniques, or whether the text at times comes dangerously close to imitating the object of its criticism, namely pornography. On this point, cf. Wilke, esp. 136–139; see also Janz (111–122), who holds that Jelinek's text succeeds in frustrating "culinary" reading strategies (113); further see Helmut Schmiedt (1993, 129–135), *Liebe, Ehe, Ehebruch: Ein Spannungsfeld in deutscher Prosa von Christian Fürchtegott Gellert bis Elfriede Jelinek*.

27. Lamb-Faffelberger (194). In the German original, Jelinek speaks of the "Gesetze ... des Marktes ..., die mir sowieso immer ein Rätsel bleiben werden." If one wanted to be cynical, one could certainly maintain that, on the content level, the greater part of Jelinek's literary texts definitely exhibits the author's knowledge of a variety of economic mechanisms and theories.

28. It seems, for instance, as already pointed out, that Allyson Fiddler (1994), in her otherwise useful study on Jelinek, does not always clearly distinguish between author and narrator, and that she lets some aspects of her interpretation of Jelinek's texts be guided by Jelinek's expressed intentions. Thus, the analysis of certain dimensions in Jelinek's texts—dimensions outside the parameters of authorial intentions—might potentially be foreclosed. See Fiddler *in toto*. See also Schmiedt (1993, 131), who likewise refers to Jelinek's intentions; as a result, the question of whether *Lust* actually succeeds in undercutting and subverting pornographic mechanisms is not discussed in as much depth as possible.

29. Lamb-Faffelberger (1992, 184–185). The German original reads as follows: "Ich muß mir den Vorwurf machen, daß ich einfach zu gutmütig bin und zu viele Fragen beantworte. Einen besonderen Höhepunkt hat das natürlich bei meinem letzten Buch, bei *Lust*, erreicht, wobei man dazu sagen muß, daß die Kunst von Frauen im Feuilleton ja viel stärker als die der Männer biographistisch behandelt wird. Die Biographie der Frauen, auch ihr biologisches Äußeres, ihr Aussehen, die Art, wie sie sich kleiden, wird sehr viel stärker zur Beurteilung ihrer Produkte herangezogen, als das bei Männern der Fall ist. Dann wurde auch bei der *Klavierspielerin*, die wirklich etwas autobiographischer ist—eigentlich eine Ausnahme von meinen sonstigen Sachen—immer wieder versucht [sic] das biographische Element, also meine Person in meine Arbeit hineinzuziehen und beide zu einem Brei zu verrühren, daß man nicht mehr wußte, was das eine und was das andere war. Ich habe mich immer sehr dagegen gewehrt. Aber in dem Bemühen [sic] mich zu wehren, bin ich immer nur tiefer hineingeschlittert."

30. A good example in this context is the history of the reception of the texts by Sophie von La Roche, an eighteenth-century German writer. The fact that Sophie von La Roche was capable of supporting herself with her writing despite adverse conditions was interesting to twentieth-century feminist critics, and hence they concerned themselves with an analysis of these conditions and of La Roche's particular life circumstances. While this research was useful, it clearly also had a negative flip side: by conducting this kind of research on La Roche, feminist critics often unwittingly perpetuated a male prejudice against La Roche's texts, namely that these texts were not truly high literature, but were rather of instructional and pedagogical value to female readers (this estimation of La Roche's texts was first put forth by Wieland, the editor of one of La Roche's novels, and was then accepted unquestioned for the longest time by later critics). Therefore, feminist critics' concentration on La Roche's biography, rather than on her texts, implicitly affirmed the judgment that La Roche's texts were not in and of themselves suitable objects of literary criticism. For relatively recent studies that still largely concern themselves with analyzing the personal and socio-historical conditions under which Sophie von La Roche lived, see, for instance, Ingrid Wiede-Behrendt (1987), *Lehrerin des Schönen, Wahren, Guten. Literatur und Frauenbildung im ausgehenden 18. Jahrhundert am Beispiel Sophie von La Roche*; also see Monika Nenon (1988), *Autorschaft und Frauenbildung: Das Beispiel Sophie von La Roche*.

31. On this point, see again Vogel *in toto*; also see Wilke, esp. 115 and 139–141.

32. This is indicated by the subtitle of the volume in which the interview is published: *Schreiben als Geschlechterkampf*. These words could be translated as "writing as a gender war."

33. Adolf-Ernst Meyer (1995, 35). The German original reads as follows: "Wie ich ja überhaupt sehr verschlüsselt in meinen Texten vorkomme. Außer der 'Klavierspielerin' habe ich ja den Zwang, so zu verschlüsseln, daß ich unkenntlich bin. Andere Autoren können ja immer nur über sich schreiben."

34. See, for instance, page 51 of the interview in question.

35. Meyer (1995, 36–37). The German original reads: "Die 'Klavierspielerin' ist Ihr autobiographischstes Buch." Jelinek replies: "Sicher." ["Sure."]

36. The German original reads as follows: "Auf jeden Fall hat meine Mutter mich phallisch besetzt, bis heute. Das wird an einer Stelle kenntlich, die mir ein Psychiater gedeutet hat und die mir selbst nicht aufgefallen wäre, wo nämlich der Vater abgeschoben wird und wo steht: 'Der Stab wird an die Tochter weitergegeben.' Der Stab ist so ein eindeutiges Bild, daß es wirklich nur aus dem Unterbewußtsein gekommen sein kann. Das wird einem klar, das ist wie beim Stafettenlauf, der Phallus wird an die Tochter übergeben, die jetzt der Vater zu sein hat. Dazu paßt ja auch die in der Literatur meines Wissens bisher noch nicht beschriebene lesbische Vergewaltigungsszene der Mutter durch die Tochter in der 'Klavierspielerin'. Die geht nur, indem die Tochter das phallische Element besetzt. Das kenne ich in der Literatur nicht, obwohl es realiter, z.B. bei der Unica Zürn vorgekommen ist. Sie ist aber von ihrer Mutter vergewaltigt worden. Es war offenbar ein so schreckliches Erlebnis, daß sie später schizophren geworden ist. Sie mußte es offenbar sehr kompliziert übertragen. Bei mir ist es wohl direkter möglich gewesen." Unfortunately, the framework of this essay is not broad enough for me to be able to debate here the particular merits of the interpretation of certain elements of *The Piano Teacher* that Jelinek presents in this passage, but it is important to note that in her statement, Jelinek mingles two approaches to her own text: a psychoanalytic-critical one, and an autobiographical-psychoanalytic one.

37. In this interview, Jelinek takes a biographical-psychoanalytic approach not just to reading her own texts or those of Unica Zürn, but also to Ingeborg Bachmann's novel *Malina*. While such an approach to texts, to be sure, can, under certain circumstances, be legitimate, one should keep in mind that this approach stems from a type of *Erkenntnisinteresse* that privileges the persona of the author as object of inquiry, rather than the body of the text.

38. For instance, in an interview that Josef-Hermann Sauter conducted with Jelinek, virtually no personal questions are posed, and the interview focuses much more exclusively on aesthetic and political questions than most others. See Josef-Hermann Sauter (1981, 99–128), "Interviews with Barbara Frischmuth, Elfriede Jelinek, and Michael Scharang." In her interview with Lamb-Faffelberger, Jelinek remarks that, in general, whenever she was interviewed by academics, especially GDR-academics, the questions that were posed to her focused much more clearly on aesthetic issues, whereas journalists, Jelinek claims, are almost exclusively interested in personal issues. See Lamb-Faffelberger (1992, 186). Of course, one has to keep in mind that the interview Sauter conducted with Jelinek took place before the publication of *The Piano Teacher*, the text that triggered the proliferation of biographical readings of Jelinek's works.

39. I would like to express my gratitude to Heidi M. Schlipphacke for her valuable comments on this essay.

Works Cited

Bartsch, Kurt, and Günther Höfler, Eds. 1991. *Elfriede Jelinek*. Graz: Droschl.

Bei, Neda and Branka Wehowski. 1984. Die Klavierspielerin: Ein Gespräch mit Elfriede Jelinek. *Die schwarze Botin* 24: 3–9 and 40–46.

Berka, Sigrid. 1993. Ein Gespräch mit Elfriede Jelinek. *Modern Austrian Literature* 26(2): 135.

Biron, Georg. 1984. Wahrscheinlich wäre ich ein Lustmörder: Ein Gespräch mit der Schriftstellerin Elfriede Jelinek. *Die Zeit* 40 (September 28): 47–48.

Fiddler, Allyson. 1994. *Rewriting Reality: An Introduction to Elfriede Jelinek*. Oxford, USA: Berg.

Foucault, Michel. 1986. What Is an Author? In *Critical Theory Since 1965*. Edited by Hazard Adams and Leroy Searle, pp. 138–148. Tallahassee: Florida State University Press.

Gürtler, Christa, Ed. 1990. *Gegen den schönen Schein: Texte zu Elfriede Jelinek*. Frankfurt am Main: Neue Kritik.

Hoesterey, Ingeborg. 1994. A Feminist "Theater of Cruelty": Surrealist and Mannerist Strategies in *Krankheit oder Moderne Frauen* and *Lust*. In *Elfriede Jelinek: Framed by Language*. Edited by Jorun B. Johns and Katherine Arens, pp. 151–165. Riverside: Ariadne.

Janz, Marlies. 1995. *Elfriede Jelinek*. Stuttgart: Metzler.

Jelinek, Elfriede. 1970. *wir sind lockvögel baby!* Reinbek bei Hamburg: Rowohlt.

Jelinek, Elfriede. 1972. *Michael. Ein Jugendbuch für die Infantilgesellschaft*. Reinbek bei Hamburg: Rowohlt.
Jelinek, Elfriede. 1975. *Die Liebhaberinnen*. Reinbek bei Hamburg: Rowohlt.
Jelinek, Elfriede. 1983. *Die Klavierspielerin*. Reinbek bei Hamburg: Rowohlt.
Jelinek, Elfriede. 1989. *Lust*. Reinbek bei Hamburg: Rowohlt.
Jelinek, Elfriede. 1992. *Krankheit oder Moderne Frauen*. In *Theaterstücke*. Reinbek bei Hamburg: Rowohlt.
Jelinek, Elfriede, Jutta Heinrich, and Adolf-Ernst Meyer. 1995. Elfriede Jelinek im Gespräch mit Adolf-Ernst Meyer. *Sturm und Zwang. Schreiben als Geschlechterkampf*. Hamburg: Ingrid Klein Verlag.
Lahann, Brigitte. 1988. Männer sehen in mir die große Domina. *Stern* 37 (September 8): 76–85.
Lahann, Brigitte. 1989. Lust statt Pornnograpie. *Rowohlt Revue* 21: 4–5.
Lamb-Faffelberger, Margarete. 1992. *Valie Export und Elfriede Jelinek im Spiegel der Presse. Zur Rezeption der feministischen Avantgarde Österreichs*. New York: Lang.
Löffler, Sigrid. 1985. Der sensible Vampir. *Emma* 10: 32–37.
Löffler, Sigrid. 1989. Ich mag Männer nicht, aber ich bin sexuell auf sie angewiesen. *Profil* 13 (March 23): 83–85.
Müller, André. 1990. Ich lebe nicht: André Müller spricht mit der Schriftstellerin Elfriede Jelinek. *Die Zeit* 26 (June 22).
Nenon, Monika. 1988. *Autorschaft und Frauenbildung: Das Beispiel Sophie von La Roche*. Würzburg: Königshausen and Neumann.
Riedle, Gabriele. 1987/88. They call her Elfie. *Literatur-Konkret* 12: 5–9.
Sauter, Josef-Hermann. 1981. Interviews mit Barbara Frischmuth, Elfriede Jelinek, Michael Scharang. *Weimarer Beiträge* 27(6): 99–128.
Schmiedt, Helmut. 1993. *Liebe, Ehe, Ehebruch: Ein Spannungsfeld in deutscher Prosa von Christian Fürchtegott Gellert bis Elfriede Jelinek*. Opladen: Westdeutscher.
Spanlang, Elisabeth. 1992. *Elfriede Jelinek: Studien zum Frühwerk*. Vienna: Verband der wissenschaftlichen Gesellschaften Österreichs.
Vogel, Juliane. 1990. Oh Bildnis, oh Schutz vor ihm. In *Gegen den schönen Schein: Texte zu Elfriede Jelinek*. Edited by Christa Gürtler, pp. 142–156. Frankfurt am Main: Neue Kritik.
Wiede-Behrendt, Ingrid. 1987. *Lehrerin des Schönen, Wahren, Guten. Literatur und Frauenbildung im ausgehenden 18. Jahrhundert am Beispiel Sophie von La Roche*. Frankfurt am Main: Peter Lang.
Wilke, Sabine. 1993. Ich bin eine Frau mit einer männlichen Anmaßung: Eine Analyse des 'bösen Blicks' in Elfriede Jelineks *Die Klavierspielerin*. *Modern Austrian Literature* 26(1): 115–144.

Vanishing in the Text: Elfriede Jelinek's Art of Self-Effacement in *The Piano Teacher* and *Children of the Dead*

Alfred Barthofer

Elfriede Jelinek, who was born in 1946, is a prominent and versatile contemporary Austrian writer whose international reputation has been growing steadily in recent years. Her literary oeuvre, comprehensive by any standards, includes poetry, radio plays, narrative prose, film scripts, essays, and political articles in journals and periodicals. Her plays have been performed with great success in major European theaters, and have aroused considerable public controversy, reminiscent of some of the plays by Thomas Bernhard, whom she greatly admires. She is the recipient of numerous literary awards and prizes and she has been an outspoken critic of political and cultural life in postwar Austria and an indefatigable advocate of women's rights for many years. Despite her high public profile in Austria and Germany, Elfriede Jelinek is a withdrawn and private person who has lived most of her life in seclusion with her mother in Vienna. Nevertheless, she has made herself freely available to the media and the numerous interviews she has given over the years highlight her accessibility and willingness to discuss private matters concerning her mother, her father, her marriage, and her own emotional problems in an open and self-critical fashion. Her candidness concerning the circumstances of her life and her quasi-psychological self-exposure have been interpreted by some critics as skillful manipulation of the media, motivated by self-interest. However, adverse experience with interviewers has changed her attitude in such matters and strengthened her determination to protect her private self from public gaze and commercially driven voyeurism: "The few things I have disclosed about myself, my childhood, and my mother have been used against me in a most despicable way, just as was the case with Bachmann. It was only after her death when it couldn't hurt her any more. In my case, it led to a kind of self-effacement, the dislike for divulging any information about myself and ultimately to a stage where I did not exist at all anymore" (Winter 1991, 10).

The personal pain and hurt of deliberate misrepresentation and distortion by the media has been responsible for an almost compulsive blotting out of herself in her works, particularly works written after *The Piano Teacher* (1986), which was the only novel with a self-confessed autobiographical background and which also triggered unprecedented public interest in her private life. Of course, it does not mean that the author's self and facets of her inner and outer life are no longer present in her works. On the contrary, her presence is to be felt everywhere, but in a less overt and conspicuous autobiographically factual form and skillfully hidden in the complexity of language and fragmented narrative structure: "In reality, I am everywhere, but encoded in such a way that one cannot find me with the exception of *The Piano Teacher*, the only book of mine which has autobiographical traits" (Winter 1991, 10).

As a matter of fact, Jelinek's narrative technique of formally sophisticated immersion, transformation, and abstraction of the self in the text is closely related to the principle of composition in music that requires the translation of ideas into a mathematical code as a prerequisite for the transfer back into music (Winter 1991, 10). It plays a particularly significant role in Jelinek's latest novel *Children of the Dead* (1995), where she appears in her works not in conspicuously overt self-representation, but rather as an author who subjects herself to linguistic self-stylization and ultimately vanishes completely in the text (Winter 1991, 9 f.). She openly admits to having used a similar strategy in interviews when answering questions concerning her private life (10), but has not been very successful as far as literary criticism is concerned, insofar as some critics have interpreted her strategy of stylized immersion in the text as self-aggrandizement (11). Elfriede Jelinek has consistently argued that autobiographical matters have, in her view, no place in literary criticism, as such an approach distracts from the text itself, which ought to be the sole concern of the critic: "I have consistently argued that the life of a writer, his biography, has no place in the critical study of a literary text; as this was the case for example with regard to Ingeborg Bachmann: to immerse her whole work retrospectively like a repro in her death in fire and to see her whole work exclusively through this single filter" (9).

In her case, the critics' preoccupation with her private life has led to publications that deal exclusively with observations she has made about herself. She is scornful of this as the ultimate perversity and deplores the critics' lack of interest in the actual texts: "There already exist papers, which focus exclusively on the way I have commented on myself, which is indeed the height of perversity. If people only studied my texts and their political messages nearly as intensively as my indeed totally uninteresting life of which perhaps my childhood is interesting as it has been demonized in a certain way" (11).

She finds a similar attitude in the reception of Ingeborg Bachmann's literary works and identifies it as unwillingness to tackle complex and disturbing texts and to seek soft options instead, or what she calls critical "feather-bedding," which allows the reader to "consume" Ingeborg Bachmann's horrific death from a safe distance in the cozy warmth of a fireplace. Biographies are poor substitutes for the serious study of demanding literary texts: "In the meantime, they have settled down comfortably in the biographies of writers, admission free, in order to avoid having to settle down in their works which are a much harder resting place" (Jelinek 1983, 149).

In full agreement with Elfriede Jelinek's understanding of literary criticism, this text does not attempt to identify and list the overt and implied autobiographical references, but rather explores them as an integral part of the narrative structure and the underlying creative process and also as markers of potential change in the author's artistic perspective. Two novels are used to highlight Jelinek's narrative strategy in confronting significant aspects of her past: *The Piano Teacher* and *Children of the Dead*. Both novels are exemplary, but in a very different way. Whereas the earlier work takes a very narrow, personal stance with a mother-daughter relationship at the center throughout the novel, the later work has a much more personally distanced manner in a much wider context of social and moral responsibility and commitment on the part of the author and her fictional representatives in the novel. In both novels, Jelinek does not follow the orthodox canon of autobiographical writing in giving a chronological account of the outer circumstances of her life, the formative forces and events that determined her career and understanding of the world around her. What she conjures up in the reader's mind is a highly complex and fragmented picture of extremely sensitive characters in an insensitive environment. The present study uses the concept of authorship in its traditional, unproblematic form and does not attempt to enter the discussion triggered by Roland Barthes's *The Death of the Author* (1977) or Michel Foucault's *What Is an Author?* (1980), nor does it pursue some of the very complex questions raised in Dorrit Cohn's *Transparent Minds* (1978). "Author" is understood here as creator of a literary work; that is, Elfriede Jelinek is the author of *The Piano Teacher* and *Children of the Dead*. However, the term must not be confused with the concept of the "narrator" as a constituent element of narrative structure as well as a possible aspect of the author's persona or inner self. Although Jelinek's technique of narrative complexity and ambiguity as practiced in *Children of the Dead* challenges the reader's interpretative capacity and literary empathy in an unprecedented way, the question of the role of the reader as raised by Roland Barthes, whose writings have greatly influenced her literary work, is not addressed in this context.

The Piano Teacher has been referred to by the author on several occasions as her one and only overtly autobiographical work and she offers as explanation for her stand in this respect—a deep-seated inhibition to talk openly about herself in a text: "I have always been very much afraid of saying 'I'. I deliberately tried to disregard myself. I turned only relatively late—in *The Piano Teacher*—to autobiographical writing" (Fiddler 1994, 140). This dislike of focusing on herself in a text applies also to discussions of her private life in the media where she uses irony and self-stylization (and aggression) as a protective shield for the purpose of safeguarding her inner self from unwanted intruders, just as her preoccupation with exquisite clothes is more or less camouflage, an attempt to hide—like Greta Garbo (Jelinek 1989, 85)—her true self from the public (1990, 58). In the interview by André Müller, Jelinek expresses the view that she had actually given away very little about her real self in the numerous interviews that had focused on her private life: "Yes, but they were statements which told them nevertheless very little about myself. I dress up since I lack a life of my own. I carry sentences like posters behind which I can hide" (1989, 82). And in a later interview with Riki Winter (1991) she again points out that people know very little about her, the ominous André Müller included: "All those who believe that they know something about me, don't know a thing, André Müller included, who had thought that he had penetrated to the roots in the *Zeit* interview, which he conducted very cleverly" (Müller 1990, 55–56; Winter 1991, 11). What the public really gets is a carefully controlled myth, a stylized persona of the author, and a few stereotypes about her past revolving around her complicated childhood, the insanity of her father, and the difficult relationship with her mother. Elfriede Jelinek finds the public's obsessive preoccupation with these matters deplorable and boring: "They ought to realize by now that they won't get any further information from me apart from that" (Biller 1990, 145).

This determination to withhold information about herself applies above all to her literary work in which she claims to be omnipresent, but not in a clumsy explicit form: "I am an author who does not simply throw up things in a scale of one to one, but somebody who subjects everything to linguistic stylization which is so strong that the author finally vanishes in the text altogether" (Winter 1991, 10). This strategy of self-effacement constitutes, therefore, a hallmark of Jelinek's narrative prose and is referred to by her almost programmatically on many occasions: "With the exception of *The Piano Teacher*, I compulsively present things in code so that I can't be recognized. Other authors are only able to write about themselves" (Jelinek 1995, 35).

The novel *The Piano Teacher* abounds in autobiographical

references and Jelinek herself has discussed this particular aspect in great detail on several occasions, particularly in the interviews with Allyson Fiddler, Elisabeth Spanlang (1992), Riki Winter, and Neda Bei and Branka Wehowski in *Die Schwarze Botin* (1984, 3–10, 40–46). There cannot be any doubt that the innumerable recollections of a very difficult and unhappy childhood and youth, scattered about in the narrative of the tragic failure of Erika Kohut as a pianist and ultimately as a woman, are to a large extent autobiographically authentic and genuine. But the novel is not designed to appeal to the reader for sympathy and emotional solidarity and understanding. On the contrary, the author seems to be trying continuously to alienate and distance the reader from what is happening to the protagonist, just as the author is apparently trying to keep a distance from the events described. The narrative technique used in *The Piano Teacher* prevents an overt emotional response by the reader, whose role is more that of a curious but otherwise indifferent voyeur, just like Erika in the peepshow or in the Prater (a Viennese amusement park), particularly with regard to the sexual and masochistic facets of the novel. The narrative presentation of autobiographical material in *The Piano Teacher*, therefore, is not that of a literary confession written primarily for a reading public interested in the intimacies of somebody's private life over a specific period of time, but is rather that of a fictional postmortem by the author of an extremely difficult and unhappy childhood, focusing above all on a troubled mother-daughter relationship and the fatal consequences resulting from it. The novel is a psychotherapeutic narrative, in which the author confronts certain aspects of her past as a precondition for inner peace and ultimate reconciliation with herself. The designation of the author's retrospective recollection and confrontation with specific aspects of her past as a "novel," that is, as a work of fiction with overt emphasis on the realistic delineation of characters and events, functions as a narrative distancing device and highlights Jelinek's endeavor to address a personal problem rather than to give an authentic description of the circumstances of her life, which seem to have an ancillary function. Another distancing device used by Jelinek is narrative perspective: the narrator presents events not from a first-person point of view, but as a third-person narrator, seemingly detached, particularly in the description of quasi-realistic detail, but involved indirectly in varying degrees of irony and satire directed against the characters and their attitudes and actions, the protagonist included. This enables the author to step outside herself and to adopt a more objective stance. Nevertheless, the novel seems to be a critical self-confrontation with the underlying desire to uncover some of the roots of the emotional difficulties in her later life. The retrospection in the narrator's recollections is canceled out by the use of the present tense throughout the novel. Thus, the immediacy of the events also underpins the immediacy of the problems with regard to the narrator and ultimately the author herself. The critical confrontation with her past self in the form of a narrative, regardless of whether directed towards herself or the reader, seems to be aiming at emotional clarification through verbalization and fictional reconstruction of painful childhood and adolescent experiences and the expected healing process resulting from it. This is indirectly supported by the innumerable psychoanalytical references in the novel, which can of course also be read as a fictionalized case study of the genesis of a sick and emotionally disturbed mind. However, the narrative technique used with great mastery by Elfriede Jelinek in this novel is not always consistent with psychoanalytical principles and seems to turn psychoanalysis into a masochistic ritual (Janz 1995, 86). Although the novel's emphasis on a mother-daughter relationship could also be interpreted as a send-up of Freud's preoccupation with the Oedipus complex, it undoubtedly has its roots in the overpowering omnipresence of Elfriede Jelinek's mother and its lasting emotional impact. Already the way she is introduced foreshadows in an ominous way that she will never be able to escape her, as confirmed at the end of the novel: "However, there already stands Mummy, huge in front of it (door), blocking her way. Calling her to account and before the firing squad, inquisitionist and firing squad in one and the same person, unanimously recognized as mother by state and family" (5).

The opening of the novel also highlights the narrator's identification with Erika Kohut, the daughter figure, and her way of seeing and experiencing the world around her. The information available to the reader is limited and is determined by the perceptiveness of the title character. However, more direct and objective access to the inner world of Erika's mother is to be found in the language she uses, which is carefully recorded and presented in direct speech throughout the novel. In *The Piano Teacher*, as well as in her other works, Jelinek demonstrates an uncanny linguistic perceptiveness and an ability to use impoverished, trite, and cliché-ridden Austrian idiolects as an effective window into the soul of her characters, reminiscent of Elias Canetti, Thomas Bernhard, and Karl Kraus. The introductory door scene can also be seen as a distant thematic allusion to Kafka's parable of the *Türhüter* (the gate keeper) and his seemingly absolute power over the man who is seeking admission (Bei and Wehowski 1984, 42).

Whereas the mother-daughter relationship forms the thematic core of the novel, the father hardly features in the parental household and in the protagonist's childhood and youth. However, the apparent absence of the father in the protagonist's awareness points to a significant problem that is not allowed to surface into consciousness for inclusion in the cathartic reconstruction of the past. The situation described in the novel corresponds indeed very closely to Elfriede Jelinek's tragic relationship with her father and her inability to come to terms with it (Spanlang 1992, 20). The autobiographical background of the difficulty of her father's situation and her own guilt feelings in relation to it are explored in the short prose text *Aggravating Circumstances or A Child's Report about a Relative* (1978, 106–111). Elfriede Jelinek has commented on the role of her father in her life on numerous occasions. Without doubt, his lack of authority in the family and his physical and mental disintegration had a traumatic impact on her as a child. She had to witness the tragic circumstances of his declining physical and mental health for years, which left her scarred for the rest of her life: "He stayed at home for a long, long time until it was simply no longer possible, as you couldn't leave him unattended for a second. But he stayed with us for a long time, and that is something I just could not cope with, something connected with the guilt feeling which I have still not overcome, something I basically have not yet been able to write about. Perhaps I shall be able to do so when I have more distance to it, when I am older myself" (Jelinek 1995, 35).

There is, of course, also an appreciation of the positive qualities of her father, the difficult times he had to go through because of his Jewish background, his strong political convictions, and the final tragedy of his insanity: "My father was an exceptionally talented scientist, but otherwise a poor devil. He had the misfortune of being highly neurotic and eventually went mad" (Schwarzer 1989, 54). It is not quite clear whether her father suffered from Alzheimer's disease or a condition caused by the toxic substances he had to handle as a chemist during the war. In any case, it led to the gradual loss of language and identity during the crucial years of his daughter's puberty and the experience lingered on for years and was traumatic, even in retrospect: "It was a long process, and when he eventually died, he was seventy years old, but in reality he had already been dead for several years" (Jelinek 1995, 35). The emotional void left by the absence of the authority of a father was quickly filled by a powerful, awe-inspiring mother who exerted total control over her husband and finally her daughter for many years to come: "I practically spent my whole puberty with a father who lost his mind, who was an indescribably weak and distant, weird, obscure and useless character, simply no father figure. My mother was phallic, she was father and mother in one person. A monstrous, totem pole–like authority. My mother is still frightening today, at the age of 86" (Schwarzer 1989, 54). The virtual absence of the father in *The Piano Teacher* underpins the overpowering omnipresence of the mother as an autobiographical reality. The terrible experience of watching her father's gradual physical and mental breakdown was, at the time the novel was written, still too early and too painful and upsetting to confront. Until recently, the author had not yet been ready to reflect upon the problem of her emotionally distant and unknown father and her relationship to him. Even in interviews, Elfriede Jelinek's rejection of her father is often overshadowed by sadness and regret. This is also the case in the novel itself, although critics have asserted the opposite: "The novel does not suppress and 'conceal' Erika's grief and love, but it diagnoses her inability to grieve and to love" (Janz 1995, 85).

Erika Kohut's relationship to her father is encapsulated in two key scenes: his trip to the nursing home in Neulengbach (94–

99) and his death (73). Most of the other references to him in the novel are of little significance with regard to this matter. However, ironic distancing is conspicuous in these passing references to him as well as a feeling of unfairness and injustice: "Only after twenty years of marriage did Erika step into this world which made him go insane and thus was kept in an institution to ensure that he couldn't do any harm to this world" (15). Both scenes reflect an underlying feeling of grief and anguish, although irony and sarcasm reminiscent of Ödön von Horváth distract from it. Perhaps it is the author's only way to cope emotionally with the tragedy of the situation, even in retrospect.

The *persona* of the cold, competent, and aggressively analytical feminist, which Elfriede Jelinek tends to project in her public appearances and in some of her writing, has been taken at face value in the media and in literary criticism at the expense of the warm and caring side of her which, carefully hidden under the surface, she is apparently considered to be incapable of. The psychoanalytical implications of her relationship to her father have been discussed at length by literary critics (Burger 1990, 17–30; Janz 1995; Hoetzer 1993). However, the assertion that Erika (or the narrator) lacks the ability to appreciate the father's plight and misfortune and to respond to it with sympathy and understanding is at best doubtful (Janz 1995, 86). The opposite seems to be the case, despite the author's inclination to suppress overt sympathy and grief. Irony is used again as a powerful instrument against succumbing to such feelings: "Father is supposed to wave good-bye to his two ladies as they depart, propped up by two involuntary warders in white coats. Daddy covers his eyes mindlessly with his hand begging not to be beaten. This shows the departing rump of a family in a terribly bad light, because Daddy had never been beaten, never ever. Where he only got that idea from, the departing torso of a family wants to know from the peaceful, good air which doesn't respond. The butcher is driving faster than before and is relieved of a dangerous person. He still wants to go to the soccer ground with his children, as it is Sunday, his rest day" (97).

The same is true of the preceding description of his arrival in the nursing home, but it conjures up in the author memories of life at home. It is also quite clear that Erika (and the narrator) are emotionally on the side of the father, particularly with regard to the profit mentality of the nursing home proprietors (95) and the "insanity industry" (94): "Father doesn't understand why he is here, as he has never felt at home here. He is forbidden many things, and what he is still allowed to do is not appreciated either. Whatever he does is wrong, but he is used to it from his wife. He is not supposed to touch anything and not supposed to move, he should fight his restlessness and lie still, this compulsive walker" (96–97).

Elfriede Jelinek's social conscience intrudes continuously in the fictionalization of her childhood memories to highlight the tragic helplessness of the underprivileged and abandoned. Her narrative presentation of a painfully experienced reality, however, is unemotional and blunt, and yet powerful and convincing in its hopelessness and brutality: "And whoever is here, will also stay here because his relatives want it. Things can only get worse: Steinhof! Gugging!" (96). The death of Erika's father is only mentioned by her in passing in the context of a concert and tinged in self-irony: "Erika expresses in soft music that her father had died in Steinhof, in complete insanity. For that reason one had to be considerate to Erika, as she had to go through difficult times. In this swanky ostentatious state of health, Erika doesn't want to talk about it any further, but she is hinting at a few things. Erika wants to get a bit of feeling out of Klemmer and she is positioning the chisel on him without mercy. Because of her anguish this woman deserves every tiny bit of male affection that can be extracted. The young man's interest awakens instantly, new and bright" (73).

In line with the tragic void that the absence of a father had created in the crucial years of Elfriede Jelinek's puberty, the central concern of *The Piano Teacher* revolves around the detailed presentation of the relationship between the thirty-year-old pianist Erika Kohut and her mother, who could be her grandmother as far as age is concerned (5), and the subsequent difficulties she experiences in her relationship with the student Walter Klemmer. The title figure's experiences are very much those of Elfriede Jelinek, as confirmed by her in several extensive interviews on this matter (Spanlang 1992; Bei and Wehowski 1984) and in a number of detailed critical studies (Fiddler 1994; Janz

1995). It took Elfriede Jelinek some fifteen years before she was ready to revisit that traumatic period of her life in order to come to terms with it. Apart from the already mentioned narrative distancing devices, such as third-person narrative perspective, the use of present tense, direct quotations, authorial voice and commentary, the use of the generic term 'the mother' or the personal pronoun 'SHE' in references to Erika, and irony and sarcasm (Fliedl 1991, 57–77), to mention only the most obvious ones, Elfriede Jelinek is provocatively candid in her cathartic review of her personal problems, her family background, and the fatal emotional dependence on her mother, which she has never been able to overcome ("I am emotionally still dependent on her"; personal communication 1984). She projects her own experiences onto Erika Kohut, whose mother fixation has fatal consequences with regard to her relationship to Walter Klemmer, who is in love with her, and other lovers: "Erika does not feel anything and has never felt anything. She is as numb as a piece of roofing felt in the rain" (77). "He is not going to try to penetrate into her home? Erika would love to crawl back into her mother's womb, sway gently in the warm fluid. So warm outside, and moist inside the body. She freezes up in front of her mother when Klemmer comes too close to her" (76).

It is hard to say how autobiographically authentic these descriptions of extremely private experiences are and to what extent Elfriede Jelinek has fictionalized or reinvented them. On the other hand, she has also acknowledged that some of the personal sexual matters have actually occurred, as for example, acts of sado-masochistic self-mutilation with razor blades (88). Significantly enough, they all are related in some way to her father: "She is very clever in the use of razor blades, as she has to shave her father, the soft cheeks of her father under his completely empty forehead which is no longer troubled by thoughts and vestiges of a will" (88). The projected authenticity of the autobiographical material explored in the novel is further supported by numerous detailed references to Vienna as the city in which Erika and her mother have lived. Even more important, though rarely mentioned in literary criticism, is Elfriede Jelinek's uncanny mastery of recreating the language spoken by the inhabitants of this city. One is immediately reminded of Therese

Krumbholz in Elias Canetti's *Die Blendung* and his concept of acoustic masks. The Austrian mentality is skillfully encapsulated in the language of these passages, which expose to the linguistically sensitive reader the inner world of the characters and the forces that motivate their behavior and actions. However, sexual self-exploration and Erika's development as an individual are observed in the context of absolute domination and control by her mother and the mechanisms developed by Erika to resist or elude them: "Mother can check up whether SHE keeps her hands on the quilt all night or not, but in order to get angst under control, she would have to break open the shell of her child's skull with a chisel first and personally scrape out her fear" (89).

In Elfriede Jelinek's masterly exploration of the comprehensive system of manipulation and psycho-terror, overt and hidden, gentle and brutal, that the protagonist is exposed to and confronted with day after day gives the novel a complexity and emotional aura that is surpassed only by Franz Kafka whose novel *Der Prozeß* (*The Trial*) is actually alluded to in *The Piano Teacher*, albeit for different reasons (Bei and Wehowski 1984, 42). In the interview by Alice Schwarzer (1989), Jelinek refers explicitly to these experiences and her expertise in psycho-terror: "I have, of course, experienced psycho-terror in its most delicate manifestations and most subtle nuances. I think I am an expert in psycho-terror" (54).

The novel abounds in bondage imagery and references to captivity, imprisonment, chains, and handcuffs, all based on Elfriede Jelinek's own childhood experiences and recollections, although Olga Jelinek, the author's mother, seems to have perceived things quite differently (see Spanlang 1992, 22). The author's physical and emotional dependence was particularly pronounced after a year of total confinement in her home due to a nervous breakdown, which is not at all touched upon in *The Piano Teacher*, highlighting the selectivity principle of the author's autobiographical fictionalization strategy: "She had to accompany me all the time, as I was unable to travel on my own. So I was even more clingy than I wanted to be. I have, so to speak, turned round myself what she had always wanted, namely to turn me into her slave, and I wildly clung to her" (Bei and Wehowski 1984, 6). There can be no doubt that Elfriede Jelinek's life with her mother must have been a nightmare at times and her novel *The Piano Teacher* reflects facets of it in a unique way. The author herself suggests in an interview that only the death of her mother will ever enable her to feel free: "Sometimes I feel that I will only be able to really live when my mother is dead. I will not be able to cope with that all my life" (45).

The system of repression, manipulation, and terror, gentle and brutal, conjured up so skillfully in *The Piano Teacher* has to be understood metaphorically (just as the novel's sexual imagery) and not in terms of an autobiographical confession, or a narrative peepshow for voyeuristic middle-class readers. What Elfriede Jelinek describes in her novel has an authentic autobiographical background, but the implications of the experiences so artistically recreated transcend the strictly personal and private sphere and point at exemplary facets of the Austrian soul, close and familiar to everyone, though invisible and rarely admitted. In this respect *The Piano Teacher* reminds the reader of Arthur Schnitzler, Franz Kafka, Elias Canetti, Karl Kraus, Thomas Bernhard, and a long tradition of Austrian writers with similar concerns and objectives, but very different narrative techniques and strategies. The autobiographical link with that tradition is the Jewish background of Elfriede Jelinek's father (Bei and Wehowski 1984, 4). In the emotional turmoil and disorientation of the adolescent self, Erika Kohut's preoccupation with herself and her mother as "absolute law" (*Über-Gesetz*) is appropriate and necessary as a prerequisite for the self's future orientation and commitment outside the narrow confines of self-interest and personal need.

This is clearly the case in Elfriede Jelinek's latest novel *Children of the Dead*, which also has a significant autobiographical dimension and a self in search of clarification, but in a wider social and historical context, in line with what Goethe with reference to *Faust II* calls "die große Welt" (the large world), and a growing preoccupation with the question of her Jewishness through the family background of her father. Again, Jelinek does not follow traditional patterns of autobiographical narration in presenting the material in autobiographical chronology and the development of a self as a sequence of causes and effects. No attempt is made in *Children of the Dead* to document the factual history of the author's self and the factors that shaped and determined its outlook on life. On the contrary, what Jelinek conjures up in her latest novel is a highly fragmented picture of an extremely complex and split self responding to a dark and sinister moral wasteland with irony and a highly selective associative memory that fluctuates in an unpredictable rhythm between past and present.

Allusions to autobiographical information are to be found above all in the female characters who constitute the center of the novel: Karin Frenzel and her overpowering mother, the student Gudrun Bichler, and the narrator who reports events with ironic distance from outside, but who also slips into the characters' hearts and minds, as is often the case in Jelinek's novels. The narrator appears in the form of a narrative I, We, and a quasi-detached, impersonal One, addresses the reader directly, and often disappears from the scene altogether. The irregularity of change in narrative perspective imbues the novel with an atmosphere of restlessness, disquiet, and unpredictability. The contours of what is actually happening are deliberately kept blurry and distorted throughout the novel in support of its major themes. The mother-daughter relationship and the problem of victimization, manipulation, and filial dependence are highlighted again as in *The Piano Teacher*, but no longer in the form of a therapeutic self-analysis or case study of adolescent self-preoccupation, but in the wider context of the self's role in a society of doubtful moral principles and an uncanny ability to block out of private and public memory the horrors of a reprehensible past. It is, above all, this dimension of moral insensitivity in the presence of evil that separates the two novels and highlights a level of maturity and social commitment on the part of the author that is missing in her previous prose work.

The narrative principle of associative memory and deliberate fuzziness and opacity make Elfriede Jelinek's latest novel much more complex and difficult in a formal sense than *The Piano Teacher*, which Jelinek called a straightforward "realistic novel." The metaphoric darkness and apocalyptic twilight imagery (reminiscent of Karl Kraus's *The Last Days of Mankind*, Hans Lebert's *Wolfshaut* (1960) or *Der Feuerkreis* (1992), Thomas Bernhard's *Frost* (1963), or Christoph Ransmayr's novel *Morbus*

Kitahara published in 1995) underline the subconscious, irrational dimension in which characters move and events occur as well as the moral intransparency and ambiguity of Austrian society, particularly with regard to its fascist past. Elfriede Jelinek applies throughout this novel what she calls the art of literary evasiveness, a strategy considered by herself as uniquely hers: "You have to try to describe things in such a roundabout way and distort them so much that they can be recognized again. This applies to Thomas Bernhard, and although he has been associated with it time and again, I believe nevertheless that I am the first one who has used it: to distort something so that it can be recognized. You have to avoid excessive unambiguity in art. You have to be evasive, you have to be implicit, you have to find images" (Jelinek 1995, 49). As a consequence, the autobiographical dimension of *Children of the Dead* is less direct and explicit than that of *The Piano Teacher*. The myriad of references throughout the novel to incidents widely reported in the Austrian media, to well-known Austrian politicians and public figures, popular television shows, sensationalized media events, and detailed descriptions of the physical background of the novel, conjure up a quasi-realistic picture of life in Austria that is, however, deceptive and misleading as it reflects a faked reality of stultifying superficiality and comfort, generated and promoted by the tourist industry and the media for the masses at the expense of the conveniently forgotten reality of the horrors of the Holocaust. (The theme of forgetting and forgetfulness runs through the whole novel like a red thread, reminiscent in many ways of Günter Grass's *Hundejahre*, published already in 1963). The themes of brutality against women and ruthless exploitation of nature are parallel and complementary themes dominating not only the author's narrative strategy, but also the narrator's personal involvement in the subject as pointed out programmatically at the beginning of the novel when the narrator admits: "We are (and we feel our presence here particularly strongly) in an Austrian village" (KDT, 7). The opening of the novel also highlights the author's language-driven, associative ironic, and parodistic stance, which Jelinek inherited from her father, "an extremely clever man who was above all a verbal genius" (Jelinek 1995, 35): "The great dead of the country, only to mention a few, are Karl Schubert, Franz Mozart, Otto Hayden, Fritz Eugen Last Breath, Zita Zitter, Maria Theresiana, and everything her Military Academy in Wiener Neustadt has produced up to 1918 and in Stalingrad in 1943 and an additional few million crushed people" (KDT, 7).

The false and contrived happiness of life in the Pension Alpenrose, where the protagonists of the novel spend their summer holidays (as the author had done on many occasions), is obviously a metaphor of Austria and the shallowness and superficiality of life there, as witnessed and commented on by the narrator. It is situated in an area of Styria that Elfriede Jelinek is more than familiar with as she used to spend the summer months there with her mother, who also owned a house nearby. In a 1995 interview by Adolf-Ernst Meyer, Elfriede Jelinek calls the region "a laboratory set up for the study of social differences" and a place of great literary significance and powerful childhood memories (Jelinek 1995, 14). Despite painstaking attention to factual accuracy and detail in *Children of the Dead*, Jelinek is not an autobiographical novelist in the traditional sense, as the factual information about herself is not primarily used for the purpose of confessional self-representation and self-illumination in the context of a truthfully reconstructed past. However, Jelinek's narrative strategy of artful integration of fragmented autobiographical facts and a fictionalized past (and present) allows the reader to come closer to the truth about the author's self than traditional autobiographical accounts. In *Children of the Dead* Jelinek is no longer preoccupied with the easily traceable external facts of her life, but rather explores her inner, less tangible growth, development, and change in search of identity. The author's growing identification with the plight of victims of the Holocaust, underpinned in the title of the novel (and its dedication) and encapsulated in the elaborate system of death and fire imagery, reflects a heightened awareness of being Jewish in a country that has practically hardly changed since the end of the war and where the acknowledgment of collective guilt is still outstanding. The dead are as "hungry" in Jelinek's latest novel as in Hans Lebert's *Die Wolfshaut* (1960), which is also set in a small village in Styria, Austria. More significant, however, is the fact that the citizenry's indifference in these matters and their refusal to come to terms with their past is very much the same: "But this country is a false mother, a woman whose skin has turned cold a long time ago and whose blood stopped flowing and thickened (this country is still too unrepentant today to be willing to admit its mistakes!). This nice, homely, tree-adorned country with its round pompoms on many of its churches, has, like a playful animal, rolled over on its back, in order to feel the steel enter its body, brutality and terror. To keep quiet in such nearness can't be expected of a woman like Karin Frenzel. Does she also want to become a terrifying? child of this country, waved to from the TV screen by the father of the people? a secret signal which at present only Karin understands. Only for her, what an honor!" (KDT, 228). And the narrator asks the question why this had to be the country of birth: "Why did we, and Karin Frenzel, only have to be born in this country which keeps pretending to unite us (plus hundreds of thousands of tourists!) with nature, or in absence of it with a hospital; well, with a place in any case, where you finally find rest" (229).

Finally, the narrator offers the following answer: "I give you an answer: The dead have to eat and digest themselves! Nobody is throwing something to eat into their coffins or wherever they might be lying. Tons of ashes are piled up here—and they all have been people too, swaying shadows of brothers and sisters, oh dear, but none of them Christians! who are setting out now in search of their unborn grandchildren, clumsy like surfers who feel that the waves under their feet have turned into ice in all the colors of sunrise and the orchard of IGLO—permafrost" (229). In a short ironic reference Elfriede Jelinek identifies explicitly with Karin Frenzel and the millions of nameless victims: "We don't want and we can't name all of them, the name Jelinek may stand for many millions, but it doesn't want to" (333). The intensity with which this question dominates the life of the narrator (and author) opens up innumerable facets of hidden emotionality and sensibility, as well as inner chaos and intransparency inaccessible to the rational mind, and canonized principles of autobiographical writing with its emphasis on factual accuracy, oblivious of the fact that in the selection and arrangement of autobiographical material, manipulation of truth must occur. The persona projected in traditional autobiographical writing is in itself a literary construction by the author in response to perceived public expectations and personal inclinations and motivation and is therefore essentially fictional. Elfriede Jelinek's narrative strategy of fictionalizing autobiographical data and transforming it by means of fragmentation, association, distortion, distancing, irony, indirect inner monologue, acoustic masks, and other fictional devices into a literary genre falls well outside positivist ideals of truthful and objective autobiographical self-presentation. Her novel *Children of the Dead* is exemplary insofar as it highlights the complexity and candidness in literary self-exploration and the fluidity in the boundaries between autobiography and fiction, and consequently the inappropriateness of the rigid barriers of traditional genre description and definition.

Fictionalized self-reflection and self-exploration, or what Thomas Bernhard (1976, 16) and Peter Handke (1976, 26) call "to come clean with oneself" (cf. Wittgenstein 1974, 57), is a major concern in *Children of the Dead*, particularly with regard to narrative structure. The numerous references to the author's past (partly already present in *The Piano Teacher*) are fragmented and dispersed over a rather long and complex narrative like a huge jigsaw puzzle with numerous missing and deliberately withheld pieces. And yet, the contours of the key characters and what they stand for become distinctly visible, not as realistic photographical pictures, but in the fashion of a Rorschach test, leaving it up to the reader to search for and find truth. Obviously, it is not the realistic and detailed photographical surface or the air of objectivity that ultimately matters, but what is beneath and behind it, just like life in Austria in *Children of the Dead*, with its glossy mask of shallow tourist brochure stereotypes on the surface and a suppressed dark side (past) underneath.

Moreover, fragments of autobiographical background information are projected in varying degrees onto the female characters of the novel: Karin Frenzel and her mother, the student Gudrun Bichler and the narrator's I, We, or One, which merge and overlap at times openly, but are also clearly autonomous on other occasions. The narrative perspective is complicated even further by the author's masterly practice of obfuscating the transition from one point of view to another. In the interview by

Meyer (Jelinek 1995), Elfriede Jelinek admits her personal interest in this matter: "I frequently use that type of objective commentary. If I ever wrote a doctoral dissertation about myself, I would probably analyze the significance of the 'we,' of auctorial commentary in the narrative, which is continuously changing its perspective. In my later works, for example in *Lust*, people are being addressed directly, or I talk about myself in the plural, there is continuous change, and you have to establish who is actually talking, which I or which You. That's where I leave the fictional level in order to make a political statement which points to the truth behind things, but one has to find out first, who, which who, is actually talking" (Jelinek 1995, 28). As mentioned earlier, the narrator identifies openly with Karin Frenzel, who also bears most of Elfriede Jelinek's autobiographical character traits, particularly with regard to the relationship with her overpowering mother, her father, her childhood, and her family background. The narrator's closeness to Karin Frenzel is highlighted in a series of encounters of Karin and the narrator and Karin and her mysterious double (or *Zweitfrau* or *Fremde*) whose existence is occasionally in doubt: "This woman probably doesn't even need air, as she does not exist, Karin thinks with great relief (she isn't a dream, otherwise she wouldn't look like me)" (104). At the same time the confrontation with the other self is a necessary prerequisite for her identity: "In this Other woman which she is at the same time, Karin wants to overcome the Other in order to become finally her own self" (103). The hallucinatory ambiguity of the situation is confirmed by the narrator's observation that it is difficult to put this ultimate self-encounter in the context of suicide actually into words: "It is, and words won't help but rather do harm, it is Karin Frenzel in person who has met herself, who has to step in front of herself in order to look at herself, look at herself in a suit" (91). On other occasions the character of Karin Frenzel (like Gudrun Bichler) is split into two halves (Karin One and Karin Two; 616), and running away from herself, warned by the narrator not to do so: "and yet she keeps running, running away from herself, Karin, heads up!" (616). The theme of the twin-sister seems to refer in a very complex and carefully camouflaged way to Elfriede Jelinek's own split between the projected persona of an aggressive feminist intellectual and her true, but hidden self (see Schwarzer 1989, 51; Winter 1991, 9).

Similarly, Gudrun Bichler is also associated in numerous references with the author's personal life (Catholicism, primary school, suicide attempts, Viennese background, life of a loner, motherhood, interest in films, television, and so forth) that are at the same time canceled out again (father's background, brother, education, murder victim). The author's interest in and affinity to this character seems to be located on a more ideological level, insofar as she tries to highlight in highly emotive language and biting irony the vulnerability of women in a world of male aggressiveness and brutality (for that purpose the narrator for a short while even enters the mind of Gudrun Bichler's murderer; 504), a problem of central importance in Elfriede Jelinek's writing, literary and nonliterary alike. In the context of the brutal murder of the young girl near the Red Army Monument on the Schwarzenbergplatz (which received great publicity in Austrian tabloids) the author also uses the narrator as a mouthpiece of her personal views on the violence of men against women. (The emotional involvement of the author in this problem is clearly reflected in the highly emotive language and imagery used in these sections; 505). The character of Gudrun Bichler also forms a major thematic link to Vienna and its shadowy past, which constitutes another major area of concern of *Children of the Dead* and Jelinek's attitude toward Austria and Austrians. The transition from fiction to reality ("Attention, at this moment the two characters created by me arrive at the wet ground of the valley"; 460) is often very abrupt and sudden, and the author's deep-seated feelings surface in the cynicism and irony of her comments (461–464). The complexity of the novel is further increased by the author's deliberate fusion of characters or conjectures concerning their identity in a clearly defined reality (490): "There comes the woman in white, white as one does not know who she is, perhaps she is the fashion model student Gudrun Bichler, swiftly disappearing like smoke from the semicircular pot at the monument" (490).

The ultimate embodiment of Elfriede Jelinek's self, however, is to be found in the narrator: not on a physical and faithfully autobiographical level, but with regard to a basic outlook on life and in the ingenious use and understanding of language. These aspects of this novel (and for that matter also of her previous one, *Oh Wildnis, Oh Schutz vor ihr*, published in 1985) tell the reader more about the author than traditional autobiographical writing with its emphasis on factual information and a narrow concept of real people and real events, the relevance of which scholarship is still reluctant to acknowledge.

In the kaleidoscopic presentation of fictional characters and events in *Children of the Dead*, a number of issues emerge around which the central characters of the novel are developed, the narrator included. They have also played a key role in Elfriede Jelinek's life. Some of them are well known due to the public stand she has taken on some of these matters and her openness in the numerous interviews she has given. They have also been reflected in her literary works, particularly in her plays (Burgtheater), which have aroused considerable discussion in the local media and anger in some sections of the Austrian population. Jelinek shows great mastery in using her special brand of literary shock therapy (sexual matters included) as an instrument of sensitizing people's political consciousness, but not as an end in itself, as frequently suggested by her opponents. Jelinek's narrative prose explores various contemporary issues, including the questions of women's rights, the exploitation and destruction of nature, the media-dominated shallowness and artificiality of life in Austria, the resurgence of fascist ideologies and their support among Austrians, the vexing question of Austria's relationship to Germany, and the attitude of Austrians to foreigners; among these, the question of being Jewish and the resulting consequence is gaining more and more importance. This is particularly true in her very latest novel *Children of the Dead* and also in *Oh Wildnis, Oh Schutz vor ihr*. Both works reflect a growing preoccupation with her family background on her father's side, which is still missing completely in *The Piano Teacher*. Jelinek's father, who is referred to briefly in *The Piano Teacher* and in *Children of the Dead*, although his invisible presence in the latter is felt throughout the novel, has a long history of Jewish ancestors, including rabbis, although he was not a practicing Jew himself. Elfriede Jelinek's paternal grandfather, however, was one of the founders of the Austrian Social Democrats and her father was a committed member of the political left. And so is the author herself. The experience of being Jewish manifested itself in the author's private life more in the form of something absent and missing than in an active identification and involvement in Jewishness. Moreover, due to her mother's Catholic background the family was unevenly split into a powerless Jewish proletarian father and a powerful Catholic middle-class mother, which had a direct bearing on Elfriede's upbringing, as reflected indirectly in *The Piano Teacher* (Jelinek 1995, 33). Most family members survived the Holocaust, but the author's father experienced severe hardship and humiliation and survived only because of his special expertise as a chemist and his marriage to an Aryan: "I think that he had carried out research in a war-related field and therefore became indispensable. I can imagine that this also had a devastating psychological impact on him" (Schwarzer 1989, 54). There are references in *Children of the Dead* to the rounding up of the narrator-I and its parents by the Nazis and the suicide of the old father, as a consequence seeming to recreate an aura of terror rather than a first-hand experience by the author (407). The author does not focus on the personal impact that the Nazi regime had on her life or that of her family, but she is haunted by the death and suffering of Jews as a group. She expresses a similar view in the interview by Alice Schwarzer (1989): "The experience of having been persecuted, that collective experience is something I have certainly been aware of" (54).

The indescribable horrors of the Holocaust nevertheless preoccupy the narrator over large sections of the novel. Parallel to the events in the Pension Alpenrose, the reader is taken on a tour through Vienna (556) that is reminiscent of the apocalyptic backdrop in Karl Kraus's *Die Letzten Tage der Menschheit*, passing infamous landmarks of Austrian political history that Thomas Bernhard had visited only shortly before (557). The horrors of the past are still alive everywhere, below the surface of the streets (493), behind the facades of the historical buildings in Vienna, in the shallow happiness of its inhabitants, and above all in their hearts, ever ready to strike again: "Tschinn. Bumm. Krach. Jörg" (564). The tragic fate of friends is alluded to ("Now you will witness how down at the Quay of the Donaukanal the truck with Ilse's grandmother and a few other grandmothers, grandfathers and children and grandchildren is driving into a bend and disappearing" (397) and Eichmann's and Mengele's horrific crimes occupy the narrator's (and the reader's) mind with relentless immediacy (394 f.). The narrator's tour through the "city of the dead" (555) takes the reader to the huge Rassensaal in the Museum of Natural History, where scandalous documents of inhumanity are being exhibited: "There is one hall after the other in which smashed bodies of human beings are exhibited. You can see what they were meant to be, before they managed to escape our insecticides. When they saw that things were not good the way they were, we, their Gods, simply smashed them to pieces, but we didn't get around any more to recreate them" (557). Here the visitor/tourist can see what you must not look like in Austria, in order to be allowed to exist (559). The hall of races must have left a feeling of outrage and pain in the author, just like another Viennese landmark of inhumanity—the huge collection of preserved brains (and other parts of the body) of mentally handicapped patients from Steinhof, an institution that Elfriede Jelinek knows very well personally as her father spent the last years of his life there (563–568; 457). Memories of the horrors of Mauthausen are triggered in the narrator at the sight of the exhibits (564); the narrator feels and identifies overtly with the Jewish people (564) and shares their anger and fear of the future in a country where not even the dead are allowed to rest in peace (490). The feelings of outrage, anger (primarily reflected in the use of irony), uneasiness, and fear recur throughout the novel, but without conspicuous appeal to the reader's emotions; closely related is the narrator's growing awareness of being different and a "stranger" in Austria and among its people, who seem to live like zombies and to adjust truth to their immediate needs (473). And yet, the narrative "we" is also a prisoner of the country's shadowy past, albeit a critical and sensitive one (452 f.). The shadows of the past are indeed visible everywhere in this "Island of the Blessed" (555), but are ignored by the majority of its people. They would rather celebrate the glory of their past (473) and immerse themselves in the world of the Pension Alpenrose, unwilling to face the truth. But truth cannot be ignored, nor can truth be a thing of the past (512). Truth must stay alive and must be passed on to future generations, even if it is difficult.

The novel is dedicated to the dead and is understood as a testimony to their suffering. But in confronting this problem, Elfriede Jelinek also examines her own past, particularly her Jewishness in the Austrian context. The references to her life in *Children of the Dead* are numerous and often candid and personal, but are never intended to be photographically realistic. Traumatic personal experiences are woven into the narrative as well as those of parents, grandparents and friends, for example her grandfather (144) or her grandmother's life as a *Fremde* in Vienna (Jelinek 1995, 33), with one major objective: to search for truth— truth about herself and the past.

The fictionalization of autobiographical detail in *Children of the Dead* turns out to be an effective instrument in this endeavor and the intensity of narrative self-presentation is a powerful testimony of courage and moral commitment.

Works Cited

Bei, Neda and Branka Wehowski. 1984. Die Klavierspielerin: Gespräch mit Elfriede Jelinek. In *Die Schwarze Botin* 24/3.

Bernhard, Thomas. 1976. *Der Keller. Eine Entziehung*. Salzburg: Residenz.

Biller, Maxim. 1990. Sind Sie lesbisch, Frau Jelinek? In *Tempo* 4.

Burger, Rudolf. 1990. Der Böse Blick der Elfriede Jelinek. In *Gegen den schönen Schein*. Edited by Christa Gürtler. Frankfurt am Main: Verlag neue Kritik.

Fiddler, Allyson. 1994. *Rewriting Reality: An Introduction to Elfriede Jelinek*. Oxford/Providence; revised dissertation of 1990.

Fliedl, Konstanze. 1991. 'Echt sind nur wir!' Realismus und Satire bei Elfriede Jelinek. In *Dossier 2. Elfriede Jelinek*. Edited by Kurt Bartsch and Günther Höfler. Graz: Droschl.

Handke, Peter. 1976. *Ich bin ein Bewohner des Elfenbeinturms*. Frankfurt am Main: Suhrkamp.

Hoetzer, Irene. 1993. *Contemporary Austrian Women's Literature: Feminist Stereotyping and Literary Self-Expression*. Newcastle: Ph.D. dissertation.

Janz, Marlies. 1995. *Elfriede Jelinek*. Stuttgart: J. B. Metzler.

Jelinek, Elfriede. 1978. Erschwerende Umstände oder Kindlicher Bericht über einen Verwandten. In *Das Lächeln meines Großvaters und andere Familiengeschichten erzählt von 47 deutschen Autoren*. Edited by Wolfgang Weyrauch. Düsseldorf: Claassen.

Jelinek, Elfriede. 1983. Der Krieg mit anderen Mitteln, Über Ingeborg Bachmann. In *Die Schwarze Botin* 21.
Jelinek, Elfriede. 1985. *Oh Wildnis, oh Schutz vor ihr. Prosa*. Reinbek bei Hamburg: Rowohlt.
Jelinek, Elfriede. 1986. *Die Klavierspielerin*. Reinbek bei Hamburg: Rowohlt.
Jelinek, Elfriede. 1989. Ich mag Männer nicht, aber ich bin sexuell auf sie angewiesen. Interview by Sigrid Löffler. *profil* 13 (March 28).
Jelinek, Elfriede. 1995. Elfriede Jelinek im Gespräch mit Adolf-Ernst Meyer. In *Sturm und Zwang. Schreiben als Geschlechterkampf*. Elfriede Jelinek, Jutta Heinrich, and Adolf-Ernst Meyer. Hamburg: Klein Verlag.
Jelinek, Elfriede. 1995. *Die Kinder der Toten*. Reinbek bei Hamburg: Rowohlt.
Jelinek, Elfriede. 1990. Ist jede Frau ein Luxusweib? Interview by Ingrit Seibert. *Elle* 12.
Müller, André. 1990. Ich lebe nicht, Gespräch mit der Schrifttellerin Elfriede Jelinek. *Die Zeit* 26.
Schwarzer, Alice. 1989. Ich bitte um Gnade: A. Schwarzer interviewt Elfriede Jelinek. *Emma* 7.
Spanlang, Elisabeth. 1992. *Elfriede Jelinek: Studien zum Frühwerk*. Wien: Dissertation Wien University, VWGÖ.
Winter, Riki. 1991. Gespräch mit Elfriede Jelinek. In *Dossier 2: Elfriede Jelinek*. Graz: Droschl.
Wittgenstein, Ludwig. 1974. *Letters to Russel, Keynes and Moore*. Oxford: Basil Blackwell.

Guiltless Confessions in Gerhard Roth's *Archives of Silence*

Pamela S. Saur

The seven books comprising Gerhard Roth's *Archives of Silence* are highly confessional: they explore in excruciating detail the perceptions and thoughts of a gallery of characters, giving the impression that no nuance of experience is shied away from, however trivial, disgusting, or abnormal, because the truth is to be revealed at all costs.[1] Form and content suggest a rigorous quest for truth. In addition to many sections told in the first person, the *Archives* contain a variety of shifts in perspective, types of text, and frame devices. Peter Ensberg (1991) has commented on the effects of such a structure: "Historical accounts, reports, diary excerpts, fairy tales, dreams, aphorisms, scientific articles and drawings illustrate the complexity and openness of reality" (41). Although these techniques frequently lend an aura of authenticity, the apparent need to include such material does give the impression that great efforts are needed to arrive at and express the truth. Roth also incorporates nonfictional elements in the *Archives*; in fact, the first and last volumes are documentary material, much of it directly or indirectly related to fictional sections of the other volumes in the cycle. Volume 1, *In Deepest Austria*, consists primarily of photographs of a rural community, and volume 7, *A Journey into the Interior of Vienna*, is a collection of factual essays enriched by some photographs and much statistical information. Volume 6, *The History of Darkness*, is a realistically told biography of a Jew who experienced and survived the Nazi period. In the introduction, we are told that this account was based on notes from interviews, on reports that "do away with the border between document and literature" (10). In an unusual technique, Roth uses these nonfictional volumes to reinforce the impression of authenticity, as well as aspects of the moods and contents of the fictional heart of the cycle. Volumes 1 and 7 provide mostly unflattering portraits of rural and urban Austria respectively, bringing out the privation and violence of the rural environment, and the weird and violent tendencies of the urban, symbolized by its underground catacombs and storage vaults that contain secrets of history. The sixth volume, along with a number of passages elsewhere in the *Archives*, represents Roth's contribution to Austria's literary confrontation with the moral questions and historical legacy surrounding the Nazi period, a movement known as "coming to terms with the past" (*Vergangenheitsbewältigung*). It is noteworthy that material on the Nazi era is presented in this documentary volume, and also in other volumes in narratives giving characters' recollections, in a realistic and straightforward manner. Perhaps by separating this material from the explorations of insanity and speculations on the relativity of justice, Roth means to avoid seeming to excuse the Nazi crimes as manifestations of cruel or insane impulses that are ordinary or ubiquitously human.

The sheer size of the seven-volume edifice also has an effect on the reader. The cycle's magnitude suggests that this author sees a need for enormous effort as well as the use of all means and methods available to communicate effectively on this topic. Although the word "silence" creates a paradox and a suggestion that even great efforts may fail, the word "archives" suggests a thorough, detailed, and documented record of truth that reaches far back into history.

No handful of summarizing words can do justice to such a monumental and complex work of art, but main themes can be identified and their descriptions formulated in various valid ways. Peter Ensberg and Helga Schreckenberger (1994) have asserted that at the center of Roth's work is always "a disturbed individual seeking a way out of alienation and identity crisis"

(10). Walter Grond (1992) has identified the "creative and the cruel" as the central theme of the main novel in the cycle, *Everyday Death* (159); Sybille Cramer calls the *Archives* "nothing less than a psychoanalysis of Austria" (1992, 116). Cramer's emphasis here is echoed in Ensberg's article, cited above, on Roth's "theme of insanity"; an intriguing aspect of this theme is that insanity is not merely explored, but apparently *endorsed* in the novels. In fact, one can argue that one of the most striking messages to emerge from the *Archives* is that life in the modern world is confusing, painful, frightening, and difficult; the most appropriate response to it by the individual is found in insanity. A compelling, fascinating case is presented that shows the reader the world through the eyes and thoughts of disoriented individuals; the result is to enlist the reader's sympathy and understanding for pathological responses. So brilliant and compelling is this vision, so dominant is the presentation and justification of insanity in the novels, that the issues of guilt and justice seem to be absent or irrelevant. Crime and murder occur often, entwined in a variety of mitigating circumstances, presented in a variety of literary fashions, and accompanied by revelations of the weakness and inadequacy of human justice systems. In fact, one could argue that the primary motivation of the *Archives* is to construct an elaborate "insanity defense." However sympathetic the reader might be to the sufferings of the criminally insane, it is hard to muster much enthusiasm for the notion that murder is justified and cannot be condemned. Must we accept this as the end result of the long and laborious search for truth that the reader pursues throughout the seven books? Reflection would suggest that sympathy for murderers cannot be our final destination. If nothing else, it is too one-sided; how can it exist without sympathy for the victims as well? We must return to the labyrinth and search again, untangling the twisted threads of insanity and crime, looking again at the literary techniques used to construct the insanity defense, and then putting it aside to look for that which it overshadows: justice, bad conscience, guilt, atonement, punishment, and sympathy for suffering that goes beyond clever courtroom arguments and runs at the deepest level of the seven books. If a prime motivation of the author seems to be constructing the insanity defense, another might be the desire to expose and reveal how vast and varied is the suffering of living creatures, and by implication, to cry out in protest.

Although Roth employs many techniques that divert the reader's attention from issues of guilt, as if it were irrelevant or nonexistent, the volumes also contain passages that illustrate how complicated and difficult it is to define, identify, or measure guilt, or to define or apply standards of justice. These passages may lead the reader to want to therefore give up the ideas of guilt and justice because of their great complexity, or to concentrate on the insanity defense, although perhaps such readings are taking the easy way out. Indications that guilt and justice exist are present in the seven volumes, although they are submerged and scattered. Five characters are of particular relevance to these issues, four of them with notably similar names: Dr. Ascher, a physician guilty of causing a death by medical malpractice; Lüscher, whose obsession with justice causes him to murder three people; Jenner, a law student and serial killer; his friend the mental patient Lindner; and Sonnenberg, a disoriented criminal investigator who has lost faith in the justice system he serves.

The first novel in the cycle is its second volume, *The Quiet Ocean*. Briefly summarized, it tells the story of Dr. Ascher, who was convicted of negligent malpractice in the city and now lives in rural isolation, providing medical services to a poor and backward community. Close at hand is the implication that he is atoning for his guilt by living apart from his wife and child and by doctoring the needy. However, this interpretation is thrown into question or undermined by a host of complicating factors.

Somewhat frustrating to the reader is the paucity of information about the actual "crime" that caused the protagonist to be in this situation. As late as page 179, we learn that Ascher had performed ten years of meritorious service as a surgeon. "Then he had made a mistake out of negligence." The consequences of the mistake are not revealed until four volumes later. Rather in passing in the introduction to a book not even about Dr. Ascher, *The History of Darkness*, we learn that the death of an eleven-year-old boy resulted, and that Ascher felt like a murderer at the time (8). Again, the information provided is spare, although it is lent credence by the context: a character is reported to have spoken to the purported author. If the readers of *The Quiet Ocean*, however, are unable to focus on the suffering of this eleven-year-old victim, because he is not even mentioned, their attention and sympathy are instead focused on the guilty doctor.

One of the complications surrounding our reactions to him is that the novel also features the story of a murderer, Lüscher; in comparison to this man's brutal murder of three people, Ascher's guilt by negligence pales. Passages on the various reactions to Lüscher's guilt also illuminate the way that Roth portrays Ascher's guilt. Ascher asks someone if he knew the man who has just committed the murders. The reply is "Who? Lüscher? You talk about him as if he had died." This passage follows:

> In fact, Ascher had thought about him as if he no longer existed. In the moment that he committed the crime, he seemed to have become a different kind of life-form, a creature no one wanted to have anything to do with ... No one would care anymore about what happened to him from now on. (*Ocean* 234)

This passage reminds us that our justice system encourages us to accept the pat conclusion that punishment need be our only response to crime and criminals; we are spared further, painful, and complicated consideration of the criminal as a person. Yet, this novel begins at the point when forgetting is desirable—the city can forget the exiled Ascher and his guilt—the rural community and the reader must only then begin to interact with him. Other passages call into question the easy answers provided by our judicial system. Early in the book, after Ascher tries to pray, he recalls that:

> In court, everyone assumed that he was responsible. And he had kept asking himself if he was really the person they were talking about. He kept being surprised at how simple everything seemed. But it was only simple in court; afterwards he was back in regular time again. The connections fell apart into a series of actions, that were given significance only after the fact. Was he guilty? (29)

The justice system will no doubt deal with Lüscher in its simplifying way as well. Since he does not deny his guilt, his punishment by imprisonment is certain. One minor character raises another issue, however, saying, "It was a mistake when they did away with the death penalty" (224). Ironically he uses the same word for mistake (*Fehler*) that was used to identify Ascher's fatal but unintended misdeed. As it turns out, Lüscher reaches an agreement with the authorities, a rather trivializing deal based on the considerations of a moment: "He signed the papers [of confession] after he was promised that he could see his wife and mother" (242).

In a much more dramatic and provocative way, however, Lüscher's situation calls the concept of justice into question. His background is succinctly described in this startling passage: "His father is said to have drowned himself in the well when he received the call to join the 'Hitler military,' as he called it. The son became known as a 'fanatic for justice'" (206). Before the readers can absorb the implications of his father's suicide, we must confront the ironic situation that three murders resulted from the son's sensitivity to injustice. The three were killed because they had been victorious in a small lawsuit that Lüscher had filed to try to get compensation for some labor he had performed for an equestrian organization he no longer belonged to. Even as a boy, Lüscher had believed deeply in law, justice, and order, and any injustice had always disturbed him greatly.

Much irony in the novel is also found in the relationships that develop between Dr. Ascher and his new community. Their many negative characteristics, including cruelty, backwardness, and in some cases allegiance to the supposedly dead Nazi ideology, even their squalid poverty, all detract from the nobility of his service to them as possible atonement for guilt. In idealistic terms, the country people's ignorance of city scandal apparently provides Ascher with a blessed fresh start. Eventually, however, several reveal that they have heard of his case, but do not care about it. Surely there are two sides to their lack of concern, which, by the way, the reader is likely to share because of the habitual tendency to identify with every protagonist. Just as Lüscher's oversensitivity to justice had two sides, the community's refusal to condemn Ascher can be viewed as depraved indifference, self-interested desire to take advantage of his skills, or high-minded mercy.

The issue of sensitivity is also relevant to Ascher's relationship with his wife. His love for her contrasts with several mentions of wife abuse in the community, and he shields her from details about hunting and killing animals so that she doesn't cry. He also is glad when she seems happy, because then "he feels less guilty" (127).

Violence against animals, which occurs throughout the volumes of the *Archives*, is prevalent in Ascher's new environment. Presented in rather vivid detail are killing mice in traps, hunting, slaughtering for meat, killing animals on the real or feigned belief that they may be rabid, and also Ascher's recollections of scientific dissections. Ascher is informed that the annual slaughter of a fattened pig used to be quite a festival for the people, because then there would be fresh meat for a while. The butcher adds, "Now slaughtering has become routine; only the old people still have a festive feeling about it" (102). Of course, the poverty of the people and their desire for meat makes this festival slaughter quite understandable; elsewhere it is also mentioned that the people had to eat cats and dogs to survive during the war and postwar years.

A connection is made, too, between violence against animals and violence against human beings in war, a major realm in which violence is considered justified by most people. The old doctor tells Ascher of his concern over the aggressive impulses of the local people, whether toward themselves, animals, or other people. He says that he finds killing repulsive, but, "There are plenty of people who enjoy killing. They can tell stories about it for hours, and this applies both to veterans of war and to hunters" (177–178). In an article about the literary functions of the many references to animals throughout the *Archives*, Helga Schreckenberger (1995) has demonstrated that Roth uses the fates of animals to reveal human "aggression, cruelty and the will to dominate" and that he "thereby calls into question the achievements of human culture and civilization. At the same time Roth shows in the nature and lives of animals positive alternatives to inauthentic human existence as shaped by social constraints and norms" (180).

Despite the many negative characteristics of the people in Ascher's new home, the old doctor also points to their tolerance of the most marginal members of their community, the insane and the returning convicts. He tells Ascher:

You see, they live together with any kind of person. If a released convict returns home, the people are willing to live with him under the same roof ... Likewise, they care whether a mentally ill person can contribute labor or not, but otherwise they don't bother about him. Naturally they are often crude, and they do make fun of the defenseless and of strange behavior, but they live together with these people. (*Ocean* 195–196)

The next volume in the Archives, *Everyday Death*, is the longest.[2] It introduces us to the two friends, Jenner and Lindner, one a criminal, one an insane man. Both appear in the next three novels in the cycle. We first meet them in a circus environment, long a kind of anti-society in European literature, although their backgrounds are revealed only gradually. The reader does not yet know the relevance to their life stories of the detail given that the circus director intentionally doesn't ask his new employees about their pasts, for they are "mostly insane or convicts" (*Everyday Death* 21). Like Ascher's community, this director, as head of the circus community, provides a fresh start for these outsiders and in turn benefits from their labor. The circus also adds a layer of animal-human associations because animals are involved in the entertainment produced, and in a sense are even artist figures. A comment by the circus director on animals and people evokes these thoughts by Jenner: "Precisely in my field, law, it is important to view things from different sides. One is forced to do so by questions of guilt ... I have come to the realization, in fact, that there are no guilty parties, also no innocent ones." The thought follows: "In a higher sense, there are just the accusers and the accused" (29–30). Although in this passage Jenner seems to bid the reader to give up the difficult quest to define or understand guilt, his assertion that there are no innocent people could reveal that he believes in the existence of guilt on some level.

Long sections of *Everyday Death* consist of writings by Lindner in the mental hospital. His various meditations, anecdotes, memories, and fantasies mirror issues found throughout the cycle, such as thoughts on insanity and institutionalization, violence and cruelty, murder, suicide, slaughter and other violence against animals, suffering and privation, ironies and injustices of war, and postwar incidents. In one passage, Lindner tells his doctor about his childhood, revealing a picture of human nature quite consistent with much of the grim content of the *Archives*. He says that his childhood was

> interdiction, oppression and violation, in a word hell ... I maintain that the fairy tale about the innocence of children is nothing but pure invention ... [A child] is—not from ignorance but from burning curiosity—primed for the bad, for the most horrible and most cruel ... and his head burns with devilish wishes ... Nor does he need to be taught to have guilt feelings ... He already has deep guilt, ... [and] feelings of joy over others' misfortunes. Children are born tormentors ... They live with fear all the time. (540–542)

One section of this volume consists of sixty-six fairy tales that were purportedly written by mental patients. The idea is fascinating, for it conjures up a special entrance to a new world of fiction, fantasy, and truth, unknown terrains, unexplored areas of thought and perception, emotion and experience, and possibly access to new kinds of secret beauty and supremely honest, unrestrained truth. Here, the environment of the asylum and the genre of the fairy tale provide a double distance that is increased even more by a frame device. The narrator claims, "Last night I dreamed I had written a book and when I woke up, I found it next to my bed" (615). The imagination of both the insane person and the often anonymous or collective author of a fairy tale is very free, released from the bonds of rationality, causality, and logic, from all rules of thought or narration; the combination of frame, fairy tale, and asylum multiplies this freedom. Neither author nor reader is responsible for the content.

These stories, like the *Archives* as a whole, contain many instances of death, murder, and suicide, as well as many interactions between human beings and animals. In these often visionary or hallucinatory tales, people may try to communicate with animals, to confess to them, to learn their language—or they may turn into animals or objects. When such things are possible, as well as magical and thinking objects, and interactions with the cosmos, society's concepts of responsibility and justice can hardly be applied.

In addition to such effects of the general context, guilt and justice are also called into question by various specific stories. For example, in "Foxglove," a mother mourns her sons, one killed by lightning and one by war (*Everyday Death* 623–624). Her third son, spurned in love, commits suicide by drinking the juice of the red foxglove plant. His mother calls the doctor (ironically called Dr. Foxglove) and kills him with an axe when he cannot revive her last son. This story, somewhat reminiscent of Dr. Ascher's guilt as a doctor, creates (within a rational world in this case) an extreme situation that leads the reader to justify the brutal murder of an innocent person.

In "The Punishment," the themes of war, animal slaughter, wife abuse, conscience and guilt, all in *The Quiet Ocean*, are brought together in condensed form. A young farmer, who had been a merciless killer during wartime, beats and overworks his wife and children. The wife prays to an angel, who turns the man into a rattlesnake. In this form he overhears his family's complaints about him and suffers remorse. When he falls into his old habits, however, the angel returns and makes him experience slaughter in the form of one of his own hogs. Again he is remorseful; again he relapses. When finally his family dies from his maltreatment, he is sorry. He drinks, and loses his memory. An angel, who turns out to be himself, appears and tells him that he will have to live his life over again, and again he will lose his memory if he is sinful. One point of interest in this story is the fact that the avenging angel is the sinful man himself. The story thus holds out hope for the existence of a conscience, but in this case the conscience is ineffectual.

Another story, "Unbelievable Explanation," yields insight into the mind of a young man accused of a series of robberies and killings. In a classic situation calling for the insanity defense, the man is warned of future deaths by the voice of a pheasant. He cannot reveal these messages because of fear that he will be suspected. Finally he witnesses one of the crimes and tries to stop the perpetrator with a knife. This story was invented by a mental patient to excuse his own crimes.

In the next book in the cycle, *At the Precipice*, the reader becomes better acquainted with Jenner and Lindner. Both offer some speculations and insights into crime and insanity, although many of their remarks point toward the conclusion that explaining either crime or insanity is difficult or impossible.

For a reader unfamiliar with the previous volumes, distance

is established immediately by introducing an unreliable narrator. Lindner reveals not only that he is a mental patient, but also that he is delusional, as seen in such statements as, "I was a witness when the earth was born on April 5, 1330 in Obergreith" (*Precipice* 15).

In the second chapter, the omniscient insane narrator introduces another animal image, a merging of animal and human. While usual assumptions of the insanity defense would suggest that a man who thinks he is a dog cannot be held to the usual human standards of justice, both fiction and mental illness are environments in which a person may actually *be* a dog. However, the metamorphosis in the chapter, "A Portrait of Alois Jenner As a Dog," may actually be a very rational attempt by Lindner to try to absolve his friend Jenner from guilt. Lindner reveals here that Jenner murdered a girl "for inexplicable reasons" (*Precipice* 19), a suggestion perhaps that reasons for violent crime are ultimately unknowable. In the next chapter, Jenner expresses regret that he confessed the murder to Lindner, even though he did it when his friend had been in the asylum more than three years and had spoken to no one but him. On the matter of conscience, Jenner asserts that it is strange (*merkwürdig*) that the thought that Lindner might betray his confidence bothers him more than the murder itself (21). Parallel to Lindner's statement on the reasons for Jenner's murder is a statement Jenner makes on Lindner's condition: "It is hard to say what the reason for his sickness is" (22). In a later chapter, a diary entry, Jenner offers a rather unconvincing explanation, "I'm convinced that sicknesses of the soul are just forms of jealousy" (48). At the end of this chapter, Jenner analyzes his own motivation to confess: "I'm not writing these lines under pressure from my conscience, but rather because I'm driven by a strange compulsion: the wish to discover myself " (24).

An interval is described during which the two friends go on a mountain-climbing trip together. Jenner seduces a waitress, and Lindner (interestingly enough acting as the conscience that Jenner seems to lack) is afraid he may kill her. Jenner is afraid too: "also he was afraid of being surprised again by that cold curiosity that had driven him to witness a person dying" (25–26). So this is his motive for the murder, cold curiosity! His fear of being overtaken by the impulse is at least a weak suggestion that he regrets his violence, although perhaps he merely fears being out of control and being governed by impulse. At any rate, he has some fear of getting caught: while mountain climbing he has fleeting thoughts of pushing his friend to his death so that he cannot betray him. Strangely, the two friends also discover a dead body while on their excursion, and they learn that it is the corpse of a man who killed himself, but no one knows the reason. The grim juxtaposition of insanity, murder, and suicide, all more or less inexplicable, is accompanied in an eerie way by Lindner's experience of beauty in nature and in his own fantasies—could insanity be a desirable condition? Just as Lindner has been portrayed as Jenner's moral superior, Lindner's rural experiences, even if largely in his own mind, contrast with the day-to-day ugliness and anxiety that Jenner experiences in the city in the chapters to follow.

In the city, Jenner befriends an old man who has fallen down and helps him return home. When the man asks him questions, however, he feels displeasure (*Unwillen*) well up in him, a rather weak motivation for his next action, a double homicide and arson. Also a contributing factor is his realization that the man and his wife are completely under his control. When the crimes are over, his reactions, like his motivations, are described in very mild terms: "A burden had been lifted from him. He sat there a while. He had no fear of fingerprints or neighbors. Nothing stirred" (36). Shortly thereafter, Jenner confronts a dog; he considers shooting him, but decides against it. Here, once again, animals are set parallel with people. This dog is a potential murder victim, but Jenner spares his life; human life seems to him to be less valuable than animal life. During the rest of the day, Jenner is somewhat disoriented, and his crimes seem almost unreal. However, he does not experience remorse. At one point, Jenner tours a slaughterhouse. He experiences "no curiosity and no guilt feelings, only a mild nausea he attributed to the smell" (67). A few days later, Jenner reads about his crime in the newspaper. No reaction is described, except that he fell asleep soon thereafter.

In a key chapter of the book, "A Moment of Truth," Lindner speaks quite rationally, stating that he knows Jenner fears his betrayal. He asks him why he is studying law, adding, "I mean, when you are indifferent to right and wrong, why ..." Jenner gives the "crazy" answer, "I am studying law precisely because I don't believe in justice" (73). After thinking about Jenner's vague, weak motivations and mild, almost indifferent responses to his own bloody crimes, this sentence may come as a relief to the puzzled reader. However, the glib and clever-sounding paradoxical statement, in the form of a quotable aphorism, does not explain his motivation to study law, his lack of belief in justice, or his criminal nature. The enigma of Jenner's pronouncement does not end Jenner's story in this volume either, for he goes on to have several sexual encounters, then to kill a woman he encounters by chance near the harbor. At another point, he thinks that truth itself, not only violence and insanity, is "as impenetrable as solid rock" (92). If here, at such a moment of profound doubt, the reader seems to have reached the bottom of the "precipice," there is more confusion and irony to come. An innocent man, Brandstetter, is arrested and tried for Jenner's murder of the woman by the harbor. Jenner "doesn't know whether to be happy or shocked. This man is only a victim of chance, so to speak the mirror image of my guilt. That is enough. Everything else [referring to the trial] will be put together by diligent officials, falsifying the facts in the usual way" (93–94). Jenner experiences a bit of remorse at the innocent man's conviction, but much more relief. During the account of the trial, it is also revealed that the innocent man had gotten away with other crimes, and secretly felt that "justice was served" by the trial (130). Other details, such as the petty thoughts and self-doubts on the part of the judge and attorneys, further undermine our perception of the effectiveness and nobility of this court and trial.

Profound doubts about the justice system are also experienced in the next chapter by Sonnenberg, the professional who serves as the protagonist and title figure of the fifth volume of the cycle, *The Investigating Officer*. On a visit to the asylum, apparently on the false presumption that Lindner may have been involved in the old couple's murder, Sonnenberg torments himself by questioning his own motivations: "Why was he so eager to solve the retired couple's murder? Was it personal ambition? Was he curious to see the perpetrator face to face? Did he want to bring the story out of sinister darkness and into the brightly lighted world of understanding?" (104). Sonnenberg recalls the confusion and doubt about justice that he experienced earlier in his career. He thinks of the attraction that violence has for some people. For the murderer, he thinks the act of murder is "the attempt to reconcile thought with deed, secret command with resistance. Seen this way, there is no guilt that can be defined by the letter of the law." Sonnenberg completes these thoughts with the statement that he regards "the prisons and asylums less as society's sadistic abuses than as its expression of customary but helpless self-defense" (106). In an ironic scene to follow, Sonnenberg encounters Jenner at a public place and hears someone say his name, but of course he has no way of knowing that he is the man he seeks. The title of this novel befits the low point that it reaches, by amassing evidence and presenting ironic situations that encourage the deepest doubt—doubt about finding the causes of murder, suicide, or insanity, about justice and order underlying society, indeed about reaching any kind of truth. In the thoughts and feelings of the various characters, there are only faint glimmers of conscience, faith in the good, longing for truth, and knowledge of right and wrong.

In the next volume, named for Sonnenberg, there is an apparent endorsement of insanity in the concluding sentence of the last page, in a reference to the "insight" we have only in "bright moments" when we "are not quite in our right minds" (*Officer* 172). The placement of this sentence at the very end of the novel gives it special weight, and the reader may be tempted to accept this thought as the "moral" of the book, to chuckle over the idea of the superiority of the insane, acceptable enough as a superficial witticism, and perhaps satisfying as an escape from some of the pain caused by experiencing Roth's fictional world.

However, if the reader considers earlier pages, the simplicity found in this solution disappears. One page earlier, we read, "Maybe a new philosophy needs to come into being, perhaps in asylums, in prisons or hospitals" (171). Although it is easy to read past it, the word "prison" ought to give one pause. Most readers would concede that it may sometimes be difficult to draw sharp lines between insanity and nonconformity, the normal and abnormal. However, fewer of us would wish to identify with outsiders whom society has labeled criminals, or to *look* to prisoners as sources of wisdom. While the book's conclusion can be read as glossing over questions of guilt, crime, and justice by folding them into an idealization of insanity and outsider figures, the book itself does not gloss over these questions, but concentrates a good deal on their complexity, beginning with the opening page.

In the first scene, the protagonist faces a fourteen-year-old who murdered his father, seriously wounded his mother, and dumped his parents in the garbage. Lindner's searing remarks on the myth of childhood innocence come to mind. Sonnenberg's thoughts are revealed:

> Never before had he had to deal with such a young murderer. Sometimes it seemed to him that an epidemic was raging, whose victims were compelled to commit crimes; other times, he thought he was trudging along an endless stream of violent deeds, on a quest for their source. Some day the secret of the stream would reveal itself clearly to him, its chemical composition and the history of its development. (7)

This provocative passage presents once again the problem of finding the causes of violence. Is violence an epidemic, a compulsion, a chemical composition, or must it be explained developmentally as a history? Whatever the causes and however eager one is to discover them, the passage implies that doing so will be long and difficult, if it is possible at all. The word "secret" suggests that efforts to uncover these causes may be futile. Throughout the events of the book—many of which take place in Sonnenberg's mind—paranoid and hallucinatory visions, such as talking dogs and sudden outbreaks of violence or obscenity, cause the reader to experience the insights of the insane. Also, the reader experiences Sonnenberg's daily experiences in the profession of justice: a world of bloody crime scenes, eerily fascinating weapons, autopsies, interactions with criminals and judicial authorities, and underlying doubts about whether the idea of justice or the way it is administered makes sense.

If the theorizing of Sonnenberg is questionable because of his cynicism and tendency to lose his grip on reality, particular authenticity is claimed for theorizing in passages authored by the narrator: he identifies himself as the omnipotent author of

Everyday Death, so the reader is led to assume that he is the author of the entire cycle, Roth himself. This figure, on learning of the suicide of an acquaintance, writes, "Suicide fills me with respect." Then, in an unusual twist of literary technique, he writes:

> I felt enjoyment when I made Ascher shoot himself with a shotgun. I admit, that I first wrote his story to the end, out of fear of being unable to keep writing the book after Ascher had died. But then, as I pictured in my mind ... him lying in bed and Lindner coming into the room, wearing bee-keeping headgear, and seeing through its veil the dead man lying in his blood, the image was enjoyable to me. On the other hand, I hate violence. True, I have experienced joy at the ... crude. Secretly, I despised the people who did it (and the ones who had it done) ... It has something to do with murder; of that I had no doubt. (28–30)

In addition to the familiar melding of violence against humans with the slaughter of an animal, and the expression of ambivalence toward violence, of interest here is the foregrounding of the fictional nature of the story and of the process of creating literary reality. The notion of an author enjoying creating a bloody scene is a short distance from the notion of the enjoyment of such a bloody scene by the reader, a detail to add to the cycle's overall emphasis on the violent nature of human beings. Sonnenberg's crime scene investigations belong to a novel that does not resemble a traditional detective story, but they are reminiscent of some of Roth's other works that are parodies of this popular genre. In a study of Roth's detective novels, Helga Schreckenberger (1993) draws a parallel with this novel:

> As he did in *How to Be a Detective*, Roth dissolves in *The Investigating Officer* the conventional opposition between perpetrator and detective ... The title figure, the examining magistrate Sonnenberg, already familiar from the earlier novel *At the Precipice*, acts more like a criminal than a detective. Again and again he is witness to crimes, but it is unclear to what extent he may be involved ... The parallels to Police Inspector Potter from *How to Be a Detective* are unmistakable. However this book is not a parody of a detective figure, but the genesis of an existential crisis. (177–178)

Sigrid Bauschinger (1987) also comments on Potter: "In Dadaistic short scenes and remarkably brief paratactic sentences he is described as literally throwing evidence out of the window; in the last installment he is shot dead before solving his non-case" (339). The detective throwing away evidence, an image so absurd as to be cartoon-like, is as striking and memorable as the aphorism, "I am studying law precisely because I don't believe in justice," and the content of these two nuggets leads in the same direction, toward the conclusion that the quest for justice is pointless.

The volume on Sonnenberg, however, is more philosophical than one would expect of a detective novel, or a parody of one. Raising the idea of justice at one point, the narrator tells of being threatened with financial ruin in a court case of his own, then goes on to say,

> It's all the same whether the sentences are prison or the death penalty—either way the state becomes a 'criminal' itself by its dispensation of justice. As a rule, only the defenseless are called to account. Obviously justice is always based on social class. It's not about 'justice,' however that is defined, but about a ritual; it's about not facts, but verbal definitions. A trial is a display of lies. (*Officer* 11)

Later the narrator comments, "I'm convinced that most crimes are simply the result of lonesomeness" (13). This theory, reminiscent of Jenner's views that insanity is caused by envy, and crime by curiosity, seems pitifully simple and inadequate. Elsewhere in this volume, the narrator theorizes, "I'm convinced that one major component of so-called mental illness is just fantasy; the other is imbecility, and the free-flowing fantasy is always violent" (48).

Sonnenberg also speculates about justice: "(All human beings are truly just only to themselves). Before the court the accused is released from self-justice, he is *forcibly* laid bare. Every trial is an exposure ... *Everyone* has something to hide. The biographies of the accused are their uncovered secrets." Next he mentions a squashed salamander he had seen, and says, "It would make just as much sense to conduct a trial over the death of this salamander" (93–94).

The end point of the volume, the apparent endorsement or glorification of insanity, is echoed at one point by the narrator: "Only in the asylum can one talk like the Pope—ex cathedra or alone to oneself." The previous sentence, however, was as follows: "That is the tragedy, that ... psychology and psychiatry, even justice *also* are right" (87). Here is one of a few glimmers of hope in the *Archives*, hope that it is not in vain to continue to search for sense and order, for a boundary between the real and unreal, for justice or the possibility of distinguishing between right and wrong. In all the injustice and senseless violence in the volumes, one can perhaps hear a submerged cry for justice and understanding.

In conclusion, one would have to say that the seven volumes of the *Archives* present evidence that human life, the suffering of human beings and animals, and human society, including its justice system, are for the most part senseless and absurd. In such a world, insanity is justified and perhaps even a superior response to life. Violence is deeply ingrained in the nature of the human species, and children, far from being innocent, have deep guilt feelings, along with a penchant for evil and attraction to seeing other creatures suffer. Yet, Roth seems to stop short of indicating here that murder is acceptable, that it is not wrong. In Sonnenberg's line, "All human beings are truly just only to themselves," cited above, a just court is conjured up, that of the individual conscience (even though this same character didn't suffer pangs of conscience over stealing an atlas from a crime scene because he was used to stealing books; *Officer* 84). In his own mind, Brandstetter secretly believes that his trial and punishment functions in a just manner because of past crimes he had committed that had gone unpunished. Here, justice exists, although it operates in secret.

Behind the meditations on insanity, crime, and justice evoked by the *Archives* is the theme of suffering and pain endured by human and animal creatures. There is surely some sympathy and mercy expressed thereby, and evoked on the part of the reader. Roth labors throughout these volumes to bring to light the secret suffering of powerless children, humble people, hallucinating mental patients, compulsively violent killers as well as their innocent victims, convicts wanting to earn a living, hogs at the moment of slaughter, dogs killed for amusement, a dead salamander lying on the road. He brings to light the privation of rural laborers so poor they cannot afford eyeglasses or false teeth, of sickly farm hands who have slept their whole lives in barns with the animals, of people eating cats and dogs to survive, of women whose experience makes them equate marriage with physical abuse, of wartime death and senseless killings just after peace has been declared. Roth does not bid us take action or reform society in this cycle of books, despite their admixture of anti-Nazi content, and yet insanity is not advocated as the only right response to suffering, and crime and violence are not really advocated at all. Dr. Ascher's solution of action, providing medical care for suffering people, despite the possibility of making a mistake, and even after doing so, is presented, and the reader can honor it even when Dr. Ascher gives up and chooses another solution, suicide. After all, his suicide was motivated externally: from the author's petty desire to create a bloody scene in order to startle a funny-looking fictional character and create a tableaux, a memorable literary moment. Other memorable moments, such as a law student uttering a paradoxical motivation for studying law, or statements about the insight of the insane or the philosophy of the asylums, prisons, and hospitals, need not be regarded as encapsulating the message of the entire cycle. An alternate approach is to place more emphasis on the evocation of sympathy for suffering, and on those indications that the search for truth and justice is worthwhile, as in the line from *The Investigating Officer*, cited above, claiming that psychology and psychiatry, "even justice ... are *also* right." The reader's journey through the lands of violence, insanity, and injustice in the cycle need not necessarily end at the bottom of an abyss of hopelessness, where only suicide and madness make sense.

Notes

1. References to the *Archives of Silence* (*Archive des Schweigens*) are to the 1992–1994 edition published in Frankfurt am Main by Fischer Taschenbuch Verlag. The volumes (1–7) are listed below with their original publication dates: (1) *Im Tiefen Österreich* (In Deepest Austria, 1990); (2) *Der Stille Ozean* (1980) translated to English by Helga Schreckenberger as *The Quiet Ocean* (Riverside: Ariadne, 1993); (3) *Landläufiger*

Tod (Everyday Death, 1984); (4) *Am Abgrund* (At the Precipice, 1986); (5) *Der Untersuchungsrichter* (The Investigating Officer, 1988); (6) *Die Geschichte der Dunkelheit* (The History of Darkness, 1991); and (7) *Eine Reise in das Innere von Wien: Essays* (A Journey into the Interior of Vienna, 1991).

2. On the translation of the term *Landläufiger Tod*, Anne L. Critchfield (1987, 71) has commented that, "the title *Landläufiger Tod* appears to have a double meaning. Death [*Tod*], is indeed *landläufig*, that is customary or common ... [and] death comes in forms related to the land; "Land," not in a bucolic or pastoral sense, but as a decidedly unidyllic finality." It is difficult to capture all these associations in an idiomatic English title, and so I have chosen *Everyday Death*.

Works Cited

Bauschinger, Sigrid. 1987. Gerhard Roth. In *Major Figures of Contemporary Austrian Literature*. Edited by Donald G. Daviau. New York: Peter Lang.

Cramer, Sybille. 1992. Das Gedächtnis ist die letzte Instanz von Moral und Recht. In *Gerhard Roth. Materialien zu "Die Archive des Schweigens."* Edited by Uwe Wittstock. Frankfurt am Main: Fischer.

Critchfield, Anne. 1987. Gerhard Roth: A Postmodern Austrian Writer? *Selecta: Journal of the Northwest Council of Foreign Languages* 8.

Ensberg, Peter. 1991. The Theme of Insanity and its Effects on Form and Style in the Work of Gerhard Roth. *Modern Austrian Literature* 24, No. 3/4.

Ensberg, Peter and Helga Schreckenberger. 1994. *Gerhard Roth: Kunst als Auflehnung gegen das Sein*. Tübingen: Stauffenburger Verlag.

Grond, Walter. 1992. Genese eines Romans: Zum Landläufigen Tod. In *Gerhard Roth: Materialien zu 'Die Archive des Schweigens.'* Edited by Uwe Wittstock. Frankfurt am Main: Fischer Taschenbuch Verlag.

Roth, Gerhard. 1992–1994. *The Archives of Silence*. Frankfurt am Main: Fischer Taschenbuch Verlag.

Schreckenberger, Helga. 1993. Parodie und Destruktion eines Schemas. Gerhard Roths Kriminalromane. *Experimente mit dem Kriminalroman. Ein Erzählmodell in der deutschsprachigen Literatur des 20. Jahrhunderts*. Frankfurt am Main: Peter Lang.

Schreckenberger, Helga. 1995. 'Man sieht an den Tieren immer die Grausamkeit des Menschen': Die Paradigmatische Funktion der Tierheit in Gerhard Roths Die Archive des Schweigens. In *Gerhard Roth*. Edited by Marianne Baltl and Christian Ehetreiber. Graz: Droschl Verlag.

Personalizing Fiction—Fictionalizing the Personal: Gerhard Roth's *The Investigating Officer*

Helga Schreckenberger

The novel *The Investigating Officer: The History of a Sketch* (1988) is the fifth of the seven works in Gerhard Roth's cycle *The Archives of Silence*. The cycle marks a shift in the author's interest from the subjective inner perspective of his earlier works to the sociopolitical reality of his native Austria. Roth examines his country's historical, political, and social structures in the context of Austrian daily life. He portrays their influence on individual lives, often those of social outsiders. The normative forces that govern society and its tendency to demand conformity from its individual members emerge in his works as the main societal ill causing alienation, aggressive behavior, and the repression or persecution of the perceived "other."

The five novels of the cycle—*The Quiet Ocean* (1980), *Everyday Death* (1984), *At the Precipice* (1986), *The Investigating Officer: The History of a Sketch* (1988), and *The History of Darkness* (1991)—are framed by the photo-essay volume *In Deepest Austria* (1990) and the essay collection *A Journey into the Interior of Vienna* (1991). These two works document the intensive research conducted by Roth in order to write his *Archives of Silence*; they constitute according to the author "the foundation of reality" of the entire cycle. In a 1995 interview, however, Roth also emphasizes the subjective, personal dimension of the *Archives of Silence*, which influenced the direction of the work as much as his empirical research. Moreover, he points specifically to the *Investigating Officer* as the work where he sought to clearly demonstrate the personal aspect of his writing:

> I realized more and more clearly that the stories I am writing are also aimed at myself, that they are my stories and that I am not someone who sees Austria only as a case study but someone who himself is part of this case study, of this story, of this environment like the rest of the Austrians.
>
> During my work I became conscious of many things that I had not noticed before. I wanted to include all these things especially in the novel *The Investigating Officer* to show that, in addition to a historical-political base, my work also has a personal one. (198–199)

With this quote, Roth suggests a breaking down of the distinctions between subjective and real, between personal and sociological in his work. He demonstrates this blurring of the fictional and the personal in his novel *The Investigating Officer* by writing himself into the text in the shape of a first-person narrator who claims to be identical with the author of the novel. Thus, *The Investigating Officer* consists of two separate but interrelated narratives: a detective story featuring an investigative judge named Sonnenberg as its protagonist, and a first-person narrative of seemingly autobiographical nature. My analysis focuses on the relationship between the two narratives. I suggest that in form and content *The Investigating Officer* works to break down distinctions between self and society, subjectivity and reality, and, most important, between autobiography and fiction. For this reason, the choice of a detective story as the doubled narrative is very purposeful, because of all narrative forms, traditional detective fiction proceeds according to clear-cut oppositions which, in Roth's text, break down. Thus, *The Investigating Officer* should be read as Roth's very personal poetics. Whereas the autobiographical narrator presents his philosophical and poetic beliefs in the first-person narrative, they are put into practice in the detective story.

"This book is a letter and not a novel. I stop when I do not want to talk about myself anymore, I invent [stories] when I feel like it. It is not a self-portrait. Not even a fragmented one" (1988,

45). This is how the narrator characterizes the novel in the fifth segment of the first-person narrative. With this characterization, the narrator not only emphasizes the autobiographical content of the first-person narrative—he is talking about himself—but also suggests the text's relationship to reality by contrasting it with the invented detective story. However, he links both narratives: together, they form one metafictional text, be it novel or letter. This indicates that the two narratives complete each other, that the text's meaning cannot be derived from just one of the narratives; both must be considered. This intricate relationship between the two narratives exists thematically as well as structurally.

The first-person narrative does not present a coherent, continuous story. Rather it proceeds in an associative, unsystematic, often disjointed manner, forming a collage that includes lines of arguments, childhood memories, recent experiences, and personal revelations. This fragmented and at times confusing narrative revolves around a central theme: the intangibility of true knowledge. For the first-person narrator, the longing for truth and the impossibility to achieve truthfulness is inherent in the human condition: "The myth of Sisyphus—the rolling rock is the interplay of insight and fallacy, of deception and the desire for truth" (12).

The narrator identifies conventional language and thought patterns as reasons for the human inability to gain true insight, as to oneself or life in general. Language, he insists, is constructed as a means of self-assertion, not of self-recognition. In this self-serving function, language will never reveal the truth. Like language, thinking has been conditioned for survival in a normative society. Under the influence of society, thinking turns into "a sort of policeman" (45), that is, a tool of self-censure, thus repressing anything that does not fit the accepted norm. The narrator rejects a way of thinking that is not able to accommodate life's contradictions as too limiting and too restrictive to allow for any form of insight: "Contradictions are inevitably an expression of life, whereas a way of thinking that is free of contradictions is not alive. Rather it is a model, an *imitation*, something *mechanical* with hinges and joints, something that is basically ponderous" (81).

The narrator extends his criticism of language and thinking to include the legal system, psychology, and philosophy—the disciplines that raise the claim of truth and insight. But according to the narrator, neither the legal system, nor psychoanalysis, nor philosophy is able to lead to true insight because of the inability of each to cope with complexity. Instead of accepting the complexity, ambiguity, and contradictions of life and all its manifestations, these disciplines seek to reduce and control them, to impose a system. The narrator rejects such an attempt as delusion: "Philosophy must sprout like plants in a meadow, it cannot be a garden. It has to run wild. There are only atoms of truth. What kind of body they form is just as unclear as the shape of the universe" (54). In the legal system, the desire to impose norms and regulations leads to deceit, not to truth or justice: "What matters is not 'justice'—whatever you understand by it—but the rite; what matters are not facts but their linguistic arrangement" (11). By pretending that there is a single truth and by its attempt to uphold it, the legal system has become criminal in itself: it produces and enforces injustice. Psychoanalysis and psychology, like the legal system, are nothing more than means of the state to carry out its norm: "Today, psychiatry and psychology serve the state, they are supposed to grant it the authority to imprison, and they are supposed to counsel which institution is possible: insane asylum or prison" (13–14). This all-encompassing tendency to enforce normality causes alienation and isolation of the individual from self and others. It leads to aggressive behavior that is directed either against self (suicide) or against others: "I am convinced that most crimes are the result of loneliness ... A crime rips up the loneliness for a short time. The act of violence, which admits the forbidden into life, is a protest against the imposed ordinariness; murder represents at the same time the murder of the world as it allegedly is, it does not matter what motivated it" (13).

The narrator's criticism of normative judgment that dominates scientific discourse corresponds to Michel Foucault's (1981) criticism of the "exorbitant singularity" of forms of knowledge. According to Foucault, each discipline "pushes a whole teratology of knowledge back beyond its margins" (60). This "unthought" remains outside of a truth that is organized and sustained by certain institutionalized, discursive rules. Because of its heterogeneous nature, the unthought is perceived as a threat to society and its norms. Foucault's theory builds upon Nietzsche's concept of man's pursuit of power. According to Nietzsche, the will for power dominates all of man's actions and achievements, including those of an intellectual nature. Knowledge is pursued not for knowledge's sake but for the sake of power. It is used selfishly for orientation in a difficult world, for deception and for evil. This notion is reflected in the narrator's assertion that thinking and language are self-serving, like everything in nature. The narrator's criticism also contains one of Foucault's most provocative theses (1979), which contends that the legal system (represented by the prison system) contributes to the delinquency it claims to eliminate (303). Instead of resocialization, the prison system produces a criminal environment that legitimizes the increasing use of control and surveillance. As a consequence, the normative and disciplinary tendencies of the legal system have evaded all spheres of life (304)—a criticism equally maintained by the first-person narrator of Roth's text.

As the references to Foucault indicate, the narrator's criticism concurs in many ways with the current debate on rationality and its role in the quest for private and public meaning.[1] However, the narrator does not refer to Foucault or any other philosopher to support his arguments.[2] Not unlike Foucault himself, the narrator presents his criticism in a highly subjective, affirmative manner, never offering any proof for the accuracy or even justification of such criticism except his own judgment, as the following example indicates:

> It does not matter whether the verdict is prison or death; the state, with the assistance of the legal system, turns itself into a "criminal." As a rule, it is the defenseless who are called to account ... A trial is a scene of lies. The defendant lies, the witnesses lie, the jury lies, the judges lie, so do the defense lawyer and the prosecutor. Most of the time, all participants, with the exception of the defendant, desire a guilty verdict from the beginning on. Even the defense lawyers work covertly or overtly toward a guilty verdict; a good defense is an exception. (11)

But later in the novel, a seemingly unrelated childhood memory backs up the assertions of the narrator. In this memory, the narrator relates how as a child he desperately tried to win the love of a teacher. To gain her admiration, he stole a valuable pin from his grandmother and turned it in at school claiming he had found it. Instead of being recommended for his honesty, he was immediately accused of theft. At home too, he quickly came under suspicion of having taken the pin. But when his parents were called to school, they denied ownership of the pin. However, the narrator never received the praise from his teacher that he had so desperately wanted. Ten years later, he saw her wearing the pin. This childhood memory can be seen as a symbolic representation of the legal system. The school's investigation resembles a trial and displays all the characteristics that the narrator had criticized earlier: Everybody involved lies and nobody is interested in the truth, just in the appearance of law and order.

The narrator's childhood memory that reflects his experience as an outsider serves the same function. Here, the narrator recalls how as a newcomer at school, he was emotionally and physically harassed because of his haircut and clothes. This experience not only reflects society's intolerance for difference but is also an example for the failure of philosophy: "In my distress I prayed in tiny short emotional thoughts to the *Unknown* hoping for help from there.[3] As long as a silent prayer is more natural than all philosophical insights, I told myself even later after having overcome my fears, that philosophy will not be more than an intellectual exercise—perceptions of a world for *sane people* written by *sane people*" (171). Philosophy fails because it does not concern itself with experiences outside of what is considered normal.

In the context of the narrator's criticism, the childhood memories take on almost parabolic character as they clearly exemplify the narrator's critical analysis of social norms, their alienating effect, and the hypocrisy of the legal process. They are especially effective because earlier the narrator has set up the child's way of thinking as a positive alternative to conventional thinking: "People only think in their childhood: As long as there are no explanations, the brain wades in a sea of equivalent concepts and perceptions. It does not play any trump cards. It fights for survival but at the same time it resists learning because learning means its destruction" (44). The narrator values the child's way of thinking because it lacks the need to judge, schematize, and categorize. Because of this, the child's insights and experiences have more claim to truth than those of adults whose thinking is already corrupted to suit the norms of society. By attributing this quality to a child's thinking, the narrator positively disposes the reader toward the accuracy of his childhood memories, which in turn assure the accuracy of his criticism.

In addition, the narrator uses memory or the difference between two memories to prove the subjectivity of truth. He reports of a visitor who talked about their common past: "He reminded me of all sorts of things, what I had said about this and that. He took everything out of context, misinterpreted everything ... Or was what he told me true? There was a grain of truth in it; he had also reminded me of things I would rather not be reminded of " (33). This suggests that there can be more truths than one, depending on the point of view of the speaker. Moreover, the narrator points to the changing of truth at any given point in history: "Did I even bear any relationship to the person I had been ten years ago?" (33). Truth, this suggests, is not a constant but rather a variable that can take different shapes according to time and point of view. Again, a seemingly unrelated experience is used to underscore the narrator's criticism of the untenable position that the legal system is in possession of the only possible truth. Thus, the novel's themes and structures enact and serve as examples of Foucault's view of how discourse functions.

But not only the memories serve to illustrate the narrator's criticism. The personal disclosures are filled with self-reproof and desperation, loneliness and longing for an escape, for a new beginning. They support the narrator's claim of the alienating repressiveness caused by society's tendency to enforce what it considers normality. They prepare the reader to accept the narrator's closing call for a more open and inclusive way of thinking:

> Like from the beginning, we must only defend the dignity of the idiot, who *longingly* tries to say what he wants, but cannot do it, because we are caught in a strategy, which we only recognize in *lucid moments*, when we *are not completely conscious*. (172)

The detective story adds yet another level of criticism to the text. In the first-person narrative, the effects of the normative forces and the ensuing criticism are framed as the real-life experiences and convictions of its author. The detective story relates similar experiences and suggests a similar criticism, but this time by means of a clearly fictional character, the investigating judge Sonnenberg. In addition, by coexisting with the autobiographical narration in the same text, the detective story enacts the breaking down of the boundaries between fiction and reality. The first-person narrator warns the reader to identify him with his fictional protagonist: "He is a little I as I myself am" (14). However, as stated in the sentence before, Sonnenberg has the narrator's ears and eyes. This underscores the personal relationship between the first-person narrator and the fictional character. While they are not identical with each other—rather one is the creator of the other—the narrator and the fictional character Sonnenberg share the same experiences. This common experience is the search for self and the impossibility of gaining true self-knowledge in a world ruled by norms and restrictions.

In the detective story, this search is framed as an identity crisis of the main character, the investigating judge Sonnenberg. Sonnenberg is increasingly losing faith in the profession that has given him his identity. The investigating judge, whose profession it is to establish truth beyond a doubt, has realized the impossibility of doing so: "Of course, what he constructed from his daily interrogations and investigations was just the model of coherence, a geometrical figure that was then put out as truth. It had to be like this if he wanted to practice his profession" (42). Thus, Sonnenberg reiterates the conviction of the first-person narrator that the justice system is interested not in truth or facts but in the appearance of justice. Sonnenberg relates his surprise in finding out that nobody was interested in solving the crime—only in arresting a guilty party. Sonnenberg's increasing incapability to solve the crimes he is confronted with, as well as his uncertainty of his own role in them, reflects his growing doubt in the justification of his work. In addition, it underscores the narrator's conviction that the current justice system is not capable of adequately understanding the complex and often irrational motivations for crimes and criminal behavior.

Sonnenberg feels increasingly alienated in a world that upholds its illusion of truth and justice by a ruthless enforcement of norms and conventions. He escapes from this world by means of imagination. Soon he cannot distinguish between his daydreams and reality. His thoughts, which start out as empirical observations, become more and more fantastic. In the first-person narrative too, imagination has a liberating effect on the narrator. From the beginning on, the narrator identifies his writings as a way to make his existence bearable. Writing is a way to overcome his loneliness, to help him deal with his aggressions: "I cannot hurt a fly, I am a desk-bound murderer without power" (13). His imagination makes his existence bearable: "I would be nothing without these independent thoughts and images; they take away the emptiness from my life. Often I am convinced they are my actual life and I despair when I see myself thrown into my existence and everything is as it is" (14). The realm of imagination offers the narrator an alternative to his otherwise empty existence. However, these images cannot be produced by "conventional thinking"—they have to be "independent," otherwise they have only a decorative function. But an independent, freely flowing imagination is necessarily abnormal and violent because it breaks the established rules. This is the case with Sonnenberg's daydreams. They are grotesque, aggressive, and often threatening:

> Sonnenberg hurried back as far as the escalator and then on to St. Stephen's Cathedral. There, instead of the giant church tower, stood an equally giant box with the logo *Knorr Soup*. It was a yellow box with red and green letters, and a piece of juicy, marbled beef was painted on it lengthwise with a carrot and an onion. And now the bell started to toll and enormous bouillon cubes wrapped in golden paper fell into the screeching crowd, where they burst open and released a cloud of powder that the beginning rain changed into a torrent of soup in which many of those who hadn't been killed by the bouillon cubes drowned. (119)

The grotesque and violent content of these hallucinations reflects Sonnenberg's alienation. They call to mind the narrator's definition of imagination: "Imagination is a survival mechanism in the brain, when thinking does not suffice, when thinking has lost control over order or itself. Only in those lives where fantasy runs wild in self-defense does it change thinking into a jungle with poisonous snakes and orchids" (48–49). However, Sonnenberg's hallucinations express his rejection of the normative order of society which he, as investigating judge, is supposed to uphold. As such, they have a positive meaning: they constitute Sonnenberg's chance to escape his conformity with the ruling order for a more meaningful existence. The contradictory statement of the first-person narrator in the autobiographical section, "Sonnenberg is least crazy at the very moment where he seems to be losing his mind" (119–120), indicates again his belief that contradictive thinking will lead to true knowledge.

Sonnenberg's losing faith in the justification and effectiveness of the legal system pushes him into the position of the outsider. His well-ordered life is interrupted and Sonnenberg is more and more drawn into a world of ambiguity, irrationality, and violence. He falls victim to violence but also his own involvement in the murders he is supposed to investigate is unclear. The boundaries between right and wrong, between detective and criminal, between hunter and hunted, are less and less clear. However, this experience gives Sonnenberg a more complete understanding of the world than the narrowly defined principles that governed his earlier life.

With the framing of his criticism as a fictional story, Roth suggests that, aside from a personal dimension, his criticism of the normative forces that shape private and public meaning also has an aesthetical dimension (or the other way around). Michel Foucault (1970) also regards art as a possibility for challenging the normative tendencies of the established orders of discourse, by creating a counter-discourse to established values, or by giving form to "the unthought" (xv–xvi). A similar idea is presented by Roth's first-person narrator:

> Art punches life on the nose, so to say; it defeats life at its own game. What else is it but the expression of the law of *change*? The unchanging style is disaster, is establishment. In its place: a fresh beginning. Art as rebellion against life as it is ... Art *resists*. It leaves its trace as it shapes the clay, the snow. Here you have been, it doesn't matter if the ground was clay or snow. You have destroyed the uniformity. (81)

Art, according to the narrator, functions as a counter-discourse to the established discourse by constantly changing its form, by breaking new ground, and thus by breaking the rules of the status quo. And breaking established rules is an objective that the narrator states at the very beginning of the work: "I will not be imprisoned by a novel, by style, by thinking" (11). A breaking of literary rules occurs in both narratives if they are compared to the conventional forms of the genres they seem to represent.

The fragmented, disjointed, and unsystematic first-person narrative contrasts sharply with the traditional notion of autobiography, which attempts a retrospective and systematic examination or rather interpretation of the narrating I's life. Again, the text undermines the notion of man as knowable unity. However, the prominent presence of a first-person narrator who claims to be identical with the author and the high degree of personal disclosure that the text suggests call to mind what Jürgen Lehmann (1988) terms "the confessing autobiography."[4] According to Lehmann, the author of such a self-revealing text is anticipating a readership committed to certain linguistic and moral norms and which will be surprised or even offended by the author's revelations (60). Thus, the author is consciously taking the risk of being censured for his disclosures. Lehmann identifies two objectives of such autobiographical confession: the author is either attempting self-liberation from certain institutional constraints or wants to present controversial beliefs or actions as alternatives to such beliefs and actions, which are restricted by norms and regulations. This, however, necessitates that the author must convince the reader of his sincerity (71).

All of these elements are present in the first-person narrative. Based on his personal experiences, the narrator develops his criticism of the established belief systems and calls for a way of thinking that offsets their normative tendencies. His attempt to liberate himself from the constraints of traditional discourse is reflected in the structure of his own discourse, which opposes the rules of traditional discourse. As to the question of sincerity, the structure of the narrative itself is meant to induce the reader into believing the claims of the narrator. Its unsystematic, seemingly free-flowing manner of representation contrasts with the tamed, systematic, and controlled discourse that the narrator has been criticizing. Rather it resembles what the narrator has defined as the thinking pattern of a child: "The most original way of thinking is that of a child, this direct grasp, this series of ideas. No hesitation. It enters into it head over heels, jumps to the next idea without delay. Imagination in contrast to effort" (21).

The same principle seems to apply to the structure of the first-person narrative, which pretends to be a spontaneous, unrestricted, uncensured representation of the narrator's thoughts. As the narrator claims, the text was initially planned as a "sum of spontaneous ideas" (44). However, later on the narrator formulates a more ambitious goal: "I don't want to reproduce my thinking; I want to match it. I want to free myself from its yoke and create something that works like it, a mixture of calculation and spontaneity" (122). Both calculation and spontaneity are present in the text, provided by the associative method of the narration. This method allows not only for a combination of seemingly unrelated material, but also for the utilization of analogical links. As the narrator's disclaimer of his ability to be sincere is based on his imprisonment by the conventional discourse, his text, which seems to defy the rules and laws of the conventional narrative, can raise the claim of sincerity.

More important still is Roth's deliberate deviation from the structure of traditional detective fiction, as it aims directly at the sociopsychological effect of that genre, its adherence to conformity and social norms. Franco Moretti (1983) defines detective fiction as follows:

> What, indeed, does detective fiction do? It creates a problem, a 'concrete effect'—the crime—and declares a sole cause relevant: the criminal. It slights other causes (why is the criminal such?) and dispels the doubt that every choice is partial and subjective. But, then, discovering that unique cause means reunifying causality and objectivity and reinstating the idea of a general interest in society, which consists in solving *that* mystery and arresting *that* individual—and no one else. In finding one solution that is valid for all—detective fiction does not permit alternative readings—society posits its unity, and, again, declares itself innocent. (144)

Moretti's criticism of conventional detective fiction corresponds exactly to the first-person narrator's criticism of the legal system. Like the legal system, detective fiction is concerned not with justice but with reinstatement of the status quo. It reduces a complex matter to a single cause with a single solution. In addition, as Moretti points out, detective fiction undermines the concept of individuality. The crime and the criminal are defined as the exception, the unnatural. Thus, innocence means conformity; guilt means individuality in the sense of being abnormal. Solving the crime, according to Moretti, is "the purge of a society no longer conceived as a 'contract' between independent entities but rather as an organism or a social body" (135). This covert ideology is subscribed in the thematic and narrative structure of the traditional detective fiction.[5] It represents a continuous, logically narrated story, directed toward a climax, the solving of the crime. There is a clear opposition between good and bad, represented by the opposition between the detective (representing society) and the criminal (the individual). Finally, it celebrates rationality in its allegorical representation by the detective. Roth's text deviates from all of these structural characteristics.

The deviation in the narrative is partly caused by the interruptions of the detective story by the first-person narrative. Often these segments come in places where the reader is fully involved in the development of the detective story and is curious to find out what will happen next. On one hand, these interruptions build up the suspense; on the other hand, Roth disappoints the expectations of his readers by not picking up the story where he left off. Thus, he not only confuses his readers but also destroys the narrative continuity and causality, which are characteristic of the traditional detective novel.

In addition, Roth's detective story lacks a clear-cut dichotomy between good and evil. His detective takes on characteristics of the criminal—it is unclear whether it was he who has committed the mysterious crimes. But as he himself is assaulted, he also takes on the role of the victim. In addition, he works against society by destroying evidence that could solve some of the mysterious murders.

Sonnenberg also constitutes a contradiction of the traditional character of the detective modeled after Edgar Allan Poe's Auguste Dupin and his "ratiocination." This type of detective, who inspired a long line of successors from Conan Doyle's Sherlock Holmes to Agatha Christie's Hercule Poirot, is seen as a representation of absolute rationality. Franco Moretti states that "since

Poe, the detective has incarnated a scientific ideal: the detective discovers the causal links between events: to unravel the mystery is to trace them back to a law" (144). Critics of the traditional detective novel aim precisely at this idealization of rationality in the form of the detective. He reduces crimes to technical problems that can be solved with logic and intellect while preserving the appearance of objectivity and impartiality. By creating a detective who reveals the arbitrariness of the investigative process, and whose thinking becomes increasingly irrational, Roth's detective story undermines this celebration of logic and rationality.

Most importantly, the mysterious crimes that occur in Roth's detective story remain unsolved or are only solved by accident. This corresponds to the first-person narrator's conviction that the legal system is not equipped to solve crimes because it lacks the ability to recognize their complexity. However, by not solving the crimes, Roth's detective story goes against the most important premise of traditional detective fiction: the confirmation of a normal, rational, and predictable world. If crime destroys this normality and harmony of the world, solving it reinstates it. By not allowing the reader the illusion that we live in a just and well-functioning or at least fixable world, Roth activates an essential function of detective fiction: it points out the contradictions caused by the way our society is organized. This makes the reader more susceptible to Roth's call for a new, more individualistically inclined society.

In both narratives, rejection of the normative order represented by the legal system is paralleled by rejection of the normative rules of literary conventions. By inverting the thematic and formal structure of the traditional detective story, Roth defies its pro status quo ideology. Indeed, the entire novel, its content and form, has to be read as a defiance of normative tendencies and clear-cut oppositions, be it in life or in art. Instead, it embraces all contradictions of a complex world in which life and fiction, subjectivity, and reality coexist.

Notes

1. Joseph Federico (1992) points out parallels in Roth's criticism to Stanley Aronowitz, Thomas Kuhn, and Paul Feyerabend (12, 66).

2. However, Roth refers to Foucault's writings in his essay "Der Narrenturm," published in volume 7 of the *Archives of Silence* (115).

3. The German, "zu dem Unbekannten gebetet, von dem ich mir Hilfe erhoffte," is ambivalent as to the gender of the "unknown." It could be masculine referring to a person or neuter referring to an abstract.

4. Lehmann (1988) distinguishes between three types of autobiographies based on the act of speech that dominates in them: confessing, narrating, and reporting. According to Lehmann, the "confessing autobiography" was most common in the eighteenth century. This is contested by Manfred Schneider (1986), who sees the twentieth century as the "epoch of confessing" (20).

5. Roth's deviations are not innovations of the author. Already during the sixties, initiated by the authors of the French *nouveau roman*, this genre was the object of many literary experimentations. The best known example in German literature is Peter Handke's *Der Hausierer* (1967). In his earlier, experimental novel *How to Be a Detective* (1976), Roth also deviated from the structure of the traditional detective story. Moreover, since the beginning of the twentieth century, the traditional detective story has been challenged repeatedly, even by many of its mainstream writers.

Works Cited

Federico, Joseph. 1992. *Confronting Modernity: Rationality, Science and Communication in German Literature of the 1980s*. Columbia, SC: Camden.

Foucault, Michel. 1970. *The Order of Things: An Archeology of the Human Sciences.* London: Travistock.

Foucault, Michel. 1979. *Discipline and Punish: The Birth of the Prison*. Translated by A. Sheridan. New York: Random House.

Foucault, Michel. 1981. The Order of Discourse. In *Untying the Text: A Poststructuralist Reader*. Edited by R. Young. London: Routledge and Kegan Paul.

Lehmann, Jürgen. 1988. *Bekennen - Erzählen - Berichten. Studien zu Theorie und Geschichte der Autobiographie.* Tübingen: Niemeyer.

Moretti, Franco. 1983. Clues. In *Signs Taken for Wonders: Essays in Sociology of Literary Forms*. Translated by Susan Fischer, David Forgacs, and David Miller. Thetford: Thetford Press.

Roth, Gerhard. 1988. *Der Untersuchungsrichter. Die Geschichte eines Entwurfs.* Frankfurt am Main: Fischer.

Roth, Gerhard. 1995. Meine Geschichten betreffen auch mich selbst. Gespräch mit Walter Vogl. In *Gerhard Roth. Das doppelköpfige Österreich. Essays. Polemiken. Interviews.* Edited by Kristina Pfoser-Schewig. Frankfurt am Main: Fischer.

Schneider, Manfred. 1986. *Die erkaltete Herzensschrift: Der autobiographische Text im 20. Jahrhundert*. München: Hanser.

Autobiographical Elements and the Search for Meaning in Peter Rosei's Novel *Persona*

Robert Acker

The eminent Austrian Germanist, Wendelin Schmidt-Dengler, once remarked (1995) that "it is the burden of the literary historian to always have to compare the incomparable" (7). This observation can be easily applied to a discussion of Peter Rosei's most recent (1995) so-called novel, *Persona*. This work actually consists of three disparate sections, all of which at first glance, or even second glance, seem to have little or nothing to do with each other. The first part is titled "Landscapes," a term laden with connotations for devoted Rosei readers, who are well acquainted with the author's penchant for detailed descriptions of natural phenomena. "Landscapes" contains seven vignettes set in eastern Canada, Triest, Crete, Salzburg, the province of Carinthia in Austria, Zurich, and Amqui in western Canada. They are the first-person narratives of an author who wants to write a murder story but who never seems to get around to doing so. The narrator is a lonely, restless traveler who is searching for an unknown and thus unobtainable goal. This first part can thus be seen as a summary or at least a reference to many of Rosei's earlier works, where the characters seek escape or redemption through travel, or eventually realize that their searching is in vain (see Acker 1989, 258–262). These stories also depict the intensity of the individual experience, ranging from sexual excess to heightened sensual perceptions. At the same time these stories are, at least partially, autobiographical, as can be easily determined by strong parallels to the author's life, for example his summer travels in Canada (see Schwarz 1994) or his admiration for the Canadian painter Emily Carr. These parallels have led some critics to dub the first part of *Persona* (borrowing a term from Rosei) a virtual autobiography (see Kopitzki 1996), trying to connect it to computer lingo. Thus the person or mask of the title might be none other than Rosei himself.

This comfortable although scientifically illegitimate equation of narrator and author might seem to disintegrate rapidly in the second part of the book, titled "Crown of Life." This is the story of two brothers, Franz and Robert Wukowar, who grow up in southern Carinthia in a one-parent household with their father, surrounded by abject poverty. Franz (a character name that Rosei has used before, which is thus, even if superficially, self-reflexive; see Rosei 1974) grows up to become a famous artist and sculptor, while his brother Robert becomes a truck driver. Franz marries Catherine LaGrande, a woman from the upper classes of Parisian society. They move to Vienna, are happy for a while, and then move to Hamburg. As Franz's fame and fortune increase, his interest in his marriage decreases. He engages in a series of hetero and homosexual affairs and becomes estranged from his wife. One day Catherine leaves with Robert in his truck to drive to Turkey, but Robert suddenly murders her, because, or so it seems, she laughed too loudly in response to one of his gestures. Franz dies soon afterward, leaving his fortune to his niece—Robert's daughter. Interspersed with this narrative is the story of Catherine's mother, Madame LaGrande, who is slowly dying of cancer in a French hospital, all the while bemoaning the fact that she was a selfish and uncaring mother. Her husband Jacques visits her faithfully in the hospital every day, but at the same time has a very belated "spring awakening": he frequents porno shops on the East Bank and begins a torrid affair with his wife's best friend, Madame Stephanie. This story of dysfunctional families ends with an ironic quote from the late Franz's notebook: "The family is the dancing pyramid on the stream of life. Even if its starting point, the ancestors, is an arbitrarily chosen one and its upper limit a transitory one because of the living, it is nevertheless form and as such brings happiness: we find security in the flight of appearances" (156).

The family, then, as the "Crown of Life?" Just as the individuals in the narrative seem unable to find any foothold or support in this venerable institution, the reader also struggles to find a foothold in the narrative, which is told in a series of nonchronological fragments, which themselves are frequently punctuated by authorial comments. A few examples of the narrator's statements: "There is a whole series of such sentences, which, however, don't accomplish very much and which decay again immediately after they have 'reminded' us. We, on the other hand, need other sentences. We want to create images that are inspired by the promise of their indestructibility" (66–67) or "We forgot to mention" (78) or "Naturally we are getting ahead of our story and promise to add the 'missing parts' later" (84) or "with a tone that one can superficially characterize as humane—what a gloomy promise!" (127) or finally "In the first part of the book we purposely narrated no more but no less than the story of a murder, together with background materials. Now we have to set to work to fill in the 'missing parts' about the actors, their circumstances, and so forth, before we can proceed with the sweep of the narrative" (139).

Why does the narrator make himself so evident in this second part of the book? Why does he often refer to missing sections? Why does he force the reader to unscramble the puzzle pieces? Why does he frequently call attention to himself and to the creative process? Perhaps the answers can be found in a certain similarity between Rosei the author and Franz the artist. Both are intimately involved in the creation of cultural products, both work long and hard while struggling with the concept of form, and both have dealt intensively with the idea of family and interpersonal relationships—Franz in this story and Rosei in a whole series of novels, particularly in the *15,000 Souls* project.[1] What Franz's wife writes to him in a letter could perhaps also be applied to Rosei the author: "Why do you work at all? I've often wondered. Good, you need money, you never have enough. You claim you'd like to know something. Good: what do you really want to do with this knowledge? Show it around? Give it away?

Keep it for yourself? ... You'd like to numb your fear, alleviate your despair, but everyone wants to do that. You will construct a kingdom of madness, a kingdom of silence for yourself, or have you already constructed it? A long time ago? That's probably the real purpose of the exercise. You are erecting a fortress for yourself consisting of plain truths. You have the power! And you are entirely for yourself" (88). Is Franz an alter ego for Rosei, a means to show the creative individual, not just as the lonesome cowboy on the road as we find in the first part of the novel, but as one who is forced to interact in a social and familial framework, as one who must justify his existence, his reason for being, not only to himself but to others, by supplying the missing truths, by improving and perfecting the artistic form? Such an equation would provide a solid link or connection to the first part, but it is a far-fetched hypothesis.

The third part of *Persona*, "Out of the Future," is a science fiction novella set in a coming century. Commissar Plokow is called upon to investigate and solve a triple murder. He never manages to do so, but in the process he has a love affair, mainly at the scenes of his former crime investigations, with the Japanese love slave of one of the managers of his brave new world, a so-called Ty (short for Tycoon). This crime is considered so heinous that it is punishable by death. The Tys have had themselves medically altered so that they can live to be extremely old. They reside in an artificial green paradise, Diamond Hill, which is isolated high above a filthy metropolis and is accessible only after passing a series of checkpoints and border crossings. Most of the other inhabitants of this society have been cloned by means of gene manipulation and live as drifters or in gulags. Emotions are controlled by means of shots and by "happiness boxes." Some additional features of this society include that there is no way to distinguish morning from evening in the dreary polluted city, individuals can be "timeshocked," that is, frozen in time, and every two weeks the shops organize sales to extract huge amounts of money from the greedy and gullible population. From this description it would be difficult to find any biographical or autobiographical connection to the author Rosei, and thus our initial speculation about the first two parts seems to collapse. It would appear that we are in a quandary.

How can one compare the incomparable? Is it possible to find some other common thread or unifying factor that would lead to some sort of cohesive interpretation?

We are not alone in our predicament. Most critics who discussed the work were equally perplexed. While an occasional voice could be found calling it a "masterpiece" or praising the "in part refreshingly successful detailed sketches," most critics called it "failed prose," "shockingly superficial," or full of clichés.[2] One of these critics (Kamann 1995) even wrote: "It happens too seldom that a dust jacket identifies not the strong points but the decisive weakness of a novel." The critic was referring to the statement on the dust jacket to the effect that the novel provides "the ultimate form of that which Rosei began in his earlier novels," and interpreted "ultimate" as "lifeless prattle." And indeed, most critics took issue with the dust jacket summary and praise, a very rare occurrence indeed. One critic (Pittler 1995) even went so far as to state that, "When reading this opus you get the impression that Rosei is under pressure from his publisher to deliver 200 pages; that's why he now got three manuscripts out of his drawer and declared with resolute boldness, that the trinity forms a larger whole." However, if we give Rosei the benefit of the doubt, if we assume that such an established and respected author would not subscribe to such a Nestroy-like ploy of playing a joke, we must seriously search for a connecting thread or unifying theme.

A good place to start would be to dare to commit the ultimate heresy according to contemporary theories, namely to look at authorial intent. When asked about his novel in an interview, Rosei said the following: "I wanted to try, as the title says, to unfold the domain of a person, in that I first begin with a virtual autobiography from an I-perspective. Then I try in the middle part to imbed the person into a 'we,' to place it within family connections, and the third part is then the dissolving of the person into the politically quantifiable, one is just a number, quantity, and size in this respect. And it's just as if we had to play these roles simultaneously" (1995). If we use this statement as a guideline to examine the three disparate parts of the novel, perhaps we can discover the missing link to help us out of our dilemma.

Following Rosei's lead, if we look at the three major persons in each of the three parts we discover some remarkable similarities. The most obvious connective theme is that of murder and death. The author in the first part wants to write a murder story, the wife of the artist in the second part is murdered by the artist's brother, and the commissar in the third part is investigating a triple murder. Also obvious in all three parts is the motif of sexual excess. The author has the wild affair on Crete, the artist has several sexual trysts, and the commissar has many extremely dangerous and forbidden encounters with the Japanese wife of the tycoon. (All of these scenes are described so graphically that one critic complained about a "continual sexual obsession of the author," which he viewed "as an obtrusive, annoying element, which forces itself into the foreground with obscene expressions and episodes"; Th.T. 1995, 3). Can this foregrounding of love-sex be explained in any way and can it somehow be related with the murder-death theme? The following considerations might give us a clue. The artist in the middle section is asked "Will death conquer love or vice versa, will love conquer death?" (147). In one of the stories of the first part, the author, who engages in such sexual excesses, also succumbs to depression and contemplates suicide. The commissar in our futuristic vision of society, even though he does not fear death because he deals with it on a daily basis, is nonetheless fascinated by it: "Strictly speaking he also felt a kind of titillation—death was one of the few things where you didn't know what it was all about. Death was exciting" (168). It would seem, then, that love and sex are viewed here just as a possible means of overcoming a person's fear of death and the recognition of one's own mortality. Drowning in sexuality seems to be a way of forgetting death. Yet all these sensual escapist escapades do not seem to matter, for they do not achieve their purpose. They are transitory and fleeting at best, and hold only empty promises for those who engage in them. Death will ultimately conquer.

How, then, can one face life? What will give meaning to life in the face of death, if not love and sex? Again, a statement from the second part provides a possible answer: "Every work of art," says Franz, "wants to conquer death" (101). It is through the creation of this nebulous thing called art that one can perhaps face death and achieve a certain type of immortality. It is no accident that creative individuals, often in crisis, are the focal points for the first two parts of the novel. Both are desperately searching for meaning in life in the face of death. Try as they might, however, love, sex, or the interaction with a family do not seem to provide the answer. Their journeys of searching are in vain, except for the products of their creative energies, which somehow seem to point the way out of this dilemma. But how can the third part be reconciled with this interpretation? The answer is simple: If the world continues on its present course there will be no need for art. One day, since he has nothing better to do, Commissar Plokow decides to visit the Museum of Antiquities—where all the artistic creations of the past are housed. He is the only visitor in the museum—art has become a dead artifact without relevance. Happiness, pleasure, and meaning, which might have once emanated from art, are supplied in this new society by chemical and electrical means, and now consist of "a quick and deep pleasure" (197). As the narrator of the third part comments: "It can no longer be our goal to find ourselves because for that we need a location. The art of living in this age consists of quickly choosing, quickly deciding, and during the pleasure to be already looking out for the next opportunity" (197). Rosei's view of the future is thus pessimistic: Where everything is scientifically manipulated and controlled, the one thing that might help make sense out of the chaos, namely the artistic product, is relegated to the junk heap of history.

Looking at the novel from this perspective, we see that our initial speculations were not too far from right. Rosei is indeed writing about himself and his craft. He is searching for meaning in life and seeking to justify his existence. He has concretely, in real life, and vicariously through the characters in his many novels, tried all avenues of approach to come to terms with this monumental question. We must not forget that Rosei turned fifty in 1996, an event that might, through some sort of midlife crisis, have added an immediate urgency to this whole question. Thus the novel *is* in many ways a culmination and summary of his work to date, as the now infamous dust jacket claims. The novel also carries Rosei's thinking one step further, for throughout this struggle Rosei sees himself threatened by a not-too-distant future, where both individual persons and the creations they produce have lost all relevance. In his aforementioned interview Rosei (1995) says the following about this future world: "In my circle there is no one who puts up a fight anymore. All are already going down the great torrent and accept all the atrocities like destruction of the environment and gene manipulation or isolation, the disintegration of the person, and so forth."

The interpretation presented so far is further reinforced by and reflected on the narrative level. A privileging of the narrative discourse over the story it tells is not a particularly popular approach for Germanists, as Patrick O'Neill points out in his recent book, *Acts of Narrative: Textual Strategies in Modern German Fiction* (1996, 12). Yet following O'Neill's lead we can see that Rosei's extremely postmodernist text does indeed overtly draw attention to itself, and invites or even forces readers to negotiate its labyrinthine structure and transform it into their own narratives. So let us briefly consider this narrative form.

As we have discussed, the book is fragmented into three very different parts. Each of these parts in turn is further fragmented: The first consists of seven mainly nonrelated stories, the second contains nonchronological units about various characters, and the third section, although most traditional in scope, contains frequent ellipses and has no real beginning or end. In all three parts the narrator comments directly on the creation of the characters and on the tentative nature of the narrative process. Rosei is here implying that totality is no longer feasible, either the totality of the narrative genre or the totality of the individual. Both are fictions in a very real sense of the word. Individual identity and autonomy, which we all cherish, is, from this perspective, nonexistent; it has dissolved into nonconnected pieces. Since individual identity is fragmented, so also must the text be fragmented that tries to represent it. The author's unwillingness or inability to provide many useful links between the parts can be seen as his resignation to the hopelessness of trying to create unity where there is none. This fragmentation makes the search for the meaning of life all the more difficult and forces a rejection, as we have seen, of most of the traditional answers to this problem. Although such insights can hardly be considered new or innovative in light of the large corpus of twentieth-century literature that deals with the same problems, they do provide a further aid in our reading of the novel and point to a new level of meaning in Rosei's oeuvre.

From another angle, the narrative level directly reflects the creative process. The first section can be read as the author's preparations for writing the novel (travel, observation of nature, gathering of experiences, encountering potential characters, and so forth) and as the origin and beginning of the narrative. The second part can be read as the end product, disconnected and incomplete though it might be, of the creative process begun in the first part, and the final section can be read as a reflection on the possible futility and meaninglessness of the first two parts. In this connotation the novel is also a reflection on itself, and on the sense or non-sense of writing for the contemporary world.

These brief thoughts on the narrative structure are congruent with my earlier comments. The author's autobiographical self and his *métier*, which were postulated as the subject matter of the novel, are themselves fragmented and illusionary. Thus the search for meaning in life through art and the attempt to defy death through creation are perhaps as transitory as the sexual act, as useless as the museum artifacts, and as fictional as the search for unity. As the end of the novel states: "We are not striving for totality. One thing exists in our souls, using the concept one last time, alongside the other things, one thing replaces the other, and even if it is there the soul is a screen upon which the circumstances play. To create totality out of plurality, how dumb. Even plurality has absolutely no meaning; it is simply there" (197). The stories that are left largely untold in the novel and the fragmented identities they portray are paradigmatic of the situation of both the contemporary reader and the contemporary author.

Notes

1. Between 1984 and 1986 Rosei wrote a series of six works centering around a thematic nexus. One of the major themes in these works is the relationship, in varying contexts, of the individual to others. These works, known collectively as the *15,000 Souls* project, are *Mann & Frau* (Man and Wife, 1984), *Komödie* (Comedy, 1984), *15000 Seelen* (15,000 Souls, 1985), *Die Wolken* (The Clouds, 1986), *Der Aufstand* (The Rebellion, 1987) and *Unser Landschaftsbericht* (Our Landscape Report, 1988).

2. Quotations are from Faltin 1995; von Trotha 1995; Kamann 1995; and Pittler 1995, p. 9, respectively. See also Fuchs 1995 or Steinlechner 1995, p. 7.

Works Cited

Acker, Robert. 1989. Peter Rosei. In *Dictionary of Literary Biography, Vol. 85: Austrian Fiction Writers after 1914*. Detroit: Gale.
Faltin, Thomas. 1995. Es gibt keine Garantie!: *Persona*, ein Meisterstück des Österreichers Peter Rosei. *Stuttgarter Nachrichten* (8 November).
Fuchs, Claudia. 1995. Lust am Experiment. Ein Roman, der keiner ist: Roseis *Persona*. *Allgemeine Zeitung* (14 October).
Kamann, Mathias. 1995. Rhapsodie der kaputten Welt: Mißlungene Prosa von Peter Rosei. *Frankfurter Rundschau* (11 October).
Kopitzki, Siegmund. 1996. Ich-Auslöschung?: *Persona*—Ein etwas anderer Roman von Peter Rosei. *Südkurier* (2 February).
O'Neill, Patrick. 1996. *Acts of Narrative: Textual Strategies in Modern German Fiction*. Toronto: University of Toronto Press.
Pittler, A. P. 1995. Uneinige Dreifaltigkeit. *Der Standard* (20 October), album insert.
Rosei, Peter. 1974. Franz und ich. In *Wege: Erzählungen*. Salzburg: Residenz.
Rosei, Peter. 1995. 'Für mich ist der Herr Haider ein Opportunist:' Ein Gespräch mit dem österreichischen Schriftsteller Peter Rosei. *Südkurier* (22 November).
Rosei, Peter. 1995. *Persona*. Stuttgart: Klett-Cotta.
Schmidt-Dengler, Wendelin. 1995. *Bruchlinien: Vorlesungen zur österreichischen Literatur 1945 bis 1990*. Salzburg: Residenz.
Schwarz, Wilhelm. 1994. *Conversations with Peter Rosei*. Translated by Christine and Thomas Tessier. Riverside: Ariadne.
Steinlechner, Gisela. 1995. Tanzstunde der Totalität. Ein Roman, der keiner sein will: *Persona* von Peter Rosei. *Wiener Zeitung* (6 October), extra insert.
Th. T. 1995. Seelische und reale Landschaften: Peter Roseis neuer Roman Persona. Der Bund (Bern; 7 October). Der kleine Bund insert.
von Trotha, Hans. 1995. Peter Rosei: *Persona*. *Zitty* 21.

Rosei's I's: The (De)Composition of the Self in Peter Rosei's Fiction

Geoffrey C. Howes

Peter Rosei's fictional texts do not strictly belong to the genre of autobiographical fiction, but many of the motifs and themes in his fiction derive from his life: places like Vienna, provincial Austria, or Quebec; milieus like the art world or the intellectual scene; and activities like travel or writing inform his life as well as his writings. Such typical intersections of life and art are not, however, the most important way that Rosei's fiction involves the question of autobiography. More significant is the fundamental question of what the self is, a question endemic to autobiography and a thematic center of almost all of Rosei's narratives.

Both classical autobiography and traditionally realist fiction depend largely on the principle of a separate and autonomous self that acts and then defines itself through its acts. Its interactions with the world are exchanges, negotiations between independent entities. The self is an agent, a subject among objects, whose will acts upon those objects. This conception of the self as "one's own person as distinct from all others"[1] is dominant in modern Western cultures, but what Rosei sees in variation after variation is that this conception does not work. It does not fit how persons interact with the world, for the self is not distinct or separate from all others. The resulting clash of expectation with reality produces a culture of bewilderment, of selves seeking to fulfill and actualize themselves under conditions where this is hardly possible. The blame for this failure is placed either on the objects (including other people)—they do not fulfill the self—or on the subjects—there is something wrong with them if they cannot fulfill themselves.

In presenting this bewilderment, Rosei does not try to solve the problem. His writing is not therapy in any immediate sense. Rather, he tries to present the problem in its fullest possible context, for it is precisely unawareness of a fuller context that condemns selves to try, and fail, at being self-sufficient and self-fulfilling, and ultimately to fail at being selves at all. The attempt to be a self is doomed because it does not even ask the right question. The question is not so much ethical as epistemological—not "how can I be myself (fulfill myself, actualize myself)?" but rather "what is my self, and what is its relationship with the world, including other selves?" We cannot very well set out to be ourselves if we have only vague, derivative, or wishful notions of what the self is.

We moderns, when we are not dwelling so much in the realm of theory that we are postmodernists, still prefer an image of personality as something integral, developing, and effective. Even Freud's fragmentation of the self into id, ego, and superego, or other variations of psychological differentiation, did not affect this predilection in a practical way. And the idea of therapy, that one can correct distortions of the personality, contributes after all to the notion of an ideal integral self, the goal of therapeutic efforts. Although many intellectuals accept in theory the idea that a self is a fiction, for example Deleuze and Guattari (1987, 27–28), who regard the supposedly individual subject as a multiplicity, nonetheless in daily life most people cling to their selves as identified by the state and the economy—as autonomous beings with a unique tax-identification number and a unique phone number and a job and a family and some money and possessions, all of which suggests very strongly that each is a singular self. But although the culture at large, including "high culture," encourages this self to consider itself autonomous and unique, in fact it is a "lonely and isolated center of being," as Alan Watts puts it (1972, 12).

This is what Rosei's protagonists have in common, whether they are stoned students, independent businessmen, teachers, housewives, tour guides, professors, lawyers, writers, traveling salesmen, prostitutes, or unemployed workers: they believe that they have integral selves, and when they inevitably encounter experiences that contradict this belief, they interpret their environment, or themselves, or both, as pathological. Rosei's fiction, at the same time that it diagnoses this pathology, indicates that the pathology is not essential, but lies in the social (and hence self-) definition of the self. By de-composing the selves of his characters, Rosei both reveals the integral self as a delusion and shows that this is cause for pessimism only if one continues to cling to the delusion, hoping that the self, like Humpty-Dumpty, can be put back together again.

That is, Rosei always implies that the disintegration of the self-as-independent-agent, while irreversible, can become a reintegration as part of a larger assemblage, a realization that through its embeddedness in a cybernetic system (as understood by Gregory Bateson and explained below), the self participates in a different sort of identity, a contingent existence from which it cannot be extricated without losing real selfhood (as opposed to the pseudo-selfhood of singular identity that is defined by this very extrication). In other words, one must abandon one's self (understood as a necessary, integral, self-sufficient, separate entity) in order to gain oneself (understood as a contingent, connected entity). This is related to the old religious idea that you cannot gain your true, godlike self until you lose yourself. For example, the *Tao Te Ching* (Mitchell 1988, 21) says: "If you want to become whole, / let yourself be partial. / If you want to become straight, / let yourself be crooked. / If you want to become full, / let yourself be empty. / If you want to be reborn, / let yourself die. / If you want to be given everything, / give everything up." Or Jesus according to Matthew (5:3): "Blessed are the poor in spirit, for theirs is the kingdom of heaven." This ancient wisdom steers away from pursuing the fullness of self, which our modern wisdom dictates is the chief goal of life, toward a different fullness of the interconnections of self and world. Here I will call the common-sense notion of the self-as-separate the "integral self," and the alternative notion of the self-as-embedded, the "contingent self."[2]

It is one thing, however, to identify self-identity, selfhood, as the problem rather than the solution; it is entirely another matter to willfully abandon one's integral self; almost everything in Western postindustrial culture militates against it. Nothing threatens the integral self more than the prospect, demonstrated in another's madness, eccentricity, or destitution, of losing itself, becoming contingent. If there were a method, a twelve-step program for overcoming the powerful cultural conditioning that imprisons us in integral selves, then Peter Rosei might have written a how-to manual, a self-help book. But it is not easy, so he tells the story, over and over again in variations, of the failure of the integral self to live up to the expectations placed upon it. He tells of those who experience the loss of their integral self as an injury without a chance for healing, for they futilely seek healing in a return to self-identity rather than in abandoning it, thereby compounding the problem. There are also those who seek escape but find no sanctuary, temporary and delusional or otherwise, who then arrive at an extremity from which there is no return. This accounts for the occurrence of suicide and murder in Rosei's stories.

Even in the pre-poststructuralist dark ages, critical thinkers often noted the overlapping of autobiography and fiction. From a positivist point of view this entailed two different games of "gotcha": In autobiographies one detected passages embellished by the writer's imagination, if not made out of whole cloth; in fiction one discovered passages taken over more or less thinly disguised from the world of actual experience and fact. Invention was so real or reality so invented that the implicit claims of genre—history is truth, autobiography is history, fiction is invention, invention is not truth—were undermined. As long as one subscribed to the "law of genre," such discoveries could be used against the autobiographer or the storyteller as proof of dishonesty or insufficient imagination, or at least as violations of the law.[3]

In fact, however, it is impossible to find pure examples of genres (Derrida 1980, 59–61). Autobiography in particular has never quite fit genre theory, as it has been regarded as both too subjective to be history and too objective to be art (Gilmore 1994, 6). In the postmodernist questioning of genre, therefore, the hybridity of autobiography has been an interesting place to explore "an enlivening instability of both text and context" (7). Hence, even if Rosei's fiction is not autobiographical in any immediate sense, and even when it is not even couched in the first person, it bears what Leigh Gilmore calls the "mark of autobiography"— "the always problematical deployment of the I" (6). In Rosei it is not only the grammatical and generic "I" that is problematical, but the entire concept of the self that calls itself "I," whether that self happens to be the first-person voice or not. In this sense, most of Rosei's fiction is autobiographical, because it has to do with selves trying to establish their identity *as selves*. Thus the bounds are broken down between fiction, which invents selves, and autobiography, which tries to establish the self as fact by constructing it, that is, by inventing or fictionalizing it. In some ways, then, the better site for "autography"— writing the self—is not self-biography, but fiction, for fiction does not depend on a preset notion of the self. Fictional autography is in no way secondary to factual autography, because the I (even when it is a she or he) is revealed as a certain sort of fiction. When acknowledged for its particular revelatory power, its insistence on experimenting but not generalizing its results, literature gains the status that Rosei likes to claim for it, as a source of knowledge parallel to, but different from, such pursuits as politics, economics, and science (BPZ 6).[4]

Just as Rosei calls into question the ontology of the self, he also calls into question the status of the genre of narrative fiction. The sense of beginning, middle, and end, the sense of a causal connection between episodes, and the sense of unity of action are often missing in Rosei's fiction, or when they are present, they are parodied (as in *15,000 Souls*, 1985). Such experiments in narrative are commonplace in poststructuralist and postmodernist writing and hence it is not surprising to find a recent author like Peter Rosei writing narratives that question the status of narrative. What is interesting in Rosei's case is that this questioning of generic conventions exactly parallels his questioning of conventions of personal identity. Just as human selves can no longer pretend to be integral, so too texts cannot rely on their own unity. We lose the assurance of narrative threads and linear causality. Rosei abandons certainty and writes in order to find out what it is possible to write about and how it is possible to write about it. "The writer (*Dichter*) forgets what he knows" (BPZ 14) so that it does not interfere with what he discovers. And further: "If we want a new art, we must not only talk about it in an erudite, well-versed, and aloof fashion, but we must also try to create it. And we can do that only by gambling everything" (BPZ 81).

Even though he abandons "what he knows," and "gambles everything," Rosei still retains many elements of past narrative conventions, romantic or realist. Landscapes, of course, figure largely; in fact one text, *Project for a World without People*, is mainly a single, sustained landscape description. Cityscapes provide the civilized counterpart to Rosei's detailed work on natural settings (e.g., Bartens 1994, 91–168). Descriptions of the day or night sky and the clouds set scenes in nearly every work. Interiors, described in minute detail, are evoked for the sense of mood they supply to the human interactions within them. The richness of description collides with the sparseness of story so that Rosei seems to be at once an inept storyteller (in the traditional sense) and an unconvinced postmodernist who allows the romantic pathetic fallacy to turn his head from postmodern skepticism about referentiality.

The critics have noted this discrepancy again and again. One speaks of "a gush of worn-out images and clumsily formulated impressions" (Kosler 1994, 319). Another writes of his "bent for the precious and maudlin image" but grants him the originality of his metaphors, only to take back this praise by noting that the result is not always precision and clarity, but sometimes a "toppling into skewed images" (Bulla 1994, 321). Reviewing *Rebus* (1990), one critic complains: "Rosei can write. Many of his books show this, especially *From Here to There*. But Rosei doesn't write *Rebus* with irony, or with tension, or with wit or poetry. His language is as boring as the things it's talking about. The same images repeat themselves endlessly" (Appelt 1994, 339). Thus the reputation that emerges from the journalistic criticism of Rosei is that of a highly skilled writer who is capable of writing hackneyed and boring stuff; of a postmodernist who cannot avoid (sometimes cheap) romanticism; and of a highly intellectual author who is often simplistic and trite.[5]

What shall we do with these paradoxes? What is Rosei up to,

if it seems both to be and not to be a good story, a self-referential text, a neoromantic portrayal of nature, and a pessimistic assessment of the postmodern condition? Does he want to have his narrative tradition and deconstruct it too? One possible resolution of this contradiction is his apparent conviction that even though the unities of self-identity and narrative identity are not tenable, the elements, the contents, of both are still with us. Experiences ranging from sunsets, to moonrises, to love in its more and less tender varieties, to breezes on the cheek, to adultery, to murders, to drug-induced hallucinations, to revolts on the street—all of these have equal validity as the elements of both the self and the narrative text. There is no doubt *that* we experience them. What needs investigating is *how* we experience them, how these experiences are related, and what it is that brings them together in myriad tiny universes: the self. In Rosei's fiction these elements are jumbled together without prejudice toward the questions of who is experiencing, how experiences are connected, or what they mean. They are also jumbled together without prejudice toward the question whether they are original, derivative, hackneyed, or uncritical. The demarcation between the self (or selves) and the text and its content is erased so that the experiences of protagonists, "secondary characters," narrators, and ultimately of readers are not kept neatly apart, nor neatly categorized. It is not always clear whether the author is using poetic language, whether a narrator is limited not only by point of view but also by powers of expression, or whether we are to take what we read as true emotion or false consciousness, as high poetry or popular triteness, though all of these do occur.

Rosei's method, however, is not to pursue mystery for its own sake in an attempt to befuddle or dazzle. Whatever clarity is lost in this mélange is gained in the probability that the real interconnections of the elements—not just the willed or manufactured ones between supposedly autonomous actors, including the writer and the reader—might begin to show through. When the law of the integral self and the law of integral genre are both abandoned, the self (or selves) and the text (or texts) are no longer fully distinguishable, but the possibilities of their interactions and interconnections are increased, along with the possibility of gaining knowledge of their shared role in a vaster system.

It was asserted earlier that Rosei's characters inevitably find that their integral selves do not function properly in the world. The root of this disappointment is very often the contradiction between pleasure, which is ample in Western experience, and amply described in Rosei's texts, and the fact that all this pleasure never adds up to anything like an accumulation of gratification. This accounts for the almost universal disappointment of Rosei's characters. Why is it that experience after experience of desire fulfilled, distress relieved, comfort provided, or appetites indulged does not result in a person who is the total of all those experiences—an overflowing tub of pleasure? It could be that pleasure is balanced or negated by pain, loss, and death, and that the self is thus a scene of more or less equilibrium between pleasure and pain, in which pain and death ultimately win. But in fact even when pleasure exceeds pain for long stretches of time, the basic sense of modern Western life, despite antibiotics, sewer systems, oranges in winter and apples in summer, exotic wines, air travel, and birth control, is somehow one of dissatisfaction. This mystery, that all our satisfactions are not satisfying, is at the center of Rosei's fiction.

What Rosei seems to be trying to show (not to argue) in his fiction is that there is a fundamental inability to incorporate either type of experience—pleasure or pain—into the integral self. If pleasure is a stream of water flowing into the bucket of the integral self, at some point the water will run over. The bucket is limited by its self-definition, its basic immurement within its surroundings, and so it will have no benefit from the overflow. Often, Rosei's protagonists experience the self, so to speak, as a bucket full of holes, and thus they interpret their loss of satisfaction as an inability to contain pleasure, rather than seeing the more fundamental problem of viewing the self as a container in the first place.

One of the best critiques of this view of the self as a container that can be filled with experiences comes from Alan Watts. Perhaps a popularizing spiritual teacher might not seem the most dependable source of a philosophical critique, but Watts's ideas, like Rosei's fictions, address the state of practice, not the state of theory. His book *The Book* problematizes the integral self, not on the forefront of theory, but in the hinterland of experience. I will quote him at some length because his generalizations about modern life seem to fit the variety of situations in which Rosei's I's find themselves:

> We suffer from a hallucination, from a false and distorted sensation of our own existence as living organisms. Most of us have the sensation that "I myself" is a separate center of feeling and action, living inside and bounded by the physical body—a center which "confronts" an "external" world of people and things, making contact through the senses with a universe both alien and strange. Everyday figures of speech reflect this illusion. "I came into this world." "You must *face* reality." "The conquest of nature."
>
> This feeling of being lonely and very temporary visitors in the universe is in flat contradiction to everything known about man (and all other living organisms) in the sciences. We do not "come into" the world; we come *out* of it, as leaves from a tree. As the ocean "waves," the universe "peoples." Every individual is an expression of the whole realm of nature, a unique action of the total universe. This fact is rarely, if ever, experienced by individuals. Even those who know it to be true in theory do not sense or feel it, but continue to be aware of themselves as isolated 'egos' inside bags of skin. (1972, 8)

Watts's critique states that the wall between self and other is an illusion. The self is part of the other, it emerges from the other, so that the very terms "self" and "other" are ultimately meaningless. But it is very hard for us to imagine and experience ultimates, and so we regard only proximates as real: here I am and out there is the world and all its contents. This illusion of integral selfhood is increased in modern postindustrial society, where the ideology and the practice of individualism isolates the self even more than in earlier times, even if it is theoretically freer.

This Cartesian dualism of mind and body, of self and other, promotes the ideology of individualism, but does not account for its failures. Within the dualistic system we are obligated to account for such failures by blaming either one pole or the other, self or nonself. But the field of cybernetics offers an alternative to this. Gregory Bateson, in a 1971 article titled "The Cybernetics of 'Self': A Theory of Alcoholism," asserts that if one blames the alcoholic's sober life (the "other") for driving him to drink, then sobriety cannot be a cure for the disease—it is the etiology (310–

311). Nor can blaming the alcoholic himself lead to a solution, because it is clear that the alcoholic alone, as an integral self, is not "strong" enough to resist drink. One must, says Bateson, consider alcoholism neither as an escape from the other, nor as a failure of the integral self, but as an escape "from [the alcoholic's] own insane premises, which are continually reinforced by the surrounding society." In other words, in a system of information exchange—the self in its interaction with society—neither the self nor the other is at fault; rather, there is a malfunction in the information system. The alcoholic may "in some way be more vulnerable or sensitive than normal to the fact that his insane (but conventional) premises lead to unsatisfying results," but Bateson stresses the idea that intoxication may be seen as an "appropriate subjective correction" for sobriety. When sober, the alcoholic confronts his absurd role in the world, the insanity of his own premises, which is supplied and supported by normal life, and he flees this madness into another kind of madness—drink.

In other words, one must view the alcoholic self and its environment as a cybernetic system, that is, as a circuit of information in which no part has unilateral control over the rest of the system or any other part of it (315). Or, to state it negatively, no one element is to blame. Bateson suggests a simple model for a cybernetic system: a man felling a tree with an axe. "Each stroke of the axe is modified or corrected, according to the shape of the cut face of the tree left by the previous stroke. This self-corrective (that is, mental) process is brought about by a total system, tree-eyes-brain-muscles-axe-stroke-tree" (317). The dominant model of the average Westerner, however, substitutes for this cybernetic system the opposition of subject and object. "He says, '*I* cut down the tree' and he even believes that there is a delimited agent, the 'self,' which performed a delimited 'purposive' action upon a delimited object" (318).

Without going further into Bateson's theory of alcoholism, suffice it to say that Rosei's numerous protagonists all suffer from something parallel to the alcoholic's problem as described here: they have become aware of the insane premises that they have adopted from their environment, and they are trying to escape in various ways: through drink, art, sex, drugs, money, work, travel, politics, or suicide. These are "appropriate subjective corrections," but these selves are frustrated because they are bound up in the Western epistemology that posits them as transcendent selves over-against the world, and so they (understandably) try to correct either the environment or themselves, but not their interconnection. They try to control one element of the system, or even the whole system, and hence are bound to fail. Let us look at some instances of the failed escape in Rosei's fictional texts.

Who Was Edgar Allan (1977) sets up some basic categories for viewing Rosei's fiction of the last twenty years. The young protagonist-narrator, a student who has switched from medicine to art history and gone from Germany to a twilight existence in the drug-saturated underworld of Venice, looks back on that time as "confused and opaque" (7). He tries to reconstruct it using his old journals, bits of his attempts at being an author, letters, bank receipts, and so forth (7). He admits to disregarding chronology and to lacing his narrative with authentic material. In other words, the simultaneous questioning of genre and self mentioned earlier is constitutive for the text, because the certainty of identity is lost over time (and in this case in the fog of drug use) and must be reconstructed using literary means.

The novel is not without its narrative conventions; near the beginning we read a letter from the narrator's father and then find out that the father died soon after sending it. It is at first unclear whether intermittent passages in the third-person singular are about the narrator or his father. Eventually it seems that they are the son's literary imaginings about the time leading up to the father's death, but no clear line is drawn between the narrator and his imagined father: whose death is being pictured here? Another confusion of identity arises as the narrator tries to figure out "who is Edgar Allan?" Is this mysterious man who claims to be American and shares the name of the father of the detective story a part of the drug ring that seems to be involved with the murders of two society women? Is he as friendly as he seems sometimes, or is he as dangerous as he appears at other times? Is he a well-groomed gentleman or a cruel murderer? The conventions of the detective novel create some narrative tension, but the increase in information is so sketchy, so fragmented, and so filtered by the narrator's altered states of consciousness that the novel does the opposite of clearing up the mystery.

The narrator's motivations for abandoning an orderly, purposeful life are never spelled out, but hints are given. Art history is nothing but "a pretext for behavior that was nothing other than an escape" (8). His inheritance gives him the freedom to live a life with only minimal structure. He indulges so much in dissipation that he feels himself "totally fall to pieces." He hears voices. "Then I went insane" (33). He has to drink three bottles of liquor just to calm himself down. "They attribute the madness to the drink, and not the drink to the madness, said Poe of his alcoholism. That's just how it was with me too" (33–34). Rosei's protagonist is thus in precisely the same position as Bateson's alcoholic: he is drinking and taking drugs and dropping out as an "appropriate subjective correction" of the sense of purposelessness that his bourgeois life, and perhaps his father's death, has instilled in him. His sense of being an integral self is radically altered in the direction of contingency: "Hadn't much of what was inside of me already been erased, simply wiped away?" (38). "I had the feeling that I consisted of shimmering particles, that I was an almost bodiless cloud of atoms" (40).

This is the decomposition of the integral self. Yet the complementary movement of reintegration into a newly conceived system is only vaguely hinted at on occasion. The narrator discovers that his self-dissolution must have a solvent, a medium, because the loss of self is not an escape from connectedness with the outer world, but on the contrary it is a breaking down of the self's borders. But at this point the only example, the only possibility, for going beyond the self and connecting with the world is the enigma Edgar Allan, whose marginal existence is both fascinating and repulsive, both an implicit critique of society and a counteractive concentration of society's worst impulses. This double function is mirrored in the Poe character Hop-Frog, whom the two discuss, who is both a critic (as court jester) and a murderer (when the humor is turned against him).

The narrator's fascination with unraveling the mystery gives him a sort of purposeless purpose and the thrill of existential risk: "Without really feeling very good, it still gave me a lot of pleasure to play with Allan, knowing that I was entering into danger, that maybe it could even be the death of me—and perhaps precisely for that reason" (88–89). The vicarious path to death that his father (or his literary alter ego) takes in his literary imagination carries this dissolution to an extreme that the narrator (who lives to tell, of course) does not experience directly, but which tells of a double torment: "At that time he had fallen into the most extreme strangeness, and he had no means at his disposal for redressing this. Everything about him was constant and excruciating perception. There was nothing else. The world went along" (96). This passage expresses the limbo of a self whose very awareness dispels it from the illusory comfort of discrete existence, yet which can see the world going by without him. He has managed to disengage himself from his integral self but not to find a new way to be.

In this regard *Who Was Edgar Allan?* is representative of the other short novels from this period, *From Here to There* (1978) and *Try Your Luck* (1980), which likewise depict selves whose circumstances lead them to doubt their preconceptions of who and what they are. The protagonist Karl in *From Here to There* uses motorcycle travel and drugs as his "appropriate subjective correction" of the absurdity of normal life, and he sells drugs as a livelihood. In *Try Your Luck* the anonymous first-person narrator does not choose his expulsion from normality, as do Karl and the narrator of *Edgar Allan*. Rather he loses his job, which he discovers was the main source of definition for his self. When this framework is gone, the anguish of trying to be an integral self without a social definition drives the protagonist to look for quick fixes ("fast luck") at the employment office, in the friendship of the cynical Bergman, and in his relationship with his girlfriend Anna. However harsh unemployment may be, Rosei's narrative does not in the first place indict the capitalist system for routinely expelling its offspring; rather he reveals the cruelty of a definition of the integral self that distorts even those who are functioning within the system, but whose distortions sometimes become apparent only when that functioning ceases.

Hence the "alternative lifestyles" in Rosei's books are actually pathetic parodies of bourgeois forms: the drug cartel in *Edgar Allan* is a mirror of big capitalism; drug pushing is a mirror of the small entrepreneur; using drugs or alcohol is a mirror of consumerism; adultery is a mirror of marriage; and prostitution is a mirror of employment. In *The Man without Qualities* (1995), Musil writes of Ulrich's courtesan Leona: "Of course, if the art of trading for money not the entire person, as usual, but only the body must be called prostitution, then Leona occasionally engaged in prostitution" (1:18). A similar topsy-turvy view, in which the supposed aberration is actually a possibly less serious form of the debasement of normal life, informs Rosei's fiction throughout.

As if to make this point, many later texts by Rosei abandon the lurid "outside" of drugs, prostitution, unemployment, and bohemianism, and move to the "inside" of society, where the selves have intact roles such as employee, spouse, businessman, parent, lover, or friend. Or the selves have such "borderline" professions as artist, writer, designer, or academic. What is striking in *The Milky Way* (1981), the six books of the cycle *15,000 Souls* (1984–88), *Rebus* (1990), *Persona* (1995), and other works since the 1970s, is how dissatisfied these people are in spite of having "selves" so defined. They seek redefinition through such self-assertive actions as divorce, affairs, travel, acquisitions, personal and commercial competition, and artistic production or enjoyment. But there are also less positive ways of asserting oneself: drinking, self-isolation, illness, violence toward others, even suicide.

One such destructive form of self-assertion that runs as a leitmotiv through Rosei's books is the use of alcohol. Without necessarily being alcoholics (though some are), Rosei's I's drink and drink: an "appropriate subjective correction," perhaps, but not a solution. In an instance from *The Milky Way*, Nora rejects the bourgeois world even as she lives in luxury with Frank. She sees this luxury as a countermeasure to pedestrian reality:

> That was good: using reality as poison! That's why she couldn't stand business people, except as victims. For these people reality was something you had to determine, to get under control. That's how they talked about it. Nora drank some more of the wine, which still held the coolness of the ice bucket. She took a big swallow. (56)

Nora's critique of commercialism opposes to it the creative, artistic life without seeing that both depend on maintaining the integral self. Her deep draught of wine is an unconscious symptom of being trapped in this pseudo-conflict.

Another character in *The Milky Way*, Buck, is alone: "Was he unhappy? Because he hardly ever talked to anyone, he couldn't find out how he was doing. It was as if he were cut off from a blood supply, and he lived on in this empty field, sustained by habit" (190–191). In this severe case of isolation the self hardly has a social definition, but persists in the form of learned responses. Buck thinks and writes, but with little seriousness. He drinks: "Actually, he wasn't supposed to drink, because of his illness, but he drank himself unconscious again and again" (191). Drinking can give him some momentary inspiration, but in time Buck's listlessness wins and he apparently commits suicide.

Murad in *Man and Woman* (1984) drinks too, and in spite of resolving to quit, he doesn't. The list of drinkers could go on; their omnipresence suggests that this "normal" activity is perhaps in fact an "appropriate subjective correction" to normal life, which is therefore revealed as fundamentally pathological. To be sure, not all of Rosei's drinkers are self-destructive or alcoholic; in fact, most are merely social drinkers. Tacitly, however, the question arises: What sort of society is it whose members need to numb themselves when they spend time together (or alone)? The implicit answer: A society that expects them to survive as integral selves.

One of the bastions of bourgeois convention is the institution of marriage. Many of Rosei's characters, especially his intellectuals, avoid marriage or escape it through affairs or divorce. But the fundamental problem is not that marriage is unfulfilling, but that integral selves cannot be fulfilled. And so Murad and Susanne in *Man and Woman* are divorced, but they do not seem to be significantly happier. They just deal with new difficulties rather than the old ones of living together, which, it turns out, was not the problem, but a symptom of the problem of the integral self. Furthermore, because the past was not the problem, leaving it behind is not a solution; the impossibility of the integral self persists. There are glimmers of awareness of this: Murad has left his wife and daughter, moved out of his old apartment, and moved to a new city, but still he cannot escape his connection to his family: "Maybe the lives of other people are actually more connected with each other than I thought" (46). Distant but bound to Murad in her thoughts, Susanne realizes that the past binds people so that it can never be fully past: "And as much as she wished at that moment that she believed that the past was over, over once and for all, she still knew that that was not how it was" (36). A subtlety of language—she does not wish the past was over, but she wishes she *believed* it was—shows Rosei's keen awareness of the contortions we go through to maintain our selfhood. To the integral self, belief is often reality, because to maintain itself it must reject knowledge of how we are not self-determined.

The ambiguous German title of this book also means *Husband and Wife*, and without being sentimental or moralistic, Rosei shows that the married condition persists whether the parties want to acknowledge it or not. Our connections with others cannot be tossed aside, lightly or otherwise, for our contingent selves are as inscrutable as others' contingent selves; hence when Murad sees a poor, old woman whose face looks "like an empty stream bed. Like an old leather satchel with nothing in it" (22), he asks himself: "Was she being pursued? Or was she fleeing? Or was she simply crazy? It wouldn't have occurred to Murad that all these questions also applied to him and his undertaking" (22). Although he can see the decomposition of the integral self written in the face of another, he cannot acknowledge it in himself. There is a similar, but more conscious moment in *The Milky Way* when Ellis sees himself reflected in an old woman:

> Her bent-over posture did not seem to be caused by anything outside of her. It came from inside, it was a contraction into the inner world where the woman still lived. The outside was empty, depopulated. The woman had abandoned it, the way you abandon property. There was even pride in this attitude. There are many things you can give up before you are lost. I'm like that old woman, thought Ellis, only I have a different deformity. (49–50)

Here is an image of an integral self cut off from the world and collapsing into the resulting inner vacuum. Ellis's similar "deformity" is his itinerant life, moving from friend to friend and place to place without a real connection.

Unfaithfulness is another alternative to conventional marriage that seems oppositional but does not elude the flawed premise of the integral self. In *The Clouds* (1986), Eva, who is married to Reinhard, commits adultery with his friend Gobbo. What is remarkable about Rosei's depictions of this and other affairs, and of sexual acts in general, is their banality. The fundamental situation of two integral selves trying to cross borders without giving them up does not change if the people are not married, and so rather than the thrill of novelty and risk, adultery is presented as the trouble that two well-meaning but insecure people have who are trying to understand each other. The unconventional moment flees, and even if it is socially significant that Gobbo and Eva are not married, phenomenologically it makes no difference whatsoever. In fact, Gobbo, whose life as an international fashion designer ought to make him sexy and interesting, has become inept at intimacy, even at the low level required of him by the affair. He seems needy and unsure of himself. This may be why Eva returns to Reinhard, though we cannot be sure. Rosei's silence about motivations shows that even though we think of motives as decisive for self-definition, they are less distinctive than we wish we could believe, and less important than the situations they get us into. What really defines our selves is not making decisions, but dealing with their consequences. Decisions cannot control the cybernetic system; they are just one element in it, but the integral self refuses this knowledge.

Eva's return to domestic stability is neither a triumph of matrimony nor an ironic commentary. Home life *is* comforting, children and others we are connected to *are* important. This doesn't mean they are easy, or exciting, or that they solve all of our problems. Simple, bourgeois satisfactions are presented as temporary, delicate states that are less notable for the presence of pleasure than the absence of pain. Hence working in Reinhard's garden brings a modicum of satisfaction that only underlines for Eva her still great dissatisfaction:

> We got a good bit of work done, Reinhard begins, I'm satisfied.
>
> She smiles. Now I ought to say I'm satisfied too, she thinks, and she says it.
>
> Good, says Reinhard.
>
> It is a kind of negotiation between the two of them.

> I'd like you to be happy, says Reinhard. And he continues: The way everybody can only imagine one kind of happiness, in their own way, the happiness that I want for you is my own.
>
> Reinhard looks at her.
>
> She has the feeling that you can see through her. As if she were hollow and transparent and maybe the most negligible thing in the world: for she has no answer; not the answer that he wants.
>
> She only has a long, confused, unclear answer, and that one doesn't count. (141)

This is a negotiation between a self (Reinhard) who still has the illusion of being intact—even his forgiving Eva bolsters his selfhood—and a self that knows that it is decomposing. The short answer ("I am satisfied") is the right move in this game, but secretly Eva is already playing another game, one in which her integral self is gone ("hollow and transparent") and in which only a long, confused answer can begin to account for her contingent self.

We find a similar domestic "happy" ending in *Persona*: "Alfred and Beate, in any case, lived happily. The little boy was their pride and joy. It was nice to live in Uhlenhorst. They were a little bit afraid of a reactor catastrophe. But at least Communism was dead" (156). There is more irony here, but not much. Rosei is not so much making fun of the content of such modest comforts as showing that this is how we piece our integral selves together: we are spouses, we are parents, we are citizens, we are afraid, we are relieved. These fragments give us identity but do not coalesce; they are beams of light, but the self is not a magnifying glass, concentrating them; it is a prism, refracting them. We only pretend that these elements of identity belong together because they accidentally collect in us.

In an apparent attempt to account for a greater number of accidental elements, to increase the pool of experiences that impinge upon the self, Rosei has gone from books with relatively few characters and a relatively unified plot (*Edgar Allan*, 1977; *From Here to There*, 1978; *Try Your Luck*, 1980) to increasingly compound structures, as in *The Milky Way* (1981), *Rebus* (1990), and *Persona* (1995).[6] The loose principle of organization in *The Milky Way* is the character Ellis, who moves casually through a series of acquaintanceships, through what we would call subplots if there were a main plot. In *Rebus* the principle of (dis-) organization is even more impersonal and accidental, the city of Vienna itself. In *Persona* any obvious principle is gone, and essay, autobiography, and various fictional genres from love story, to *Künstlerroman* (novel of the artist), to futuristic detective story, are jumbled together to create a fictional mask (persona) defined only by its contingency. The broader the perspective, the less sense we have of the integral self and the integral genre, and the more sense we have of personal and generic fortuity.

Peter Ensberg criticizes Rosei's fiction in general for not portraying the historical, social, and political contingencies, the outward causes, of the disintegration of the self (1994, 55–57). Their absence, however, is a clue that Rosei is not concerned in the first place with portraying the disintegration of identity as the result of impersonal forces. Instead he is showing that the personal-impersonal polarity is false, and the modern individual's problem is not simply a loss of identity or personality at the mercy of outward forces. The concept of personality—the integral self—is itself part of the problem. Identity promises what it cannot deliver and therefore frustrates Rosei's I's, who turn to destructive and self-destructive behavior.

Rosei concentrates, therefore, on describing "subjective-arbitrary" reality (Ensberg 1994, 53) in order to show the integral self for the trap that it is. One can criticize him for neglecting political, historical, and social forces, but he portrays, from their subjective perspective, people who are themselves not aware of these forces. His fiction is to historical-realist fiction as autobiography is to history; that is, it consciously selects a limited point of view. Unlike traditional autobiography, however, it does so to show the limits of the point of view on its own terms. In this way he is like Kafka, who also did little to show the political, historical, and social forces at work on his protagonists. This is not a qualitative comparison—no one does it like Kafka, of course—but Rosei does evince some of the claustrophobia of Kafka's protagonists, who are trapped between the way they think the world should be and the way the world is. Their attempts to gain personal advantage (to assert their integral selves) in spite of this discrepancy resemble some of the "appropriate subjective corrections" of Rosei's characters. Both Kafka and

Rosei rely on their readers' knowledge of the world to put these restricted attitudes in a greater perspective, but both of them also rely on their readers' unconscious commitment to the integral self, which draws them into the story so that they empathize with the characters right up to the point where the basis of their empathy—the embattled integral self—is found wanting.

If overarching political and historical awareness were given to an authorial narrator, then Rosei would be creating something that his experience tells him does not exist: a self who has it figured out, whose self *as a self* and not just as an intellect, in fact and not just in theory, surmounts its surroundings. Ensberg takes Rosei to task for merely showing and not interpreting, and asking the reader to do the work (1994, 54). But the narrator or author is not coyly withholding information like a Socratic examiner. If he were, he could show just how outward forces deprive people of identity, and abet their struggles to get identity back. He could write a self-help book in fictional form. But Rosei does not know how people might get their identity back. In fact, he is not sure they should. He simply accompanies them, again and again, to the point where the self-assertion of the integral self fails. Rosei is not bemoaning a society that has deprived us of our selfhood; he is showing that selfhood itself is part of the scam. Until we get beyond the delusion that the integral self is a good that is being withheld from us rather than the thing that, in collusion with the social, economic, and political systems, is doing the withholding, we will not grasp Rosei's criticism.

The implicit social criticism of Rosei's bohemians, dropouts, artists, divorcees, madmen, and silent, lonely sufferers, then, is that the premises upon which they live are insane, and the proof of this is that the premises drive all of them, in varying degrees, to madness ranging from mild neurosis to suicidal depression. We must resist a false polarity in which we automatically assume that because society is hypocritical, dropping out is a solution; because marriage can be unsatisfying, divorce is a solution; because sobriety is stiff and painful, inebriation is a solution; because commercialism and consumerism are dehumanizing, bohemianism and nonconformity are solutions. Such a critique ignores the bigger context, shared by all of Rosei's selves, that is, the cybernetic function of these actions and reactions.

There is no intoxication without sobriety, there is no divorce without marriage, there is no bohemian without the bourgeois. These truisms have serious implications for our topic, because they describe the systems (in Bateson's sense) by which Rosei's selves are bound. Like the alcoholic who seeks to survive his sober life by getting drunk, the bohemian seeks to survive his bourgeois life by being weird, the wife (in *The Clouds*) seeks to survive her married life by having an affair, her lover seeks to survive his unmarried life by having an affair, the lonely man (in *Comedy*) seeks to survive his loneliness by adopting a child, and the drug dealer seeks to escape social restraints by setting himself up in business. Whereas each alternative can be seen as a means of taking personal control of the situation, of asserting one's sovereign self, such control is an illusion when viewed in the context of a system (Bateson) of social constraint–rebellion or withdrawal–social censure–further rebellion or withdrawal. This cycle will be repeated indefinitely, even if it leads to violent reactions like suicide or murder, which change the elements of the system but not its mental (cybernetic) functioning.

As Rosei's I's are ground down in their struggles within greater assemblages, they usually become aware that their selves are fragmentary, defective, disintegrated. But only occasionally do they question the premise of an integral, "functioning" self that deserves rewards, happiness, and freedom. They persist in seeing the failure of the self either as objectively determined (resulting in antisocial and asocial responses) or as subjectively determined (resulting in self-destructive responses), but they do not see the third alternative between the two. What we are able to see as careful readers is the system in which the self and the other are inextricably bound. We are encouraged to identify with neither the "establishment" that wants people to get jobs, buy things, get married, obey authority, stay clean, and enjoy ourselves to death; nor the "anti-establishment" that rejects self-definition through work, consumerism, social institutions, Puritanism, or thoughtless hedonism.

Rosei is no moralist who wants to imply that his characters would necessarily be better off if they stayed married, sober, diligent, and faithful. He simply shows that they are not much better off divorced, drunk, indolent, and adulterous. The only slight improvement in their condition is that they become aware—how aware varies widely from case to case—that their integral selves do not work. But the question why they do not function is too complex to be answered by a quick placement of blame.

This distancing of the text from political or ethical issues of right and wrong accounts for the uncanny lack of affect, the indifference, of much of Rosei's narrative texts. It is not that he does not want us to know how the narrator or characters feel; rather, he does not want us to be swayed by this knowledge. He knows that the ideology of the integral self encourages us to take the side of the "little guy" against the "establishment," and that we like to identify with the protagonists' selves. To identify too much with their integral selves, however, would be to keep our finger on our side of the scales, so we are not found wanting. But we should not sacrifice our patient search for knowledge of the world in favor of our wish to believe that we can prevail; that would be indulging our selves at the cost of knowledge of the world. Like his mentor Franz Kafka, Peter Rosei knows: "In the fight between you and the world, back the world" (Kafka 1946, 290).

The "world" whose side Kafka suggests we take is not the world in the narrow sense of the particular social or political or economic system one finds oneself embedded in. He is not suggesting that we take the side of the Law against Josef K in *The Trial*, unless one takes the Law to be a metaphor for the world in an inclusive sense. This inclusive world can be understood as the entire cybernetic system of the universe, something like the Tao in Lao Tse: "The Tao doesn't take sides; / it gives birth to both good and evil" (*Tao Te Ching* 5). The only real way we can take our own side in the struggle between ourselves and the world is to give up asserting our existence separate from the world. If we back the world, we also back ourselves. This does not mean accepting passively the political, social, or economic status quo, but does mean recognizing that both one's self and the status quo are part of the world in the larger sense, and are subject to its Way (Tao).

At several points in various texts, Rosei offers metaphors for alternatives to picturing the self as integral and separate. In *Who*

Was Edgar Allan? the protagonist wishes to be "like a drop of water within a standing body of water" (97). Bergman considers the jellyfish as a similar image in *Try Your Luck*: "Just imagine, he said, they consist almost entirely of water. Propelled by currents, they drift around in the sea. There they also appear to have bodies" (TL 6; DR 184). These tropes share the quality of a self that is somehow defined (a drop, a body), yet whose suspension within the environment is more important than its individual existence. These hints at the actual, contingent position of the self are sprinkled about, and sometimes they come from very unlikely sources. Neither the protagonist in *Who Was Edgar Allan?* nor Bergman is a philosopher, but nonetheless their loss of integral self has the authority of profound experience.

There are many other metaphorical expressions of the contingency of the self, including one that virtually permeates Rosei's work: the cloud. Peter Ensberg (1994) notes the frequency of cloud images and warns that their constant recurrence threatens to make Rosei's fiction predictable and ultimately boring (60). At the same time he notes that he does not want to refute the symbolic function of any particular application of the metaphor (60), which he identifies as marking the "fleeting, provisional, uncertain character of life" (59). Without in turn refuting the possibility that the repeated usage of cloud metaphors might become tedious, I would nonetheless like to suggest that as tropes the clouds do not symbolize the provisional nature of life (that is, the fragility of the integral self) as something negative, but rather they offer an alternative model for the self, one that acknowledges its essential contingency, one that "backs the world."

A cloud is, to be sure, an individual thing; it is discrete, discernible, and describable. But its nature is ephemeral. We are not surprised when clouds change shape, break up, dissipate, move away. Clouds are individual entities whose individuality is completely accidental. Their formation is governed by rules that are entirely external to their individual existence. They have no singular identity, no selfhood, so to speak. There is no inner principle of organization, just the arbitrary concatenation of weather conditions that makes them arise. We like to see shapes in them, the way we make shapes out of the patterns of stars that are seen—arbitrarily—from earth. We like to assign them temporary integral selves.

Rosei implies that human personalities are much more like clouds than we are happy believing, that what we take to be personality—the rule of an inner law, with a force of necessity akin to the necessity of laws of nature—is in fact as arbitrary as the temporary arrangement of water vapor molecules that is a cloud. We like to see shapes in human personalities, but if we could see a human life speeded up so that it resembled a cloud's existence, the shape of the personality might appear much more like the shape of a cloud—arbitrary, mutable, fleeting.

Furthermore, clouds are not the only such tropes in Rosei's writing. There are other phenomena that exemplify the contingent, temporary, systemic existence of what only seem to be stable individuals. To paraphrase Alan Watts, these phenomena do not come into the world, they come out of it. I have already mentioned stars, and it is significant that Rosei names one novel after clouds and one after the Milky Way, not only a formation that dwarfs human existence in time and space, but also one in which even such huge and enduring entities as stars are contingent, temporary, and dependent on their position in the system for the fact and meaning of their existence.

Stars are not merely symbols of our contingency; they are reminders that we and the clouds are in fact part of the same system. "In the sky a gap between the clouds had opened up, where the stars stood bright, and as silent points" (Wo 152). A flock of birds is a similar system of contingent selves: "The crows rose singly out of the impoverished, ash-strewn front yards and assembled in the pale, airy freedom into an excitedly glittering cloud" (R 37). Anyone who has watched a school of fish knows the strange sense that the entire assemblage has a mind of its own, like a cybernetic system in which an individual fish is only one element: "As they sailed into the harbor, a school of large fish swam alongside the now slowly gliding ship. Their backs flashed out of the depths. Look! Stars! The swarm was left behind" (M 85). Here the connection with the similar phenomenon of stars is made both visually and conceptually. Ocean waves, rivers, mountains, and forests, all of which are described throughout Rosei's fiction, are similar assemblages. Furthermore, not only natural formations have this effect; the city is also a system in which individuals are subordinate: "The city went on, thumping and percolating, off into the haze" (M 128).

What is striking about most of these descriptions is that they are merely juxtaposed to the story. They provide the backdrop before which the characters act, but usually it is unclear whether the characters are even aware of them in any critical way. The narrator himself usually refrains from suggesting a way for us to react, to integrate the background and the foreground. This is because the role of nature in our lives does not depend on our subjective reaction to it. It is simply there. Whether we find it fantastic is irrelevant; the beauty of nature is not enhanced by our enjoyment, and we are not ennobled by our enjoyment of nature. The awareness of ourselves as part of nature is not the awareness of how special we are, nor even of how special nature is. It is the awareness of our contingency. In *Project for a World without People*, Rosei writes:

> The superiority that we usually feel in the face of the imperfect natural formation suddenly changes into the knowledge that the lack of ability and limitation have not only been on the side of nature, that that which we are accustomed to seeing and esteeming as something perfect is only one case of all possible cases, but not at all an extraordinary one, as we have always assumed, but one that is just as indifferent and accidental as all the other ones are. Nature knows no deficiency, nothing is too long or two short, too wide or too narrow, everything is already in the right proportion, everything is just simply as it is. (67–68)

Nature is not marvelous—it just is. Life is good not *for* us but *with* us, and its goodness is ultimately impersonal and enjoyable, paradoxically, only in an impersonal way. The direction of enjoyment leads away from the self; it is a form of nonattachment, to use the Buddhist term. An aphorism of Kafka's puts it succinctly: "How can one be happy about the world except by fleeing toward it?"[7] If a cloud derives its beauty from the fact of our seeing it, if it needs the emotions of a self for its beauty to be realized, then its beauty is as tragic as our lives. The cloud's beauty, thus understood, will die when we stop paying attention, or when it moves off or dissipates. All clouds will lose their beauty when we die. This subjective conception of the beauty and goodness of the world is doomed to pessimism, the sort of pessimism or resignation shared by many of Rosei's characters, because it ends when the self ends.

But another version of beauty, one that is often present in Rosei, and that because of its inherent optimism can be mistaken for sentimentality, though it isn't, is the beauty that we find in clouds because we are like clouds. This is the opposite of subjectivism, for it is not finding cloud-like features in ourselves that delights us, but finding self-like features in clouds. Even if one of those features is ephemerality, it presents grounds for optimism because we can recognize ourselves as part of a bigger pattern, just as we accept clouds as products of meteorological patterns. The demise of a single cloud is not unjust or sad; it just *is*. Likewise the demise of a single person is not unjust or sad; it just *is*.

The narrator of *The Milky Way* describes our tendency to use a subjective, egotistical standard for justice:

> If we love the world, then only in triumph. As victors. We do not want to lose the spoils; we say of dying that it is unjust. But it is not unjust; it is different. Whoever is vanquished dies gladly. He wishes to face death. How many different creatures and butterflies are in the afternoon air! (95)

This reflection, which denies the integral self that plunders the world, replacing it with a self that accepts both its limits and its infinite connectedness, ends in an image of contingent existence reminiscent of clouds, birds, and fish: a swarm of insects.

In a way, Rosei's approach is the opposite of a strictly understood naturalism grounded in positivism. The detailed descriptions of settings (weather, landscape, interiors) do not show that the characters' actions depend on or are determined by their milieu. Rather, Rosei subscribes to a sort of stochastic naturalism: persons are not determined by their surroundings, rather they participate in the same processes as their surroundings, and everything, stage and actors alike, is subject to the laws of probability and entropy. Waves roll, break, and die away; clouds move past, metamorphose, and dissipate; a school of fish is temporarily organized, but always ready to disintegrate; so is a flock of birds. Trees bear leaves, shed them, and eventually die. Cities are highly organized in their centers but disperse in the direction of chaos at their edges. Galaxies, apparently like the universe itself, are dispersing over vast space and time. Likewise personalities are dynamic and threatened always by disintegration. Nature always puts everything individual at risk: it kills stars, waves, clouds, trees, and fish in the course of making galaxies, oceans, skies, forests, and schools.

Thus Rosei's clouds are not symbols of the transience of human life; they are examples of how this transience is part of a larger completeness, of which we are also a part. The seeming disjuncture between "beautiful" landscapes and disturbed humans in Rosei's fiction is the clash between complete nature and incomplete people. In his fiction Rosei restores the shock of misery amid beauty, returns us to the moment when Adam and Eve turn around to look at Eden one last time—a moment we are privileged and doomed to repeat daily, hourly, every minute. To quote from Kafka a final time, if we are always leaving Paradise, then we are always at once inside and outside of it:

> The expulsion from Paradise is in its main significance eternal: Consequently the expulsion from Paradise is final, and life in this world is irrevocable, but the eternal nature of the occurrence (or, temporally expressed, the eternal recapitulation of the occurrence) makes it nevertheless possible that not only could we live continuously in Paradise, but that we are continuously there in actual fact, whether we know it here or not. (1946, 293)

The continuous loss of unity with nature—the continuous separation of the integral self from the world—may account for the repetition of natural images in Rosei. Whether this repetition is more monotonous than the repetitions of nature in real life, that is, whether or not Rosei succeeds in applying his principle aesthetically, I leave up to the experience and taste of his readers.

Rosei's protagonists experience the self as fragmented, yet the ideology of the self as an integrated, individuated unit is so strong that they ignore their experience and seek the roots of the problem elsewhere. They use various ways to compensate for the disappointment that they are not fulfilled: sex, love, drink, drugs, nature, travel, conversation, the pursuit of money or power, art, and politics. The loss of identity has been duly noted in the literature. Peter Ensberg, for example, writes: "The 'rip through the world' also cleaves the inner world of the protagonists. The narrator in *Try Your Luck* recognizes his lack of orientation ('I didn't have a center') and asks, full of self-doubt: 'Is being solid something worth striving for?'" (1993, 207). What I have tried to suggest here is that Rosei indicates through his characters' insights, his narrators' comments, and especially through the juxtaposition of dysfunctional selves and functional environments, that being something solid is not something worth striving for, because it denies the fact, recognized by science, spiritual wisdom, and postmodern theory, but rarely experienced directly by individuals, that we are not solid. In spite of the generally accepted Western model of the self as "a separate center of feeling and action, living inside and bounded by the physical body" (Alan Watts), each self is actually "an expression of the whole realm of nature, a unique action of the total universe" (Watts again). The integral-self model fails repeatedly for Rosei's I's; his fiction decomposes them. Yet the continuous presence of images that do not so much symbolize as exemplify "the whole realm of nature"—clouds, swarms, galaxies—suggests an alternative conception, the contingent self. Perhaps this explains the aesthetic contradiction between the profound and the banal in his fiction. What we take to be profound, the suffering self, when seen as part of the "whole realm," is banal. Conversely, what we take to be banal, simple images of nature, when seen no longer as the contents of individual consciousness, but likewise as part of the "whole realm," are profound. As the narrator of *Try Your Luck* says about a moment of altered perception: "Yes, I knew about these bouts of insanity, but they were new to me. You could say: I'm yearning for a different world than this one. But it *is* this one; I only see it differently. That was the heart of my delusion, you could say, but more and more I thought to myself, this isn't madness, you're right" (SG 191–192).[8]

Notes

1. Second definition of "self" in *Webster's* (1982, 1291).

2. Well into my project I came across additional useful terminology for this distinction. Peter McLaren and Henry A. Giroux (1997) make the distinction between "identity" (the integral self) and "subjectivity," a term that "suggests an individual presence without essence. It under-

scores the contingency of identity and the fact that individuals consist of a decentered flux of subject positions, highly dependent upon discourse, social structure, repetition, memory, and affective investment to maintain a sense of coherence in a world of constant change" (24–25). I maintain my own terminology because it is more immediately descriptive, though I welcome a set of technical terms to describe what Watts, Bateson, Deleuze and Guattari, Lao Tse, and Jesus of Nazareth have already recognized. I also do not think that McLaren and Giroux would be comfortable with the implications of transcendence in the way I am defining these terms, but I think they are there in Rosei, as long as one understands this as a spiritual and physical transcendence, and not simply as a metaphysical one.

3. This law, "that genres are not to be mixed," undergoes a considerable critique by Jacques Derrida (1981, 51–77), who notes that the "law of the law of genre," which demands order and purity, has been naturalized, but because its demands cannot be met, the history of genre is a demonstration of the "madness" of genre, which nonetheless stays in control because it supplies the terms of the conflict (76–77). This parallels exactly the role of the integral self in Rosei's works—the principle of the integral self as madness, yet this principle supplies the terms of the conflict.

4. Some of Rosei's works are cited in the text by abbreviations. Except where indicated, I have provided the translations. BPZ, *Beiträge zu einer Poesie der Zukunft. Grazer Poetikvorlesung* (Contributions to a Literature of the Future. Graz Lectures on Poetics). DR, *Drei Romane*. M, *Die Milchstrasse* (The Milky Way). R, *Rebus*. SG, Das schnelle Glück. In *Wer war Edgar Allan? Von Hier nach Dort. Das schnelle Glück*. English version = TL, *Try Your Luck!* Wo, *Die Wolken* (The Clouds).

5. The contradictory reception of Rosei has been noted by Peter Ensberg (1994, 52), whose article attempts, like this one, to "shed some light" on this puzzling circumstance, with different results, as will be seen. Fuchs and Höfler's 1994 collection of academic and journalistic criticism gives a good sense of how the critics have responded to Rosei over the years. See especially Part III, "Kritiken," 255–346.

6. Peter Ensberg points out, however, that compound structures are not necessarily more intricate structures: "Rosei has not again achieved a complex structure like that in the *Edgar Allan* novel, not even in *The Milky Way* or *Rebus*" (1994, 57).

7. My translation, which I think grasps the sense slightly better than the Muirs', reads: "How can one be glad of the world, unless one is flying to it for refuge?" (Kafka 1946, 283). By explaining too much, "flying to it for refuge" eliminates the ironic surprise of fleeing *to* something

rather than from it. The original is: "Wie kann man sich über die Welt freuen, ausser wenn man zu ihr flüchtet?"

8. My translation. The published translation by Kathleen Thorpe (1994, 14), rendering "Anwandlungen von Verrücktheit" as the rather mild "flights of fancy," does not capture the connection between this phrase and the phrase "but it isn't madness." Also, "Ich sehne mich nach einer anderen Welt als dieser. Aber es ist diese; ich sehe sie nur anders" is given as "I long for a world other than this one. But it's like this: I only see things differently." This misses the point, crucial to my use of the passage, that we do not need another world, we need to see this one in a different way.

Works Cited

Appelt, Hedwig. 1994. Wie nasse Seife: Peter Roseis *Rebus*. In *Peter Rosei*. Edited by Gerhard Fuchs & Günther A. Höfler. Graz-Wien: Droschl. (Orig. *Stuttgarter Zeitung* 1/19/90.)

Bartens, Daniela. 1994. Stadt ist, wo noch keiner war. Stadt und städtische Strukturen im Werk Peter Roseis. In *Peter Rosei*. Edited by Gerhard Fuchs and Günther A. Höfler. Graz-Wien: Droschl.

Bateson, Gregory. 1972. The Cybernetics of 'Self': A Theory of Alcoholism. In *Steps to an Ecology of Mind*. New York: Ballantine Books.

Bulla, Hans Georg. 1994. Eine einfache Geschichte bemüht erzählt: Peter Roseis neues Buch *Mann and Frau*. In *Peter Rosei*. Edited by Gerhard Fuchs and Günther A. Höfler. Graz-Wien: Droschl. (Orig. *Neue Zürcher Zeitung* 10/12/84.)

Deleuze, Giles and Félix Guattari. 1987. *A Thousand Plateaus: Capitalism and Schizophrenia*. Translation and foreword by Brian Massumi. Minneapolis: University of Minnesota Press.

Derrida, Jacques. 1981. The Law of Genre. In *On Narrative*. Edited by W. J. T. Mitchell. Chicago: University of Chicago Press.

Ensberg, Peter. 1993. Poe auf der Spur. Wer war Edgar Allan? von Peter Rosei. In *Experimente mit dem Kriminalroman. Ein Erzählmodell in der deutschsprachigen Literatur des 20. Jahrhunderts*. Edited by Wolfgang Düsing. Frankfurt: Peter Lang.

Ensberg, Peter. 1994. 'Einfach unterwegs sein': Zur Wahrnehmungsproblematik und zum Problematischen der Wahrnehmung bei Peter Rosei. In *Peter Rosei*. Edited by Gerhard Fuchs and Günther A. Höfler. Graz-Wien: Droschl.

Gilmore, Leigh. 1994. The Mark of Autobiography: Postmodernism, Autobiography, and Genre. In *Autobiography and Postmodernism*. Edited by Kathleen Ashley, Leigh Gilmore, and Gerald Peters. Amherst: University of Massachusetts Press.

Kafka, Franz. 1946. *The Great Wall of China: Stories and Reflections*. Translated by Willa and Edwin Muir. New York: Schocken Books.

Kafka, Franz. 1992. *Nachgelassene Schriften und Fragmente*, Vol. 2. Edited by Jost Schillemeit. Frankfurt am Main: Fischer.

Kosler, Hans Christian. 1994. Zwei rechts, zwei links: *Komödie*—Prosa des Österreichers Peter Rosei. In *Peter Rosei*. Edited by Gerhard Fuchs and Günther A. Höfler. Graz-Wien: Droschl. (Orig. *Frankfurter Allgemeine Zeitung* 5/24/84.)

McLaren, Peter and Henry A. Giroux. 1997. Writing from the Margins: Geographies of Identity, Pedagogy, and Power. In *Revolutionary Multiculturalism: Pedagogies of Dissent for the New Millennium*. Boulder, CO: Westview Press.

Mitchell, Stephen. 1988. *Tao Te Ching*, a New English Version (with foreword and notes). New York: HarperCollins.

Musil, Robert. 1995. *The Man Without Qualities*. Translated by Sophie Wilkins; editorial consultant Burton Pike. New York: Knopf.

The New Oxford Annotated Bible. 1973. Revised Standard Edition. New York: Oxford University Press.

Rosei, Peter. 1989. *Mann und Frau* (Man and Woman). Frankfurt am Main: Fischer Taschenbuch Verlag.

Rosei, Peter. 1989. *Komödie* (Comedy). Frankfurt am Main: Fischer Taschenbuch Verlag.

Rosei, Peter. 1989. *Entwurf für eine Welt ohne Menschen* (Project for a World Without People). Stuttgart: Klett-Cotta.

Rosei, Peter. 1990. *Die Wolken* (The Clouds). Frankfurt am Main: Fischer Taschenbuch Verlag.

Rosei, Peter. 1990. *15000 Seelen* (15,000 Souls). Frankfurt am Main: Fischer Taschenbuch Verlag.

Rosei, Peter. 1990. Der Aufstand. In *Der Aufstand. Unser Landschaftsbericht*. Frankfurt am Main: Fischer Taschenbuch Verlag.

Rosei, Peter. 1991. *Die Milchstrasse* (The Milky Way). Sieben Bücher. Frankfurt am Main: Fischer.

Rosei, Peter. 1992. Von Hier nach Dort. In *Wer war Edgar Allan? Von Hier nach Dort. Das schnelle Glück. Drei Romane*. Stuttgart: Klett-Cotta. English version *From Here to There*. Translated by Kathleen Thorpe. 1991. Riverside, CA: Ariadne Press.

Rosei, Peter. 1992. Das schnelle Glück. In *Wer war Edgar Allan? Von Hier nach Dort. Das schnelle Glück. Drei Romane*. Stuttgart: Klett-Cotta. English version *Try Your Luck!* Translated by Kathleen Thorpe. 1994. Riverside, CA: Ariadne Press.

Rosei, Peter. 1992. Wer war Edgar Allan? (Who Was Edgar Allan?). In *Wer war Edgar Allan? Von Hier nach Dort. Das schnelle Glück*. Drei Romane. Stuttgart: Klett-Cotta.

Rosei, Peter. 1995. *Beiträge zu einer Poesie der Zukunft: Grazer Poetikvorlesung* (Contributions to a Literature of the Future: Graz Lectures on Poetics). Graz-Wien: Literaturverlag Droschl.

Watts, Alan. 1972. *The Book: On the Taboo against Knowing Who You Are*. New York: Vintage Books.

Webster's New World Dictionary of the American Language. 1982. New York: Simon & Shuster.

Fred Wander's Semi-Autobiographical Narrative, *The Seventh Well*— "Such stories I never heard again"

Jörg Thunecke

The twelve short stories by Jewish-born author Fred Wander (*1917)[1] collected in a slim volume titled *The Seventh Well* (1971)[2] can be classed—alongside Elie Wiesel's *Night* (1958), Tadeusz Borowski's *This Way for the Gas, Ladies and Gentlemen* (1959), Jorge Semprun's *The Long Voyage* (1963), Jurek Becker's *Jacob the Liar* (1978), Primo Levi's *Moments of Reprieve* (1981), Liana Millu's *Smoke over Birkenau* (1986), and Binjamin Wilkomirski's *Fragments* (1995)—among the few masterpieces of postwar fiction about life and death in German labor and extermination camps in the East.[3]

Vienna-born Wander fled his home country Austria after the *Anschluß* in 1938, escaping via Switzerland to France where he resided in Paris until the outbreak of World War II at the beginning of September 1939, a period vividly described in *The Room in Paris* (1975). Following Nazi Germany's imminent attack on the Low Countries and France—which eventually took place in May and June of 1940—Wander, along with thousands of German-speaking refugees in France, was interned and sent to various camps in the northwestern part of that country. Subsequent to the occupation of the northern half of France by the Germans, and the establishment of so-called Vichy-France in the southern half, Wander managed to escape to Marseilles, where he eked out a living as an exile (described in *Hotel Baalbek*, 1991), until Nazi occupation of that part of France in November 1942 (cf. Burrin 1996) forced him to once more flee, only to be turned back by the Swiss and handed over to the French authorities in the autumn of that year, to be imprisoned in the notorious Rivesaltes camp near Perpignan, and to be deported via Drancy (near Paris) to Auschwitz, Groß-Rosen, and eventually Buchenwald (near Weimar) at the end of that year.[4]

Fred Wander has told his own story in a recent autobiography (not yet available in English) titled *Das gute Leben* (*The Good Life*, 1996), the first part of which covers his exile existence in France, but the story breaks off at the very point when he arrives in Auschwitz-Birkenau and is subsequently moved to one of the satellite camps of Groß-Rosen. It seems—this at least is the author's view today[5]—that he could (and can) only write about the horrors of his camp existence in a fictionalized (or semi-fictionalized) form, and consequently had to exclude this period from his autobiographical account.[6] Chapters 15–17 of his memoirs are in fact the closest Wander gets to speaking *directly* about his initial encounter with Auschwitz (75–89), the minutae of which one therefore has to glean from the pages of *The Seventh Well* (and partly also from *Hotel Baalbek*, 198–199):

> And now to the arrival *there*. Following a period of deafening silence suddenly music could be heard. Then a hellish noise started, the doors were pulled open, and SS men jumped onto the cattle cars shouting: "All the men off!" And then they began to beat the prisoners with rifle butts. The women clung to the men, but the Jackboots beat them until blood began to splatter: "All the men oofff!" They even bashed the children over the head. The little ones, who clung to their fathers.... And immediately the weak and the sick were separated from the rest, one lot to the left, the other to the right. The weak and the sick were allowed back onto the cars, rejoining the women, the children, and the elderly. We did notice that we were on the edge of a huge camp.... Then the men capable of work were loaded onto another waiting train and driven away to a satellite camp of Groß-Rosen, as we discovered later. None of the deportees survived the next day. And following another longish journey we arrived in yet another camp, where we were subjected to the same hellish reception. The newly

arrived slave-laborers were distributed to different camps according to the demands of German industry.... The brutality and terror meted out to the deportees immediately after their arrival ... was a piece of sophisticated devilry: The intention was to paralyze the victims through sheer fear so that they would acquiesce in their fate and not offer any resistance. In this way a dozen guards were able to control thousands of prisoners. This is the only explanation of the question time and again put to the survivors: "Why did you allow yourself to be taken like sheep to the slaughter without offering any resistance?" But how is one to communicate things like that? Anybody who did not experience such events himself cannot possibly comprehend them.[7]

The question raised here by Wander partially explains why the author seems to have been unable to give a straightforward autobiographical account of his camp experiences: because all those who did not encounter such horrors first hand must find it difficult, if not impossible, to fully understand what happened. And yet Wander wanted to somehow tell *his* story; for he wholeheartedly shared Primo Levi's sentiments voiced in the opening lines of *Moments of Reprieve*: "And till my ghastly tale is told, / This heart within me burns" (13).

Consequently, in a case like Wander's, the author's narrative stance (*Erzählhaltung*) is of prime importance, as emphasized by Wander himself in a recent self-appraisal:

The stories you tell in your books obviously relate episodes of your own life, or is this not so? Did you experience everything yourself?

The answer is yes and no. In all of my writings autobiographical details can be found, but many things are purely fictitious. A fictional character can be much more appealing to the author than a character portrayal copied truthfully from reality. Fictional characters assume a life of their own, they kind of elude the author, they gain an independence of their own. And sometimes they do things, unknown even to the author himself prior to committing it to paper. That is a truly creative moment in the production of literature: the point when his own creativity overtakes the author and pulls him along. An author's real talent only reveals itself when he exceeds his own limitations and produces something the novelty of which surprises even him.[8]

The author's narrative stance gave rise to various critical evaluations, above all the one by the once highly acclaimed GDR authoress Christa Wolf, who maintained—as early as 1972, reprinted in an afterword to the first West Germany edition of *The Seventh Well* in 1985—that:

> Wander made the problem of story-telling, of talking per se, in historical circumstances like these, the main motif of his book. Starting with the first chapter ... he ponders the preconditions of human language, of addressing and of talking to another person—especially if such fundamental issues ... are subject to severe punishment. For not just sophisticated language, not just literature ... but every single word, quietly and truthfully uttered, constitutes a danger for the system if it opposes the crazy irrationality of dumb criminals. (Wolf 1972, 863)

Wander—in an interview with Wolfgang Tampe in 1971, following the publication of *The Seventh Well* that year in the GDR—gave two reasons for the twenty-five-year delay in writing down his holocaust stories: On the one hand, he insisted, he first had to *personally* come to grips with the horrific experiences of the immediate past, and on the other he had to find an adequate literary form for such stories (Tampe 1971). The form he eventually adopted was that of Chassidic narratives (cf. Reiter 1996), as the author told Stephan Steiner and Judith Veichtlbauer in an interview in 1997: "I consider myself a story-teller in an age-old Jewish tradition, going from village to village, talking to people, listening to their tales or inventing some myself" (Steiner and Veichtlbauer 1997, 47), a point expanded by Andrea Reiter:

> Fred Wander's premise "How do I communicate what I have to say?" dominates the first chapter of *Der siebente Brunnen*, a series of narrations arranged approximately in chronological order. In "Wie erzählt man eine Geschichte" the first-person narrator is taught by his fellow inmate Mendel Teichmann; at the same time this is also a story within a story—demonstrating that it is not so much the factual detail which is important as the atmosphere that must be recreated. It is these poetological guidelines which Wander adheres to not only in *Der siebente Brunnen* but also, and even more to the point, in *Hotel Baalbek* where he actually describes a house and its inhabitants in the fashion suggested by Teichmann. (Reiter 1996, 6)

But story-telling in Wander's case—as with the other authors mentioned above—also became a way to survive during the postwar era, as the author explained in the same interview: "One way to survive is telling stories."[9] However, as emphasized by Reiter, Wander offers little insight into his *personal* survival at Buchenwald and its satellite camps, where the majority of stories are situated: "Instead he confines himself to recording the fate of his fellow inmates.... Following the Chassidic tradition of story-telling he lets some of them talk themselves—each of them temporarily assuming the role of a *Batlen*, a jester, philosopher and story-teller" (Reiter 1996, 6), an issue also taken up by novelist Hans-Josef Ortheil in a review of *The Good Life*:

> Story-telling referred Wander back to the years he had spent in concentration camps: it rekindled in him memories of how to survive on the brink of death, of how to mirror and capture in his stories life's infinite variety. The heir to an ancient Chassidic tradition, whose last witnesses Wander had met in Auschwitz and Buchenwald. (Ortheil 1996, 33)

The specificity of Wander's narratives about German concentration camps is in fact an attempt to supersede and replace Nazi policies of annihilation, as argued by Steiner and Veichtlbauer (1997):

> The physical and mental destruction survives in the memory of his dead friends; at the same time, the possibility of an ultimate Nazi victory is fiercely denied by making life, not death, the center of camp activities.

This last statement also explains why in the past various critics labeled Wander's early collection of Holocaust stories a response (*Gegenentwurf*) to the NS extermination camps,[10] turning these camps into literary loci, which—above and beyond the horror scenario—reveal glimpses of humanity among the torture and destruction (cf. Grünzweig 1996, 11). Or, as the reviewer of the *Salzburger Nachrichten* put it: "He adopts a different moral viewpoint. He tries to commemorate the victims, not by showing them at their lowest point, the result of constant demoralization and humiliation, but by presenting them as dignified human beings" (Thuswaldner 1986, 9). To this end Wander did not allow himself to be wallowing in pity for the victims who suffered and died in the concentration camps, nor did he permit himself to be overwhelmed by self-pity. By maintaining a certain distance Wander in fact tried to paint a more differentiated picture of those who are often presented (and sometimes misrepresented) as pitiable victims:

> The comrades of these bitter years are presented neither as saints, untouched by filth and illness, nor as supermen, able to cope with every situation. They are scholars, traders, artisans, intellectuals, peasants, laborers; people of varying individuality, ideas, attitudes, character, joined together by their will to survive and ... in the dignity of their final hours. (Czollek 1971, 157)

Similarly, Christa Wolf, in her early review of *The Seventh Well*, stressed the variety of individuals—eighteen in all, listed on the cover of the 1985 Luchterhand edition—depicted by Wander in his twelve stories: "Strong and weak ones, rebellious and passive ones, proud and humble ones, pious and impious ones, young and old ones, Jews from all over Europe as well as Frenchmen, Russians, Ukrainians, and Poles" (Wolf 863).

Fred Wander's narrative approach in *The Seventh Well* is twofold: he is telling stories about the fate of fellow camp inmates, while at the same time he is giving some of these very inmates the opportunity to relate their own stories (cf. Bächli 1985, 26). As a kind of reader's guidance, the author's overall approach adopted in this collection is outlined in the opening tale, titled "How to Tell a Story," where a Jewish prisoner, Mendel Teichmann, described as a magician of the word, is being portrayed as capable of performing miracles with his stories on fellow inmates by captivating their minds and, at least for short periods of time, allowing them to forget their hardships (Reiter 7):[11] "The word, scarcely heard, resounded, made men turn pallid, it transformed them, turned them inwards, made them pour forth tears and laughter, scourged them, made them sigh and even sweat" (12). And it seems to have been this very Mendel Teichmann who induced Wander to take up the business of story-telling, albeit with a twenty-five-year delay, with tales that reflect his *own* experiences in various concentration camps, but merely at a *semi-*autobiographical level: for it was never the author's intention to examine himself under extreme conditions (Reiter 6). Allowing a quarter of a century to pass before putting pen to paper seems to have had quite a maturing effect on the author's creativity though, because in the opening story of *The Seventh Well* the narrator still reveals a youthful lack of insight into the art of story-telling, for which he is rebuked by Teichmann, the master craftsman:

> So you've understood nothing. I talk and talk and you don't understand me.... There are powers concealed in people, but they don't know it. They waste away, crippled. Their pores are stopped up, their eyes are blind, but life rushes on, all this force, which they don't know what to do with, breaks its shell, breaks out of its house and laws, lashes out without direction. (16–17)

So story-telling has its problems, and Wander elaborates on these difficulties in the tale that immediately follows the opening one, giving vent to ideas that could well be reflecting the author's *own* position during his years in Buchenwald and other camps. "What does man live on?" the narrator asks, venturing the following answer:

> His humiliated soul withdraws deep into unexplored places ... He observes his fellow prisoners ... But he is withdrawn, ... searches for the forgotten traces of beauty in his life ... He intoxicates himself with the past ... He must scream it out: I am a human being. He wanted to say, I was respected, I was loved, I had a home, a wife and children and friends. I helped people and demanded no thanks for it ... There was nothing I couldn't have achieved and if I had not achieved it, it was only because I didn't know, had no idea ... He wanted to call all that out, to shine, to brag, to argue, breathless. But the words failed him, the art failed him. (20–21)

However, "man lives from the hope that the dream of his lost beautiful life, of freedom, and of purity of the heart has not died out"; and consequently three inmates—de Groot, the Jewish tailor from Amsterdam; Tschukran, the Turkish Jew from Tours; and Feinberg, the resistance fighter from Paris—are shown in Chapter 2 ("What Man Lives On") to vie with each other in telling the story of their lives, passing details from person to person much the same way as they pass heavy logs from man to man at the labor camp attached to a cellulose factory near Phrixa in the Riesengebirge (24). "Those who were fulfilled," the narrator informs his readers, "stayed alive, those who wanted to drink of life to the last drop—even if it be a cup of poison." He concludes rather emphatically (32): "The dream was not dead!"[12] Wolfgang Tampe, commenting on Wander's technique of characterization, thought that the protagonists in *The Seventh Well* do not necessarily leave an indelible imprint in the reader's imagination: "They don't seem to have any special traits, any outstanding qualities, which one immediately recalls and feels inclined to imitate." They just tell their own life story, which for the most part becomes submerged in the reader's subconsciousness: "But what becomes submerged of these fictitious stories forms a layer on which one can build, which may not always be readily available, but which slowly grows on us, and which can be added to the fountain of useful ideas about human existence" (Tampe 1972, 381–382).

"Writing for Wander always meant story-telling, and in such circumstances the revival and transmission of stories about past lives and events becomes a means of survival" (Wieghaus 2; cf. Renolder 1987), as already mentioned above. This is particularly well illustrated in the title story "The Seventh Well," the fifth in the sequence, in which East European Jews are portrayed as fantasizing about their past lives, which they will never be able to resume:

> No more exciting stories from the life never to be again, chassidic sophistry, *bonkes* and memories; a train with nought but dreams, feverish traveling through somber German forests. Dreams of melancholy-gay Warsaw and sunburned Provence, dreams of Vienna and Paris, and the black coal fields of Charleroi. (45)

"I know the stories of the dead lying there on the front platform," the narrator informs his readers during the fatal train journey back to Buchenwald from a previous camp near the Riesengebirge area. He defers to Meir Bernstein, the Ukrainian peasant, who always starts his tales with the phrase "It's a story, I want to tell" (47),[13] or to Mendel Teichmann, the Polish Jew mentioned earlier, after which both of them in turn proceed to tell stories in Yiddish of the *shtetl*, conjuring up a world irretrievably lost:

> Meir Berstein and Mendel Teichmann had taken turns telling

stories, had reveled in words, had conjured up the aroma that pervades the narrow alleys on *yom tov*, in front of the houses of the refined Jews, enticing the poor who stand at the doors waiting for a donation. The aroma of roasted veal and fish, of onions and wine vinegar, raisin-cake and bitter oranges. The shining eyes of children, singing and roguish laughter, and the giggling of the little girls. (51)

By constantly being exposed to the tales of his Jewish fellow inmates from all over Europe, the first-person narrator becomes intimately familiar with some of the continent's main cultural centers he has never visited: "Without ever having been to Odessa, in Granada, in Riga, Lemberg or Kursk," he admits, "I got to know the smell of the old cities, in the barracks black at night, from sporadic, restless words, melancholy confessions, declarations of love to a place, a suburban street, a scanty backyard garden with a pear tree, the mossy steps in a quiet garden, a small house" (91), a personal experience that the author—in a pronounced autobiographical passage (Chapter 9, titled "The Smell of the Old Cities")—revives in the stories of the Parisian Jew Feinberg, who for forty years lived in the Rue des Rosiers, a Jewish alley, just like in Poltava where he originated: "An alley full of miserable dreamers, who curse at you if you don't treat them like a bourgeois! With fools and thieves in all old cities, visionaries, artless speculators, who'd like to sell you the blue sky if you're a stranger and are insulted if you don't trust their honesty" (91–92). A street where Moische Kuhn sells fish, Chaim Silberstein repairs shoes, and Jitzchok Lemberger collects old newspapers. "A back alley full of crazy things, full of suffering and small joys," where you "don't mind the external appearances, the noise, the stench, the dealers who pester you, the pale bewildered faces with the perplexed eyes, the obscure execrations, the exaggerations, the fantastic notions" (93), where—while an ocean rages at the surface—you must look into the depths to find a Jewish watchmaker who has sacrificed his whole life for an invention, but is too sick now to benefit from it; or a Jewish hospital attendant-cum-poet who never published a single line but read out his poems aloud to his patients and told them stories—stories, as the narrator claims, the likes of which he will never hear again in his life.

What Wander tries to achieve in stories like these is to immortalize—fictionally or semi-fictionally—European Jews from all walks of life, good ones and bad ones, rich ones and poor ones, who perished in the Holocaust, *not* as an act of revenge, and *not* as a way of getting even with the perpetrators, but as a way of *personally* coming to terms with the past, of purging himself, as conveyed in the words of Rabbi Löw at the end of Chapter 5 (51): "The seventh well—water of pureness, / freed of all impurities; / impervious to pollution and turbidness; / of immaculate transparence; / ready for future generations, / that they might alight from the darkness, / their eyes clear, their hearts freed,"[14] and as explained in the author's open letters to fellow Italian writer and camp inmate, Primo Levi:

> The expurgation of our past, the coming to grips with and reappraisal of it cannot be accomplished by political decisions, decrees, or might, but can only be achieved through one's daily struggle with oneself, or, to quote Goethe, through the "insatiable desire to be purified!" (Wander 1982, 23)

Only in this way, it seems, was Fred Wander able to come to terms with the past, his own past included; he could tell stories "without being overwhelmed by them or recounting them in an unacceptable conciliatory fashion" (Wolf 863). A good example of this purifying process can be found in Chapter 8 ("Blues for Five Fingers on a Board"); here the narrator—in this instance undoubtedly recounting the author's very *own* experience—is telling Pépé, a political prisoner and former French resistance fighter, the story of Erich Pechmann while they are lying in their bunks at night in block sixteen at Buchenwald camp: "The pictures descended upon me and I got a lump in my throat" (83), the narrator recalls, and then proceeds to tell the story of their imprisonment at Rivesaltes near Perpignan, a moving tale of camp life in Southern France in late 1942, of the community spirit, of a love affair and its sad ending, of separation, deportation, and broken spirits. "I had been talking for some time," the narrator informs his readers, "while all around in block sixteen in Buchenwald everything was asleep.... But Pépé didn't grow weary of listening. He crawled over to me, put his ear almost in my mouth and asked: And then what, where did you see Pechmann again? And did he find his Marina there?—No, I whispered, he didn't find Marina again" (90).

The stories in *The Seventh Well* also pay special attention to various strategies for staying alive (*Überlebensstrategien;* Wieghaus 4) designed by camp inmates, focusing not so much on the desperate battle for survival but on possible ways of developing responses (*Gegenentwürfe*) that allow glimpses of humanity in a world of atrocities. One such response can be gleaned in Chapter 6 in the personal valor of the youthful sick-bay attendant Karel (54–65), who—while maintaining that "sentimentality is a Jewish sickness" (56)—was capable of performing merciful operations on fellow inmates that the physician in charge, Dr. Lewin, was unable to carry out. Another and even better example of such survival strategies (in Chapter 10, titled "Forest"[15]), was Tadeusz Moll, the boy from Auschwitz, whom the narrator first met in the Crawinkel camp near Arnstadt in Thuringia. "I ask myself," he marvels, "what inexhaustible strength of mind must dwell in this young person. How could a sixteen-year-old endure the gas chamber without suffering damage?" (105). Moll, who obviously had a guardian angel (110), and who survived Auschwitz, not to mention various other assaults on his life, seems to have fascinated Wander: it is one of those tales in which he merged facts and fiction, turning it into a prime example of a *realistisches Zeitdokument* in which the author managed to "absorb fictitious characters and elements, to 'encapsulate' history in stories."[16] Wander himself—as he stressed in more than one interview—constantly designed survival strategies for himself during his camp years, and consequently seems to have been especially interested in those cases where an inmate's will is shown to break, his reflexes become paralyzed, and the fight for survival ceases, as happened with Tadeusz Moll—who was "at that point in that dangerous condition of struggle on the razor's edge between the will to live and the growing longing for peace. Simply give up and sink down" (112)—and as it happened also in the case of a Ukrainian farmer in the penultimate chapter of *The Seventh Well*, titled "Faces":

> The face of a Ukrainian peasant plodding along with sore feet. A face like a beet field, brown and tanned with deep furrows and two watery blue eyes, clear, bright and open, like the sky above. It has doubtless never known any leisure days. Work

has hardened it. No muscle in it, made for deceiving, and yet cunning too.... On the evening of the first day on this convoy ... his eyes lost all color. They became white and looked at things from a terrifying distance.... His steps got heavier and heavier. The languor of salvation hovered above his figure which bent over more and more, and the tension in his face loosened. (129)

This man's will to continue as a human being quite obviously had gone—but in *The Seventh Well* such a mental decline does not necessarily go hand in glove with an equivalent physical deterioration; instead a "process of etherealization" (*Prozeß der Vergeistigung*) sets in:

> You've never seen such great solemnity, composure and dignity in him. How was he able to hide it? But then you grasp it: the face of man is millennia old. The few years of life have fallen away, all that is superfluous and weak. There remains but the face of mankind. (129)

Thus, even in the face of death, Wander's voice is free from hatred (cf. Wolf 862), and he is seen to be extolling the benefits of staying alive whenever feasible: "Why did one savor a life to the last drop that had nothing to offer but humiliation and suffering?" the narrator wonders: "Or did it have something else to offer? Did it have a value hidden to us survivors?" (118) "When a human being is about to die, he discovers the magic of existence" (123) is the author's tentative conclusion, reminiscent of the narrator's defiant words following the execution of Tadeusz Moll and four other inmates: "Hold out children, life is beautiful" (106), a sentiment further underpinned in the following simile: "The rock lives forever, it suns itself, bathes in crystal water, all the splendor on earth is forever its. Does it know that? It doesn't. But man knows and pays with his life!" (122)

In an interview with Stephan Steiner and Judith Veichtlbauer cited earlier, Fred Wander claimed that everything he had written up to that point in time was the story of his own life: "Im Grunde ist das ganze ein Buch: mein Leben." In another, earlier interview with Wolfgang Tampe he maintained that his main literary theme was "the process of becoming a human being," of which *The Seventh Well* was but an excerpt (Tampe 1971). However, looking at the final episode of *The Seventh Well* ("Joschko and his Brothers"), one is struck by the glances of Buchenwald children and begins to wonder to what extent the author in fact succeeded in supplying evidence for such a process of humanization: "His [Joschko's] face is dark and serious. The cold and tragic seriousness of a stalked animal.... Questioning but without emotion his eyes penetrate me. A deep wrinkle above his nose indented his boyish forehead." "In vain," the narrator laments, "I sought the bloom of childhood in his glance. Had these little human animals once lived in rooms, slept in beds, been fed by mothers' breasts?" (136). "Many a person might say that the camp, the bestial conditions of the camp had destroyed their human substance" (139–140).

At the zero point of the Third Reich and the hour of liberation of Buchenwald camp on 11 April 1945, "the wall of Jericho had fallen, but Joschko and his brothers hadn't heard the trumpet. They didn't see the open gate to freedom because they didn't know what freedom was." "A kind of ecstasy," the narrator admits, "had taken hold of me; I alone seemed to know what this hour meant."

> But it wasn't the victory screams of the fellow prisoners ... which penetrated to us in a muffled form, nor the whizzing sound of bullets from the rifles in the hands of prisoners, nor the dim singsong of the Allied air squadrons above us, the thundering of the tanks, that wasn't the jubilation that filled me ... It was the face of Joschko and his brothers! These simple faces madly greedy for food and life. (139)

In response to what seems quite a justified question, a decisive reply is given: No, it is not true, the children's human substance has not been destroyed! "At ten Joschko was already father and tribe-elder. The way he guarded the little brother, never let him out of his sight, the wild seriousness of his care, the angry determination to see the youngest one through—wasn't that the whole greatness and dignity of mankind?" (140).

> The way they sat there now, round about the iron stove, close to one another, dirty, scrawny, worn down to the bone, the way they turned over the slices of potatoes, the crackling, steaming potatoes and at the same time eyed everyone else mistrustfully while slyly taking care not to excite the attention of the others; the way they then distributed among themselves

Jörg Thunecke 255

the miserable booty, the tiny portions, as if it were a ritual meal of delicious smelling food, the way they greedily shoved the burning hot potato slivers into their mouths, the way Joschko patiently fed his brother Naftali so weak, he wanted to sleep, the way he kept him awake, fed him the hot smelling stuff of life, and the way their eyes glowed and sparkled. (140)

"I knew then," the narrator concludes: "that nothing is lost!" (140). This is Fred Wander's ultimate message, at the end of *The Seventh Well*, the upshot of his "plea for survival."[17] "A world turned upside-down," as Christa Wolf insisted, "returns to normality" (Wolf 865). Watching, and talking to the author today raises slight suspicion whether such sentiments apply to Fred Wander himself, and one wonders if they have a genuine autobiographical base, or whether they are not merely the result of wishful thinking, the fiction of the author's imagination. After all, reflecting—like Brecht in his famous poem "Was sind das für Zeiten"—on the crimes committed in the camps of the Thuringian forests, quite a different picture emerges:

> The smell of the forest, the picture of the forest, the quietness of the deep wood, the rustling in the treetops, the majestic swaying of the towering trees in the wind—for all time for me the fragrance of the forest will be mixed with the smell of burning and with the picture of the poison white smoke over the naked bodies of the dead. (113)

While it may be impossible to say much about the death of six million Jews, it is unquestionably true that "one could tell a story about three or four of them";[18] and it is also true that Fred Wander made a valiant attempt to capture the unspeakable in *The Seventh Well* (cf. Gauß 1996, 6). The question remains though: what sort of story! For in the last resort even the narrator—and that surely means the author himself—seems unsure. The best example of this is the story of Lubitsch (in Chapter 7, titled "Ezekiel and the City"), the only genuine intellectual in *The Seventh Well*, who declaims verses of Baudelaire in French (37) and sets up a debating society to maintain his sanity in the inferno surrounding him (74–75). Ultimately, serious doubt is cast on Lubitsch's efforts, and a big question mark remains whether this is the right kind of "demonstration against barbarism" (76). So, despite the positive note on which the twelfth and final story of

Wander's collection ends, one wonders if deep down the author does not feel more in tune with the ambiguous ending of Jurek Becker's *Jacob the Liar*, leaving the decision of the overall message to his readers.

Notes

1. Cf. 425–426 in *Katalog-Lexikon der öesterreichischen Literature des 20. Jahrhunderts*, edited by IG Autoren-Solidaritaet (Wien); cf. also Georg Wieghaus (1985, pp. 1–5), "Fred Wander." See also the bibliography A–C on Wander by Michael Töteberg and Georg Wieghaus.

2. In the German original, the passage I have used in the title reads: "solche Geschichten hab ich nie wieder gehört" (94).

3. Cf. Matthias Brand (1981, pp. 133–142); cf. also Kay Seyffahrt's comment in "Die Welt vom Tiefparterre aus gesehen" (1996, p. 6), calling *The Seventh Well* "one of the most important literary testimonies of life and death in concentration camps"; and Erich Hackl, "Ich gehörte niemals irgendwo dazu" (1996, p. 67).

4. This part of Wander's story is authentic (cf. Chapter 26 of *Hotel Baalbek*, pp. 197–199).

5. In an interview with Fred Wander in Vienna on 20 July 1998.

6. Cf. Ulrich Weinzierl's criticism of *Das gute Leben* in a review in the *Frankfurter Allgemeine Zeitung* 3 December 1996: "Nonchalant mißachtet der Autor die Regeln, die perfekte 'Erinnerungen' verbürgen."

7. *Das gute Leben*, pp. 82–84 (all translations in this paper are by the author).

8. Fred Wander (1995, 40), "Nicht jeder braucht eine Heimat. Selbstbefragung 1994." Cf. also Klemens Renolder (1994, 101), "Über Fred Wander."

9. Tampe (1971); cf. also *Das gute Leben*, p. 76.

10. Cf. for example Werner Brettschneider (1979, 35), *Zorn und Trauer. Aspekte der deutschen Gegenwartsliteratur*; cf. also Christa Wolf's comment: "In this response [*Gegenentwurf*] the author does not contrast love and hatred, goodness and sadism, gentleness and violence, or even forgiveness and crime, but justice and injustice" (p. 863).

11. All references are from the 1976 English translation; page numbers follow in brackets.

12. Cf. Otto Gotsche's (1972, 988) comment, who knew Wander personally during his GDR days: "He said it all very quietly but quite emphatically, and the truth it conveyed rose like a sad song, encompassing the whole being."

13. "Hert mich ojss [...] well ich ajch dazejln a majsse" (46–47).

14. Cf. citation from *The Seven-Well-Heads* by Rabbi Löw, Judah ben

Bezalel (Prague, 1520–1609), preceding *The Seventh Well* as a motto.

15. This is a poor translation of the original German chapter heading, "Woran erinnert dich Wald?" (Memories of the Forest).

16. Anita Pollak (1992, 52): "fiktive Personen und Elemente verarbeitet, Geschichte in Geschichten 'verdichtete'."

17. Cf. Hannes Krauss, "Plädoyer für das Überleben." In: "Reise-Erinnerungen—die nachgetragenen Exilerfahrungen Fred Wanders." Paper delivered at the International Conference on the Aesthetics of Exile at the University of Vermont, Burlington, on 19 September 1998.

18. *Das gute Leben*, p. 100.

Works Cited

Bächli, Samuel. 1985. Das Lachen der Gestiefelten. In *Frankfurter Allgemeine Zeitung* 17 April.

Becker, Jurek. 1986. *Jacob the Liar*. New York: Arcade.

Borowski, Tadeusz. 1967. *This Way for the Gas, Ladies and Gentlemen; and Other Stories*. New York: Viking.

Brand, Matthias. 1981. Stacheldrahtleben. Literatur und Konzentrationslager. In *Sammlung. Jahrbuch für antifaschistische Literatur* 4.

Brettschneider, Werner. 1979. *Zorn und Trauer. Aspekte der deutschen Gegenwartsliteratur*. Berlin: E. Schmidt.

Burrin, Philippe. 1996. *France under the Germans*. New York: The New Press.

Czollek, Walter. 1971. Begegnung mit der Vergangenheit. In *neue deutsche literatur*, Pt. 12; reprinted as "Im Inferno des Faschismus" in *Die Tat* 16 October 1971.

Gauß, Karl-Markus. 1996. Ein Außenseiter. In *Die Zeit* 8 November.

Gotsche, Otto. 1972. Ein Vierteljahrhundert danach. In *Die Weltbühne* 1 August.

Grünzweig, Walter. 1996. Die Parallelen von Himmel und Hölle. In *Der Standard* (Wien) 31 October/1 November.

Hackl, Erich. 1996. Ich gehörte niemals irgendwo dazu. In *Weltwoche* (Zürich) 31 October.

Levi, Primo. 1988. *Moments of Reprieve*. London: Abacus.

Millu, Liana. 1991. *Smoke over Birkenau*. Philadelphia: The Jewish Publication Society.

Ortheil, Hans-Josef. 1996. Skizziertes Leben. In *Neue Zürcher Zeitung* 26 November.

Pollak, Anita. 1992. Vergangenheit dichten. In *Kurier* (Wien) 15 February.

Reiter, Andrea. 1996 (Summer). "Was mich entmenschlicht hat, ist Ware geworden, die ich feilhalte": Concentration Camp Experience of Jean Améry and Fred Wander. In *The Journal of Holocaust Education* 5.

Renolder, Klemens. 1987. Spät heim nach Wien. In *Die Presse* (Wien) 10/11 January.
Renolder, Klemens. 1994. Über Fred Wander. In *Literatur und Kritik* 283/284.
Semprun, Jorge. 1964. *The Long Voyage*. New York: Schocken.
Seyffahrt, Kay. 1996. Die Welt vom Tiefparterre aus gesehen. *Jüdische Allgemeine Zeitung* 27 December.
Steiner, Stephan and Judith Veichtlbauer. 1997. "Ein besessenes Wachsein." In *Falter* (Wien) 1 February.
Tampe, Wolfgang. 1971. Fred Wander: "Der siebente Brunnen." In *Sonntag* 16 May.
Tampe, Wolfgang. 1972. Episoden. In Annie Vogtländer, Ed. *Liebes- und andere Erklärungen*. Berlin: Aufbau.
Thuswaldner, Anton. 1986. Schreiben gegen den Unverstand. In *Salzburger Nachrichten* 15 January.
Wander, Fred. 1976. *The Seventh Well*. New York: International. (Original German version: *Der siebente Brunnen. Erzählung*. Berlin: Aufbau, 1971).
Wander, Fred. 1982. Brief an Primo Levi. In *Sammlung. Jahrbuch für antifaschistische Literatur* 5.
Wander, Fred. 1994. *Hotel Baalbek. Roman*. Frankfurt am Main: S. Fischer; 1991.
Wander, Fred. 1995. Nicht jeder braucht eine Heimat. Selbstbefragung 1994. In *Literatur und Kritik* 293/294.
Wander, Fred. 1995. *Ein Zimmer in Paris Erzählungen*. Frankfurt am Main: S. Fischer; 1975.
Wander, Fred. 1996. *Das gute Leben. Erinnerungen*. München: Carl Hanser.
Wieghaus, Georg. 1985. Fred Wander. In Heinz-Ludwig Arnold, Ed. *Kritisches Lexikon zur deutschsprachigen Gegenwartsliteratur* Bd. 3. München.
Wiesel, Elie. 1960. *Night*. New York: Hill & Wang.
Wilkomirski, Binjamin. 1995. *Fragments: Memories of a Wartime Childhood*. New York: Schocken 1996.
Wolf, Christa. 1972. Gedächtnis und Gedenken. In *Sinn und Form*, Pt. 4. (Reprinted in Christa Wolf's [1985, 153] "Nachwort" to *Der siebente Brunnen*. Darmstadt: Luchterhand.)

The I as Fiction: A Conversation with Peter Rosei

The following interview took place on June 15, 1997, in Taos, New Mexico, where Peter Rosei was Guest Artist in Residence at the Deutsche Sommerschule. Interviewers were Karl Doerry and Nicholas J. Meyerhofer.

NJM: Peter, it's somewhat customary in these situations to begin with biographical questions that you have no doubt answered many times before in other interviews. But these are important questions for American readers who may not be terribly familiar with you and your writing. So once again: tell us a bit about your childhood and how you came to be a writer.

PR: In Europe these kinds of questions still come up all the time, too. All of this has been dealt with in some detail before, in German in the Literaturverlag Droschl edition *Peter Rosei*, and in English in Wilhelm Schwarz's *Conversations with Peter Rosei*.

NJM: As an American, it's my distinct impression that in our culture and society a "writer" is somehow a bit more exotic than in Austria or in Europe in general, and for this reason biographical questions are of great interest.

PR: I think you're right about that, and it probably has to do with the different economic situation over here. In Austria the "free-lance writer" as a type or as a special breed is dying out, simply because it's becoming more and more difficult to make a living as a writer if one doesn't have other employment or regular assistance from the television industry or whatever. So what we have in the long run is an evolution into two different kinds of writers who can still make it: either as someone churning out best sellers or as a university professor.

KD: And that's considered normal or typical over here where a professor directs, say, a Creative Writing Program at a university and therefore has a regular income and secure existence as a result of his or her writing talent.

PR: Right, and you see this binary evolution in the publishing industry over here too, where you've got giant publishing houses that print the best sellers, and then you've got the smaller university presses who take their chances on a different kind of writing. Or else you're a Wallace Stevens, who's an insurance agent or whatever by day and a lyric poet by night. Or who was this other poet, the doctor in New Jersey? What's his name again—he's really one of my favorite poets.

KD: You mean William Carlos Williams?

PR: Exactly, that's him, he continued to work as a doctor in New Jersey his entire life. I mean, the fact that you're born an artist doesn't necessarily mean you're going to make a living doing this.

KD: And I think that an important difference between America and Europe is to be seen in the conception of what an artist is. In Europe an artist is a kind of "ornament," if you will, and familiarity with art and artists is simply seen as part of being educated or civilized.

PR: This is dying out in Europe now, too.

KD: Probably, but it still strikes me as part of the middle class lifestyle over there.

PR: No no, I really think this has all but died out now. And I think this has to do with the influence of the Left from the sixties, where literature and art in this bourgeois sense were called into question. That's how it was for us as artists in the seventies, where we saw ourselves as the ones who were to proclaim a new lifestyle. I mean, that's the way it was for me, too. I completed my law degree but never practiced law, since I wanted a different lifestyle.

NJM: And it was never your intention to earn your living as a lawyer?

PR: No, even while I was studying law it was clear that this couldn't lead to a profession for me—law, with its emphasis on power and exercising force. I mean, to practice law is also to speak a particular language, and of course it's advantageous to know this language, since knowing it can be helpful if one is interested in analyzing society. Just as it's an advantage to know the technical jargon of business, for example. But to constantly pass judgment on people, to practice law as a profession or be a judge, no.

KD: And the law has its own definition of truth: truth is that for which you can find at least two witnesses.

PR: Yes, that was probably part of it, too.

KD: And when you've got two witnesses, then you can pass judgment.

NJM: So was it always your intention to become a writer?

PR: Well, of course I started writing at an early age, but you have to remember it was different in those days than it is now. Back then jobs were plentiful; young people had fewer problems than today. I had lots of friends, for instance, who were involved in theater. They simply did this and weren't too concerned about tomorrow. I probably started writing in order to articulate problems, societal problems as I saw them through the eyes of a young person. And I felt that I was faced with the choice of supporting either those who were in power or those who were politically involved in challenging the power elite. Neither choice particularly appealed to me, since it seemed to me I'd be losing my freedom of movement either way. Of course I'm looking back at this now with the benefit of hindsight, but that's the way I think I felt back then. Those were hard times for me, because I didn't like to be faced with this difficult choice. So I became a private secretary for a painter, Ernst Fuchs, and worked as an art dealer.

NJM: And you did this for two years?

PR: Yes, a bit longer. He was really taking off in popularity, and we made deals for millions. And for me this was good experience, as I became acquainted with art and the art market from its more cynical side.

NJM: How do you mean that?

PR: Well, you know, you've got this conception of artists as geniuses on Mt. Olympus and so on, and now you see the marketing side of the operation and how things are pushed and publicized and so on, especially with respect to the markets in America and Japan at that time. And the second wave of those who were interested in this art were lots of hippies, since it was so-called psychedelic art. And so this experience for me was a good baptism by fire, to experience this marketing side of the art industry.

KD: And it's precisely this aspect of art that is repressed in bourgeois culture.

PR: Yes, completely. Even more so in petite bourgeois society.

NJM: Did you start by writing poetry or prose?

PR: With prose, but most of the early stuff I threw away. I've continued to throw away lots of my writing over the years.

KD: Do you mean thrown away for good, or simply revised later?

PR: Both. Some of it thrown away for good. For instance, everything I've written here in America has wound up getting thrown out. It's been useful to be here, to experience America and do my thinking over here, but with the single exception of the notes on poetics that appear in the Droschl book, I haven't kept anything I've written here.

KD: When I read *Der Fluß der Gedanken durch den Kopf. Logbücher* [The Flow of Thoughts Through the Mind: Logbooks, 1976], I was amazed to see the Ulenspiegel figure.

PR: You mean that he goes to America?

KD: No, I mean I know him from my own youth in north Germany, where he was a popular figure, and I was wondering if he's also a traditional figure in the folklore of Austria or in the country's mythological consciousness.

PR: No, there was a different reason behind this. It had to do with language and with what Ulenspiegel does with it, how he reacts to those in power by twisting semantic meanings and then doing exactly the opposite of what he was told to do. It's of course a strategy for remaining true to yourself in difficult circumstances. That's what interested me in this Ulenspiegel; maybe I felt a certain kinship to him. It all has to do with the old adage that "Knowledge is power." But you see, the powerless have knowledge too, but they're not able to act on it, and Ulenspiegel had a strategy for doing this. And he does so without overtly taking sides; he's completely an individual anarchist.

NJM: The classic court jester.

PR: Yes, but not really, either, since he liberates himself from this setting. He's more the communal fool. And I saw a certain affinity between Ulenspiegel and my own circle of friends, Artmann and the others—they were all practically individual anarchists, too. They weren't part of a movement as such, but were more interested in self-realization. But this has its political dimension, too, because others read you and can compare their situation to yours.

KD: But in contrast to Artmann and those of that generation, you seem to be more private.

PR: What do you mean by "private?"

KD: Oh, I suppose I mean a Thomas Bernhard and more "spectacular" pieces that create a furor.

PR: Well, his was a more radical position, you could say, and this has something to do with one's personality, as well. Also, I'm essentially someone who writes prose, and prose authors have to lead a rather lonely life in order to produce. Prose is extremely demanding in terms of lots of quiet time.

NJM: Since you've mentioned Artmann, I wonder if he could be cited as an early influence on you, and if the same might be said of Wittgenstein or even Oswald Wiener, whose "novel" *Die Verbesserung von Mitteleuropa* (The Improvement of Middle Europe) I read many years ago. He seems to be completely forgotten now, wouldn't you say?

PR: Ossi? Not at all!

NJM: No? Where's he living now?

PR: He's living north of here in the Yukon Territory. And I would say that Ossi had more influence on Austrian art than anyone else from the group. [Editor's note: Rosei is here referring to the so-called Wiener Gruppe, a group of avant-garde Viennese writers active during the fifties and early sixties. The most significant members of the coterie were H. C. Artmann, G. Rühm, Karl Bayer, and Oswald Wiener.] He is incredibly intelligent and is a wonderful discussion partner, especially because he often takes a position different from mine. Over the years, Ossi has given me hours of productive frustration, so to speak. We argue a lot, but you'll seldom find a person as stimulating as Wiener.

NJM: Have you spent much time involving yourself with literary theory, or isn't this very important to you?

PR: No, I haven't read much literary theory as such, I was always more interested in philosophy and other disciplines, as a result of which you could say I have distilled my own literary theory.

KD: But you're familiar enough with literary theory to poke fun of it on occasion, its fads and fashions of the moment.

NJM: The latest "isms," as it were.

PR: Yes, of course I've poked fun at this, since it was always clear to me that, when all is said and done, the most valuable aspect of art is that which cannot be explained. Of course it's wonderful to have rational explanations for everything, and I'm not against discussion and theoretical discourse, but it has its limits. And as an artist you realize at times that it's simply best to destroy your original approach, abandon the plan you started with and even contradict it. That's how you move forward, how you progress. And that's why I've on occasion played the Ulenspiegel to a theoretician who holds forth with his thesis or whatever, and I'll say "Oh, how interesting" and "Oh yes, of course you're right," all the while knowing he's an idiot who doesn't have the foggiest notion of what art is.

NJM: Are there particular authors whom you would mention as influences on you? I believe Kafka is one whom you've cited in this respect in the past.

PR: There's no doubt that Kafka represents my point of departure, he was my teacher; his metaphoric approach, it's where I started. Kafka's attempt to explain reality via parables, that's certainly also how I wrote in the beginning. And I attempted to improve upon this method until basically I destroyed it. That's how it usually is in these matters: you add and add some more to an original approach, and finally you've developed a new one for yourself. You see this already in my *Entwurf für eine Welt ohne Menschen* [Project for a World without People, 1975]—the parables disappear entirely under the weight of the many details. And so gradually I departed from Kafka.

NJM: And foreign authors who might have influenced you in the beginning?

PR: Actually there are quite a few. The Russians, of course, all of them, but basically the typical literary canon that one reads at the university, along with the study of ethnology. Also Freud and Malinowski.

NJM: Malinowski, not Majakowski?

PR: No no, Bronislaw K. Malinowski, a Polish-born anthropologist who taught at the London School of Economics for many years. He did ethnological research on a remote group of Pacific islands. He was an Austrian from the old monarchy.

NJM: Speaking of which: do you consider yourself an Austrian writer?

PR: That's the cause of much debate. Of course in a normative sense I am completely an Austrian, since that's where I was born and where I grew up. This beginning influences one's basic sense of perceiving the world, what's cold or hot, what's a nice day or a less nice day—all of this is rather determined by the formative experiences of childhood. But on the other hand, of course, I have almost nothing to do with Austria today. I mean, I like to spend time in Austria, but it doesn't preoccupy me in any sense.

NJM: Then you wouldn't say, to quote your literary colleague: "The fat I'm choking on, it's known as Austria."

PR: Well, you could probably also quote Handke for more positive assertions about Austria. You know, when someone asks you where you're from and you say, "Austria," the response is usually a bland "Oh, really." But if you come from Denmark, for instance, they'll say "Oh, the country of lyric poets" or something equally inappropriate. It's probably the same for the United States. I mean, what's the response of foreigners if you tell them you're from Montana? But Austria, I mean it's certainly made its share of contributions to world culture.

KD: More than its share, I'd say, if you look at the size of the country!

PR: Yes, that's no exaggeration.

KD: And I'd say that if you look at German literature today, then it's also true that "little" Austria is disproportionately represented with respect to interesting authors.

PR: And in that sense it's nice to be included in this so-called tradition of Austrian writers, but perhaps it's not without its disadvantages, either. I mean, it's as though Austrians themselves don't know their own cultural heritage; Freud and Wittgenstein and Musil are basically unknown in Austria today, that's the strange thing about Austrians. Or maybe it's not so strange. Let me ask you: is the average American familiar with these names and what they signify?

KD: Well, maybe not the statistically "average" American, but the educated American, yes.

PR: Interesting. You know, Austria in the nineteenth and early twentieth century was involved in this grand project of emancipation, Freud and all the others who attempted to liberate humanity from self-imprisonment, and all of this seems to be forgotten today. Not so for Hitler—another Austrian—and the legacy of Fascism, whose shadow still darkens the country. But as for liberators like Broch and Musil and Freud—and the list could go on and on …

KD: Kafka as well.

PR: Yes of course, the list could be almost endless, Canetti and all the others who threw open the gates of prison and said: "Look, this is power and this is how to escape the dominion of oppression, this is the human psyche and how it operates, understand these things and you can free yourselves." And today, who is aware of these people in Austria anymore?

KD: And one wonders whether this phenomenon might be explained in terms of nostalgia for the so-called good old days, the monarchy and Kaiser Franz Josef and all that, and the representative buildings that still hearken back to these times, and so forth.

PR: No, I wouldn't describe it in this way, that would be an exaggeration. Every country has its "cultural burden," so to speak. I mean, to live in Austria is to live in a museum, where every cornerstone has historical significance, and so-and-so stayed overnight in this hotel on this date, or whatever. It's not easy to escape this reality. But that doesn't really have bearing on what I'm talking about. What I'm referring to is the fact, say, that a Wittgenstein could long since be seen in England and America as a giant in the field of twentieth-century philosophy, but remain almost unknown as such in his homeland.

Or take the situation of reparations for Jews who had to flee Austria in the face of Hitler and Nazism. Austria has been very slow to respond to these demands.

KD: Right, take the case of a Billy Wilder or all the other artists like him who fled to Hollywood—who remembers anymore that Wilder was an Austrian?

PR: Slowly, perhaps, people are beginning to become aware of this today. And who knows, perhaps the Austrians will finally begin to reclaim their cultural heritage of emancipation and exploration, as it is amply represented in so many major figures of the nineteenth and twentieth centuries. And so it's for this reason, coming back to your original question, that I look upon the designation of "Austrian writer" with some mixed feelings and ambiguity.

NJM: Perhaps at this point you'll pardon a rather banal question: Do you have a set routine, a daily pattern for work, say à la Thomas Mann?

PR: I'm not sure anyone is that disciplined and ambitious anymore! But to answer your question: Regardless of where I am, I basically dedicate the morning to work.

NJM: And you work without a computer?

PR: I own a computer but I prefer to write out most everything by hand. And besides, most of my working time is dedicated to thinking, not to writing. If I write a page at a time, I consider that a lot.

KD: That's of course an advantage in terms of revisions. I mean, if things are well thought out before putting them on paper, you don't have to spend as much time on revising what you've written. And then a computer, which makes revisions so easily and quickly, isn't nearly as valuable.

PR: I suppose that's true. But the thing I want to stress is this: to write a novel such as *Rebus*, for example, demands an incredible amount of time for thinking, for meditation. To engage in such a project means that you don't mind being alone, being super lonely.

NJM: How does this work when you are home with the family?

PR: I never write at home; that wouldn't work with a young son, who of course wants to play with me whenever I'm there. I've got my own apartment for working, it's just for me and it's where I can hide away, as it were.

KD: Many people say that having a family brings with it ineluctable changes. Has it had this effect on you, I mean, has it affected your work or changed your attitude toward life?

PR: No, I don't think so. I mean, having a child of course changes the basic atmosphere, your mentality. But I was never the type of person who believed that life is to be lived entirely in the head, I was never a complete rationalist [*Vernünftler*]. And when all of a sudden you've got this incredible bundle of energy and self-assertion next to you, in a way it relativizes you and your situation. But I am used to this, since I have always believed in relativizing my own situation anyway.

KD: Of course I'm speaking a bit from my own experience here, as well. When one is younger, one is a bit more radical in one's convictions and political commitments. But then all at once the family is there, and then one starts to be less direct and less willing to put one's career or whatever in jeopardy as a result of political convictions. Of course if you are beholden to no one, perhaps you can afford to be as risky as you wish.

PR: Well, how should I put it, I guess my attitude is that when one writes as much as I do, then people don't consider a single work or book in this regard, but rather one's entire output. Of course people wonder why I write as much as I do. "Does the man really have so much to say?" and so on. But in my case it's simply that I am trying to progress, to move forward, by calling into question that which I've previously posited, not in the sense of despising this earlier approach to reality [*Wirklichkeitszug*], but by breaking it open and considering it anew from a different perspective. It is a constant calling into question of that which has already been achieved, it's not being content, it's the need to move forward.

KD: Right. There are certainly authors who, shall we say, basically keep writing the same book over and over.

NJM: And so logically one can conclude that your writing project, if I may use the term, can never be brought to conclusion, that you will never be able, unlike your friend Oswald Wiener, to stop writing.

PR: But he hasn't really stopped writing, he's researching and writing about artificial intelligence at the moment. And who knows, perhaps I'll one day depart radically from the kind of writing I'm doing now and move on to some other kind of artistic expression—as was common with certain members of the Wiener Gruppe, for example, the interest in "Actionism" and so on.

KD: Certainly there are many examples in the history of literature of people who fell prey to the attempt to make their lives into a work of art, and the attempt resulted in a poor work of art, so to speak.

PR: Well, how should I put it, these attempts on the part of certain members of the Wiener Gruppe were quite understandable in the context of the times in which they were generated. It was a conscious decision not to participate in a discursive debate, but to react to certain negative societal realities in a completely different way. And as for Ossi, he still has my complete respect, and Artmann, well he's probably still my best friend, although he has a completely different attitude toward life than I do. We still get together nearly every week, and this has been going on for over twenty-five years now. I'm really almost a polar opposite of him, but this has never hurt our friendship in any way.

NJM: You already know that a translation of this conversation will appear in a book I am editing called *The Fiction of the I: Contemporary Austrian Authors and Autobiography*. Yet the autobiographical aspects of your work are not often mentioned in the secondary literature on Peter Rosei, and I was wondering what your reaction to this is.

PR: Narrowly defined, I would not describe my works as autobiographical. Of course, nothing appears in my writing that hasn't in some sense been filtered through my own "I," that's only logical. But this "I" is problematic, I mean does it exist and if so, in what sense? This "I" is only recognizable in light of certain patterns of actions and thoughts [*Denkkomplexe*]. It's only in this sense that we can recognize ourselves, that in certain situations we will respond in a predictable manner.

NJM: Hence the "fiction" of the I?

PR: Precisely—that's the fiction of the I. And back then we adopted this position against, say, the traditional conception of the I as propagated by the Catholic Church. You know, where every individual is comprised of a body and unique soul and so on. So we took the position in the sixties and seventies that such a definition of the I was anything but a self-evident truth, regardless of whether this position was based on Hume or on someone much earlier who wasn't Catholic or even Christian at all. The Nominalists were, in this sense, our first friends, against this cult of the I with its soul, as preached by the Platonists and Catholics. Today this alternative conception of the I is not seen—at least in intellectual circles—as radical at all, but in those days it was viewed as positively evil even by the so-called guardians of public order [*Ordnungshüter*]. And I mean, well, as a result of this position the next step is to experiment with just what one's conception of one's "I" is. And in this sense my work is most certainly autobiographical, in that I've always enjoyed experimenting with myself, with my "I." I have a dictum related to this that I consider really important: "Thinking doesn't mean playing at thinking, but rather being willing to risk everything." And I really mean that. It means that one is really willing to cast one's I out of one's secure intellectual niche [*das sichere intellektuelle Häusl*]. Who knows what the result of something like this might be?

KD: Yes you're right, that's not necessarily a pleasant experience. But it leads me to something else, related in a way, since it has to do with Kafka once again. Max Brod once related the anecdote that when Kafka used to read from his work to a group of close friends, he frequently had to quit, because he broke out in hysterical laughter. This is certainly an aspect of Kafka's work that has been terribly ignored by the critics.

PR: You're right about that.

KD: Kafka scholarship is traditionally so incredibly serious or humorless, if you will. And I mention this because sometimes I have the suspicion that it's similar for Peter Rosei, that when he's reading from his work—whether to friends or to himself—he also has to laugh at his characters, and if not laugh, then at least smile. They're laughable or ridiculous, or perhaps funny in a horrible sort of way.

PR: Horribly funny is an accurate description, I'd say. This has to do with the dynamics of moving forward that I mentioned earlier; the author not as acolyte to, but as destroyer of his own works. *Rebus*, for example, is certainly a "horribly" funny work, it's chock full of black—the blackest—humor.

KD: Wouldn't you say that this black or gallows humor is in keeping with a venerable Austrian tradition?

PR: Well, certainly my approach stands in contrast to the American tradition of pragmatism, for example. It's speculative, but since it's based on experience it's also to be taken very seriously. On the other hand, of course, the tradition of literary self-relativization, whether couched in Austrian humor or not, is an ancient one. Wittgenstein had a wonderful aphorism in this regard, something along the lines of: "You must remember that the world got along very well before you had your most recent breakthrough." I mean, the coffee machine is certainly a great invention, but the world enjoyed coffee for centuries before the advent of the coffee machine, too. And the same is true of books and theories, no matter how interesting.

KD: And after Freud, we simply had new names for the problems that existed earlier. So where's the progress?

PR: Well, that's the $24,000 question, isn't it? All of us wonder about this at times, especially since progress always initially assumes that it's more important than it really is, as Wittgenstein suggested. So perhaps our motto is: "Work hard, because there's little progress to be made." And hence the humor, sometimes the black humor, when analyzing the human condition.

NJM: Perhaps back to the question of the I and self-identity for just a moment, "post-modern self-identity," if you will.

PR: That's a wonderful concept, isn't it?

NJM: It certainly is! At any rate, a critic wrote about you some years back, and I'm quoting now: "Rosei is an author who is primarily engaged in a search for self-discovery." Do you find this statement to be an oversimplification, or is it in essence accurate?

PR: Actually, you know, I said this once about myself many years ago, so this statement was originally a quote from me! And anyway, a basic component of any artistic activity is certainly self-discovery, whether on a conscious or subconscious level.

NJM: The artistic product as self-realization?

PR: Yes, perhaps. But we have to come back to the question of what the I is in the first place. Where is the I and what or where are its borders, that is, where isn't it? Where does the I stop? The I comes into contact with unknown surroundings and thereby expands, so to speak. The self is a kind of journey where it is confronted with certain constants, and everything else is mobile.

NJM: This is a different literary strategy and self-conception than that of the Russian writer Mikhail Bakhtin, who once stated something like "I am only conscious of myself while revealing myself for another, through another and with the help of another." What are the constants you refer to?

PR: The basic self-calibration connected to perception, I suppose.

KD: While this search for the self is an integral part of all literature to some degree, it doesn't seem to be nearly as prominent in modern Russian literature.

PR: Well, if not prominent, then at least present. In Tolstoy, for instance, it's certainly a literary motor, albeit subsumed perhaps by religious or societal issues. This search for the self is typically disguised or structurally integrated into the other thematics of any literary work. All of these blend together: the search for the self, political expression, the need to explain, and the desire to achieve clarity. The latter is particularly attractive to me as a writer, the simple desire to make something clearly understood. There's probably something pedagogical about this impulse, but at the same time I am certainly not a pedagogue and I do not consider myself a didactic writer.

NJM: Do you consider yourself a political writer?

PR: In a larger sense I am a totally political writer. I'm not political in a superficial sense, although I have been politically involved whenever it has appeared to me that this was called for or appropriate.

NJM: Let's take a concrete example, in order to better understand what you mean. Is *Rebus*, for example, a political book?

PR: For me, absolutely. First, because it's a model for a democratic book, since it's not me, but rather it's the reader who must determine the meaning of the work. I mean, as the writer I certainly have my own understanding of what the work might mean, that's clear. But if I place my interpretation so much in the background that the reader's initial impression is: "I'm not at all certain what this means," then it's up to him to impart meaning to the entire construct. So the reader is involved in something initially set up by me, but in a work such as *Rebus* the reader has complete freedom to determine for himself what the meaning of the work is. In this sense it is democratic literature in the truest sense of the term. The opposite of this would be an agitprop book, where the reader is beaten over the head with the writer's political convictions, whether it be "Woe is you if you smoke cigarettes!" or whatever. Not that agitprop books are automatically bad, mind you—there are some good ones, too, as in the case of Innerhofer, for example. He is always trying to convince the reader of something or other, whereas I'd prefer that the reader come to convictions on his own.

NJM: And for me this leads to the question: Who in Austria buys Peter Rosei's books? What is your understanding of your readership in the German-speaking world? For example, last evening we happened to have dinner with a visiting soccer player from Germany, and we fell into conversation with this young man. Now, I cannot imagine that this soccer player would ever walk into a bookstore at home and purchase a work such as *Rebus*.

PR: What you're asking, of course, is what the literary reception of such an "abstruse" work is. Well, there's always the possibility that a book like *Rebus* will be purchased by mistake, if for instance it's marketed as a "novel of Vienna" or a "roman à clef" or something along these lines [laughter all around].

KD: If I may interject an opinion here: I'd expect that, say, people who subscribe to *Die Zeit* would be typical or representative of people who would buy a work such as *Rebus*, wouldn't you agree?

PR: I don't really concern myself with these questions.

KD: But your publisher certainly does.

PR: Well, I don't know about that, but I do know that the publisher of a work such as *Rebus* can count on strong critical reaction, in any event, and that by publishing it, he can count on—how should I put this?—being a member in good standing of the National Culture Club, so to speak. And since cultural elitism is alive and well in Austria, this is not unimportant to my publisher.

KD: And if *Rebus* is representative of democratic literature, then it is to be hoped that it will gradually win acceptance by the cultural elite, as well.

PR: I suppose, but in the final analysis all I can do is to offer my literary model and then not worry about its literary reception.

KD: We didn't ask him, but it would have been interesting yesterday to ask the football player if he even understood the meaning of the term "rebus."

NJM: I seriously doubt he would have—I mean it's unlikely he ever studied Latin.

PR: Well, perhaps he would have understood the meaning from seeing "rebus" in the newspaper. But as for the book: you've got to remember that when *The Interpretation of Dreams* was published, it wasn't exactly a best seller for Freud, either!

KD: Of course. There's a process involved in the reception of any work such as this. First, it wins gradual acceptance by the aforementioned cultural elite, then it's "banalized" or popularized, and it thereby wins general cultural acceptance.

PR: That's a fairly accurate description of the matter.

KD: And with respect to *Rebus*: wouldn't you say that it's directly related to a narrative or literary parable tradition? And isn't a parable something that has to be puzzled out [*enträtselt*]?

PR: Perhaps, but *Rebus* is not burdened, if I may put it this way, with a metaphoric crust that needs to be split open. The metaphoric level of *Rebus* is strictly a question of mental mobility and flexibility, and while one could argue that metaphoric interpretation is possible for any literary work, *Rebus* as a totality was not conceived of as a metaphor. The incessant and insistent details of the work make this approach all but impossible.

KD: I suppose the fundamental question here is whether there can be any work of literature that does not have this metaphoric level.

PR: Perhaps *Rebus* is a possible answer to your basic question, since in reading the book, you no sooner think you've got a handle on what is happening or being stated than this certainty slips through your fingers. It's not unrelated, if you will, to an essentially Dadaistic approach to meaning.

[after a break]

KD: In beginning this next phase of our conversation, I'd like to ask you about your conception of language, of words. Do you consider yourself, perhaps à la Austrian literati affected by the *Sprachkrise* [language crisis] earlier in the twentieth century, in any way suspicious of language?

NJM: And if I may piggy-back onto this question one of my own: certain critics in the past have actually accused you of being too facile with language, of writing too much, too easily and too beautifully. What's your reaction to this rather unusual accusation?

PR: Actually these two questions are very much related for me. Your reference to those for whom the meaning of words was put into question by a *Sprachkrise* really doesn't apply to me; if anything, the language crisis of my youth was generated by the Nazis and their destruction of language. And in any event, my answer to the "problem" of language and the meaning of words would be different from that of, say, the Wiener Gruppe and of Ossi. I never question the utility of language as a tool. It was always clear to me that language was a tool, albeit a tool with its own laws and idiosyncrasies. Hence I've always worked with language as a tool and I've never problematized language as such, at least never in a fashion as radical as the members of the Wiener Gruppe. Besides, it's always seemed more appropriate to me to thematize my own methodical limitations [*methodische Bedingtheit*] more than the inherent limitations of language. This is quite clear in a work such as *Rebus*.

NJM: And what about the accusation that you write too quickly and too easily and too beautifully?

PR: Well, first of all, it seems to me that this "accusation" was really made some years back, in reference to works such as *From Here to There*. And second, I think it had something to do with the fact that I never got involved with the vulgar Marxist debate in literary circles. My writing was always perceived to be lacking in social engagement, unlike most of the mainstream stuff of the seventies and early eighties. And hence the criticism that my writing was "too beautiful."

NJM: I think that's probably a pretty fair and accurate response on your part.

PR: Don't misunderstand me: I have nothing against a Max von der Grün or a Peter Turrini or an Innerhofer. It's just that I don't wish to see one particular approach absolutized and held out for all as the norm. And the irony about all this is that whereas I was considered right of center years back, recently I've come to be seen as left of center by reviewers and critics. I don't think I've changed in my opinions, it's simply that the mainstream today isn't what or where it was fifteen years ago. I try to be consistent, which is to say, true to myself and the problems that my approach addresses. But you know, I'd never flatter myself with the opinion that something like this happens only to me in critical circles. I mean, look at Handke; he's been held up as the champion or apologist of both the Left and the Right.

KD: Allow me to return to the question of Peter Rosei and his use of language for just a moment. And I'm thinking now specifically about certain theoretical formulations you've made in the past, phrases or turns of speech you use that are both sonorous and clever; you drew our attention to the difference between *Verklärungsversuche* and *Verklarungsversuche* a bit earlier in this conversation, and that's an example of what I'm talking about. German lends itself to such word plays better than many other languages, it seems to me, and I'm wondering whether you see giving in to this kind of linguistic play as somehow dangerous or at least distracting in making, say, poetic formulations. [Ed. note: This is a pun based on the verbs *verklären*, to transfigure, and *verklaren*, to spell out.]

PR: I understand perfectly the danger you're alluding to, but I'm not really the type who puts a great deal of stock in the precision of his poetic formulations; the structure of my poetic formulations undermines my own statements. I say something ad hoc and it immediately dissolves my previous statement. I cannot think of a more anarchistic approach!

KD: So you don't see yourself as held hostage to your formulations in any way?

PR: Not at all. I'm led to think of Joseph Roth's statement, when he was shown a photo of himself and said: "Yes, that's really me: drunk and vile, but clever!" [laughter all around]. And of course if you are indeed clever, then you're particularly happy about your clever formulations. But to be aware of this is to take a step beyond this kind of self-satisfaction and move toward the next stage of development. In a way this all has to do with an essential dilemma or contradiction, one that seems to be insoluble, namely: How can I say something to my fellow human beings without being didactic?

NJM: Some might suggest that the answer to this question lies in poetry. Do you still write lyric poetry?

PR: Yes, as a matter of fact I have quite a bit of it lying around.

NJM: But you don't publish it anymore?

PR: Well, you know the old saying, sometimes things are better off in the wastebasket! [laughter all around]. No, seriously, I suppose I'm just too busy with other projects to devote much time to my poetry at the moment.

NJM: Which German-language poets do you especially like? I've personally always felt that Brecht, for example, was a better poet than dramatist, but you may not share this opinion.

PR: Artmann is the first name that comes to mind, since he takes the formal possibilities of the German language to new limits. Somehow he gets beyond form to the essence of language and its life. I know that he enjoys reading grammars and dictionaries in his spare time, and in his poems he exhausts and expands the grammatical possibilities of his mother tongue. I especially like his poems in dialect. As for other poets, a number of the Russians come to mind, especially Mandelstam—in Celan's translations, of course.

NJM: At the moment there's a fascinating Celan exhibit called "Celan as Translator" in the Schillermuseum at Marbach am Neckar. I look forward to seeing it in a couple of weeks.

PR: Every poem that Celan translated became in fact a new Celan poem. His was such a strong and unique poetic voice that this is simply the way it was. He was a tremendous talent. As for other poets whom I treasure, certain Americans such as Wallace Stevens, mentioned earlier, and then Robert Lowell, too. Most of Stevens's powerful and essentially autobiographical poetry exists in good translations in German.

NJM: Are you happy about the fact that more and more of your works are now being translated?

PR: That's an easy question to answer: Who wouldn't be? [laughter all around].

NJM: Certainly, but I was also referring to the quality of the translations. Are you happy with these?

PR: I'm not certain I'm in a position to judge that so well. It's almost a childlike joy, of course, to see your work appear in a good translation, say in American English. But the really important question here is: Who in the American cultural context is actually reading Peter Rosei in translation? And the same would apply to French or whatever.

NJM: Have you ever tried your hand at writing in a language other than German?

PR: No, not really. My English isn't that good, and it's Oxford English in any event. Perhaps if I had started something like this as a child ... But you know, real art is always a response to something in a concrete cultural context, and for me this could only be a question of working with German. To analogize: take the paintings of your Georgia O'Keefe that are on display here in the museums of New Mexico. For me, they say too little, since they concentrate on only one pattern, as it were. But apparently they are an adequate response for this cultural context.

KD: Yes, but the inevitable extension of her art in the American cultural context is popularization, which is to say, banalization. And this shouldn't be mistaken for her artistic talent.

PR: Certainly, but I still consider her art to be essentially a sexualization of nature. It's inevitable that something like this would be popularized.

KD: Yes, but for her time, her approach and her depictions were downright shocking, and they represent a breakthrough of sorts, even though today it's become a stylized cliché.

PR: Perhaps, but it seems to me that her work lends itself to becoming a cliché, simply because there's not enough there, it's not layered or rich enough.

NJM: Both of us interviewers, if I'm not mistaken, have written down a number of quotes from your work, statements that we found interesting or provocative or both. We'd like to read a couple of these aloud and have you respond to them, if you don't mind.

PR: Sure—fire away.

NJM: For example, you once wrote: "Writing is really tantamount to a kind of massive refusal" [*eine Art massive Verweigerung*]. What does that mean?

PR: That's what I was referring to earlier when I said that I was refusing to be a participant in the dominant literary discourse of the time, Marxism and the jargon attendant to it. One simply isn't obligated, as a writer, to assume the critical stance that the majority chooses as its own. I am free to concentrate on problems or issues that I consider essential, and to do so in the manner that I choose to adopt as my own.

KD: Fine, but isn't it at the same time the obligation of every writer to be involved in problems of his or her society? Perhaps no group of writers exemplifies this more than the modern Russian authors, many of whom took this Messianic obligation, if you will, quite seriously.

PR: Yes, Dostoevsky especially.

KD: Not to mention Solzhenitsyn!

PR: Right, that's the type of writer you mean, but I do not view this approach as my personal obligation. And besides, good books always outlive their writers, and if my books are good they won't be as ephemeral as a particular political point of view that's popular at the moment.

KD: Earlier you mentioned that art arises not in a vacuum, but in response to something, against or in contradistinction to something, as it were. What are you responding to at the moment, perhaps in the cultural context of Austria?

PR: Well in Austria, you know, it's usually the same old topic, coming to grips with the past and all that. More recently, it has to do with racism and discrimination against foreigners. The latter is an important topic, and it's one that everybody in Austria should be involved in.

KD: Personally involved in, or through your works?

PR: I'd say personal involvement is called for here.

NJM: Weren't you actively involved with Turrini in the so-called Waldheim affair?

PR: Yes, that's correct. When I first heard about Waldheim I was in Canada, where I was walking in Toronto one day and happened to read the newspaper headlines, "Waldheim: War Criminal." And shortly thereafter I returned to Austria and the attitude there was: "Oh, this is really nothing at all, it will all blow over in a couple of weeks." But it was immediately clear to me that this wouldn't go away, that it would stain Austria for decades, since those who previously didn't even know that Austria existed now would have this as their image of us: a country with a president who is accused of being a war criminal. So it was obvious to me that as a country Austria had to insist on the entire truth coming out, and that it shouldn't be repressed in any way, despite accusations of "denigrators of your country" [*Nestbeschmutzer*] against me and the others who took this position.

KD: And is this the type of resistance you were referring to, when you said that art arises in response to something?

PR: You have to remember that I'm not just an artist, but also a citizen, and this was a civic response more than an artistic one. But as an artist, too, I could safely be described as a classic case of one who likes to stir the pot [*ein klassischer Unterwühler*]. Of course, the inevitable result is that one wouldn't win any popularity contests.

NJM: And back to the topic of prejudice against foreigners that you mentioned a few minutes ago: do you consider this an acute problem in Austria today?

PR: Let's say it's something that one constantly has to keep an eye on.

KD: Even in a country as small as Austria?

PR: It doesn't have much to do with the size of the country, and besides, there's always the danger of exporting such nonsense. Let's not forget that Hitler was Austrian. In any industrialized country today, you've got winners and losers, and the losers are especially susceptible to this kind of talk against foreigners. It's imperative that those in the most conservative political circles who propagate this rubbish never come into power or exercise too much influence on the young.

NJM: This conversation has already gone on for perhaps longer than anyone anticipated, but I'd like to read one last rather long Rosei quote, if I may.

PR: Sure, we've still got time for that.

NJM: It takes us back to your artistic *modus operandi* and in a sense back to the topic of the "I" once more, so it's a good way to bring this interview to its natural conclusion. I quote at some length and would ask you to respond: "I might put it this way: I am a programmer, that is to say, I create software that runs through the heads of my readers. Better still, I am a computer operator, I create and combine programs and in part determine the rules according to which they are used. But on the other hand and for the most part, I am a hacker, one who invades systems that already exist, who takes what he wants and what he can use and who then constructs his own programs. Destroying and building. Often destruction is the best kind of building."

PR: Well, it's what I alluded to earlier in the conversation. By destruction I mean to destroy a position or level that has already been achieved, to progress.

NJM: Always on the move.

PR: Well, always on the move in the sense of changing parameters, not intending to destroy the original strategy, but changing parameters to the extent that in the end the result is different. And in my smaller books, such as *From Here to There*, I had a rather porous approach; the same is true of *The Milky Way*. And I achieve this porosity in *The Milky Way*, for example, by means of a basic outline consisting of the following: six books of one story each, with a given number of pages per book. So I force myself to follow a totally open strategy, such that meaning is destroyed by this prescribed approach. But there are different ways to destroy when writing; for instance, humor is a type of narrative destruction. In *Rebus*, for example, the author himself becomes the object of the laughter; I couldn't possibly be any more radical in attacking myself. This kind of strategy you can find rather frequently in my works.

NJM: It's a variation on what the literary critics used to call "Romantic irony."

PR: Yes, except that it's even more radical; I'm standing on ice that is much thinner.

KD: And what are you working on at the moment?

PR: Well, I'm "carrying on," as you say in English. It's likely that *Persona* is the beginning of a larger project that will occupy me for some time. And beyond this, who knows: maybe I'll start writing other things under a different name.

NJM: Under a different name?

PR: Why not? Many authors do this. And besides, I think the most important thing in life is to hold oneself open [*das Offene bewahren*]. We'll just have to see ...

NJM: All right then. Peter, we both thank you very sincerely for this conversation. It's covered a lot of territory, and I'm certain that it will be read with great interest when it appears in print!

PR: You're very welcome! It was lively and interesting for me, as well, and I look forward to reading it in English.

Contributors

Robert Acker is Professor of German at the University of Montana in Missoula. His areas of research include pedagogy, German film, avant-garde literature, and modern German, Swiss, and Austrian writers.

Alfred Barthofer is Professor of German Language and Literature at the University of Newcastle, Australia. He has written widely on nineteenth and twentieth century Austrian literature, with particular reference to Grillparzer, Bernhard, and Austrian Drama from 1945 to the present.

Gerald Chapple is Associate Professor of German at McMaster University in Hamilton, Ontario (Canada). His main area of research is contemporary Austrian literature, and he has co-translated two of Barbara Frischmuth's novels.

Linda C. DeMeritt is Professor of German and Chairperson of the Modern Languages Department at Allegheny College in Pennsylvania. Her research emphasis is on contemporary Austrian writers, with special attention to Handke, Reichart, G. Roth, and Jelinek. Other publications include a book on the literature of New Subjectivity and a German grammar text.

Karl Doerry is Associate Professor of English and Director of International Studies at Northern Arizona University in Flagstaff. His publications are on the modern European novel, and his particular research interest is Karl May.

Ingeborg Hoesterey is Professor of German at Indiana University in Bloomington. She has published extensively on Austrian and Swiss literature and culture, contemporary German film, critical theory, and comparative arts. Her recent publications have given special attention to the intertextuality of cultural discourses.

Geoffrey Howes is Professor of German at Bowling Green State University in Ohio. He publishes primarily on twentieth-century German and Austrian literature, with particular interests in Musil, Roth, Rosei, and Canetti.

Imke Meyer is Associate Professor of German at Bryn Mawr College in Pennsylvania. Her research areas are early twentieth century Austrian culture, and contemporary German and Austrian literature. Her particular interest is in contemporary Austrian women writers, especially Bachmann and Jelinek.

Nicholas J. Meyerhofer is Professor of German at Northern Arizona University in Flagstaff. His several books and many articles focus chiefly on contemporary Austrian literature and on Holocaust Studies.

Jennifer Michaels is Samuel R. and Marie-Louise Rosenthal Professor of Humanities and Professor of German at Grinnell College in Iowa, where she is chairperson of the Department of German. She has published four books and numerous articles on twentieth century German and Austrian literature.

Michael Ossar is Professor of German at Kansas State University in Manhattan. He has published widely on twentieth century Swiss, German, and Austrian writers, with special emphasis on Expressionism.

Bianca Rosenthal is Professor of German and French Language and Literature and Interdisciplinary Humanities at California Polytechnic State University, San Luis Obispo, where she also chairs the Modern Languages and Literature Department. She has written extensively on French and German philosophers and writers of the nineteenth and twentieth centuries, with special emphasis on Paul Celan.

Pamela S. Saur is Professor of English and German at Lamar University in Beaumont, Texas. Her publications focus on Women's Studies issues and on figures in contemporary Austrian literature, with special attention to Barbara Frischmuth, Joseph Roth, Herbert Zand, and Franz Kafka.

Helga Schreckenberger is Associate Professor of German at the University of Vermont in Burlington. Her chief research interests are Exile literature, modern German prose, and contemporary Austrian literature. The latter involves special attention to G. Roth, whose novel *The Calm Ocean* she has also translated.

Jörg Thunecke is Professor of German at the Fachhochschule in Cologne, Germany and also at Nottingham Trent University in England. His several books and numerous articles focus on Exile literature and on a variety of modern Austrian authors, with particular interest in Paul Celan.

Index

Adorno, Theodor 1, 2, 51
Anti-Semitism 65, 71, 72, 80, 94–98
Autobiography vii, 1, 3, 10–12, 15, 18–20, 47, 48, 51, 53, 55, 56, 61, 62, 65, 76, 90, 103, 112, 116, 156, 185, 194, 201, 204, 210, 213, 214, 228, 243, 270
Bateson, Gregory 212, 218, 219, 221, 230, 238
Bernhard, Thomas 3, 138, 145, 151–153, 156, 160, 263
Borges, Jorge Luis 1
Cervantes, Miguel de 2
Deleuze, Giles 9, 211, 238
Derrida, Jacques 213, 238, 239
Freud, Sigmund 8, 49, 144, 211, 265, 266, 272, 275
Frischmuth, Barbara 1–3, 10–33
   Amoral Children's Rattle 20, 31
   Amy or the Metamorphosis 34, 43, 46
   Chasing after the Wind: Four Stories 21, 31
   Days and Years 20, 31
   Heart of a Witch: Stories 22, 23, 32
   Kai and the Love for Models 37, 45
   Never Mind 22, 26, 32
   The Convent School 3, 14, 19, 20, 31
   The Dream of Literature—The Literature of Dreams 18, 32
   The Mystification of Sophie Silber 3, 34, 36, 38, 40, 41, 46
   The Script of the Friend 24, 26, 32
   The Shadow Disappears in the Sun 3, 20, 23, 24, 31
   Water Sprites 15, 22

Goethe, Johann Wolfgang von vii, 12, 50, 151, 251
Guattari, Félix 211, 238
Handke, Peter 1–4, 8, 47–59, 265, 277
   Essay on the Successful Day 55, 56, 58
   Essay on Tiredness 50–53, 55
   The Afternoon of a Writer 48, 59
   The Jukebox and Other Essays on Storytelling 47, 52–54, 59
Henisch, Peter 1, 2, 4, 61–79, 80–100
   Bali or Swoboda Drops Out 76, 78, 81, 99
   May Is Gone 77, 80, 88, 93
   Mixed Profiles 62, 63
   Negatives of My Father 65, 66, 70, 71, 78
   Stein's Paranoia 65, 70, 78, 80, 93, 94, 99
   The Small Figure of My Father 80–83, 93 (see *Negatives of My Father*)
Hilsenrath, Edgar 1, 2, 5, 101–115
   Bronsky's Confession 102, 109, 111, 113, 114
   Jossel Wassermann's Homecoming 101, 103, 105, 109, 115
   Night 101–104, 110, 111, 114
   The Adventures of Ruben Jablonski 102, 107, 109, 111, 113–115
   The Fairy Tale of the Last Thought 101, 112, 114
   The Nazi and the Barber 101–103, 106, 114
Hofmannsthal, Hugo von 10, 14, 28
Hogarth, William 4, 58

Jelinek, Elfriede 1, 2, 5, 6, 116–137, 138–163
  Aggravating Circumstances or A Child's Report about a Relative 145, 162
  Children of the Dead 138, 139, 141, 151, 153, 154, 156, 158, 159, 160, 162, 163
  Lust 121–123, 130, 133, 134, 137, 157
  Michael. A Children's Book for the Infantile Society 117, 137
  Sickness of Modern Women 116, 130, 137
  The Piano Teacher 117, 119, 122, 124–127, 130–132, 135–139, 141–143, 145, 146, 148, 150–153, 156, 159, 160, 162, 163
  we are decoys baby! 117, 136
  Women as Lovers 117, 137
Kafka, Franz 35, 109, 145, 150, 151, 228, 231, 234, 236, 238, 264, 266, 271
Kundera, Milan 51, 59
Mann, Thomas 11, 28, 32, 267
Merleau-Ponty, Maurice 49, 59
Montaigne, Michel de 2, 47, 50, 53
Mörike, Eduard 52
Musil, Robert 48, 59, 223, 240, 266
Rosei, Peter 1, 2, 7, 200–209, 210–241, 259–283
  15,000 Souls 202, 208, 214, 223, 240
  From Here to There 215, 222, 227, 240
  Husband and Wife 208
  Persona 200, 201, 203, 209, 223, 227, 228
  Project for a World without People 215, 234, 240
  Rebus 215, 223, 227, 228, 238, 239
Roth, Gerhard 1, 2, 6, 7, 164–183, 184–199, 277
  A Journey into the Interior of Vienna 164, 183, 184
  Archives of Silence 164,–166, 170–172, 181–184, 198
  At the Precipice 173, 174, 179, 183, 184
  Everyday Death 166, 171, 173, 179, 183, 184
  In Deepest Austria 164, 182, 184
  The History of Darkness 164, 167, 183, 184
  The Investigating Officer: The History of a Sketch 176, 179, 182–185
  The Quiet Ocean 167, 168, 171, 173, 182, 184
Rousseau, Jean-Jacques vii, 12, 50, 54, 59
Schizophrenia 6, 9, 61, 63, 74, 76, 239
Self-decomposition 7
Self-effacement 6, 138, 139, 142
Self-identity viii, 64, 212, 216, 272
Wander, Fred 1, 2, 7, 8, 242–258
  Hotel Baalbek 243, 245, 256, 258
  The Good Life 243, 246, 258
  The Room in Paris 242, 258
  The Seventh Well 242
Watts, Alan 211, 217, 218, 233, 237, 238